# Pearson Edexcel GCSE (9–1)

# German

## Second Edition

## Revision Guide

T0351702

Series Consultant: Harry Smith

Author: Harriette Lanzer

## A note from the publisher

In order to ensure that this resource offers high-quality support for the associated Pearson qualification, it has been through a review process by the awarding body. This process confirms that this resource fully covers the teaching and learning content of the specification or part of a specification at which it is aimed. It also confirms that it demonstrates an appropriate balance between the development of subject skills, knowledge and understanding, in addition to preparation for assessment.

Endorsement does not cover any guidance on assessment activities or processes (e.g. practice questions or advice on how to answer assessment questions), included in the resource nor does it prescribe any particular approach to the teaching or delivery of a related course.

While the publishers have made every attempt to ensure that advice on the qualification and its assessment

is accurate, the official specification and associated assessment guidance materials are the only authoritative source of information and should always be referred to for definitive guidance.

Pearson examiners have not contributed to any sections in this resource relevant to examination papers for which they have responsibility.

Examiners will not use endorsed resources as a source of material for any assessment set by Pearson.

Endorsement of a resource does not mean that the resource is required to achieve this Pearson qualification, nor does it mean that it is the only suitable material available to support the qualification, and any resource lists produced by the awarding body shall include this and other appropriate resources.

**For the full range of Pearson revision titles across KS2, 11+, KS3, GCSE, Functional Skills, AS/A Level and BTEC visit:**
www.pearsonschools.co.uk/revise

A small bit of small print

Pearson Edexcel publishes Sample Assessment Material and the Specification on its website. This is the official content and this book should be used in conjunction with it. The worked examples and questions in this book have been written to help you practise the topics in the specification, and to help you prepare for your exams. Remember that the real exam questions may not look like this, and the questions in this book will not appear in your exams.

# Contents

**1-to-1** page match with the German Revision Workbook ISBN 9781292412269

### AUDIO

Audio files for the listening exercises in this book can be accessed by using the QR codes or hotlinks, or going to www.pearsonschools.co.uk/mflrevisionaudio throughout the book.

**Listen to the recording**

### A small bit of small print

Pearson Edexcel publishes Sample Assessment Material and the Specification on its website. This is the official content and this book should be used in conjunction with it. The questions in Now try this have been written to help you practise every topic in the book. Remember: the real exam questions may not look like this.

# Physical descriptions

You will need to describe people in the photo task of the Speaking exam, so make sure you have lots of this handy vocabulary at your fingertips!

## Wie sieht er / sie aus?

| Er / Sie hat … Haare. | He / She has … hair. |
|---|---|
| blonde | graue |
| braune | schwarze |
| dunkle / helle | dark / light |
| glatte / lockige | straight / curly |
| kurze / lange | short / long |

Sie hat (blaue) Augen.    She has (blue) eyes.
Er trägt eine Brille.    He is wearing glasses.
Sie trägt große Ohrringe.    She is wearing / wears big earrings.
Er hat einen Bart / Schnurrbart.    He's got a beard / moustache.
Sie hat ein rundes / hübsches Gesicht.    She has a round / pretty face.
Er hat eine Glatze.    He is bald.

## Comparing things

> Grammar page 90

- For regular comparatives add -er to the adjective:

| attraktiv ➡ | attraktiver |
|---|---|
| dick(er) | fat(ter) |
| hässlich(er) | ugly (uglier) |
| hübsch(er) | pretty (prettier) |
| schlank(er) | slim(mer) |
| schön(er) | (more) beautiful |

- The following are irregular:

| alt ➡ | älter | (old / older) |
|---|---|---|
| groß ➡ | größer | (big / bigger) |
| gut ➡ | besser | (good / better) |
| hoch ➡ | höher | (high / higher) |
| jung ➡ | jünger | (young / younger) |

- Use als to compare:

Ich bin älter als du. I am older than you.

---

## Worked example

**Person gesucht**
Lies den Bericht.

### Person gesucht

Die Polizei sucht dringend einen Kerl. Können Sie uns helfen, ihn zu finden? Der Jugendliche ist im Alter von 17–18 Jahren mit langen, dunkelbraunen und ziemlich lockigen Haaren. Er trägt einen kleinen Ohrring im linken Ohr und hat eine bunte Tätowierung am rechten Arm. Er trägt eine blaue Jeans und ein schwarzes T-Shirt und vielleicht trägt er auch eine grüne Mütze. Er ist sehr gefährlich – bitte rufen Sie sofort bei der Polizei an, falls Sie ihn sehen.

◀ Gender gives you a clue here – the police are looking for **einen Kerl** (masculine accusative) and **der Jugendliche** (masculine nominative) – so the answer cannot be **ein Mädchen** as that is neuter. It has to be **einen Mann** – a male person.

Füll die Lücke in jedem Satz mit einem Wort oder Wörtern aus dem Kasten. Es gibt mehr Wörter als Lücken.

Beispiel: Die Polizei sucht <u>einen Mann</u>

## Exam alert

◀ Remember – just because a word is mentioned in the text does not mean that it is the right answer! Read the passage carefully to ensure you understand correctly.

| sprechen | Hobbys | ein Piercing | lang | Kleidung | sechzehn |
|---|---|---|---|---|---|
| ~~einen Mann~~ | zwanzig | glatt | ein Mädchen | weglaufen | eine Glatze |

---

## Now try this

Now complete the reading activity.

**(a)** Der Mann ist jünger als …………… Jahre alt. **(1 mark)**

**(b)** Seine Haare sind …………… **(1 mark)**

**(c)** Er hat …………… **(1 mark)**

**(d)** Die Polizei beschreibt seine …………… **(1 mark)**

**(e)** Man soll mit dem Mann nicht …………… **(1 mark)**

# Character descriptions

To talk about character, you need to be confident with the verb sein and know plenty of adjectives to go with it!

## Charakterbeschreibung

| Ich bin ... | I am ... |
|---|---|
| altmodisch | old-fashioned |
| blöd | silly |
| böse | angry / cross |
| egoistisch | selfish |
| ehrlich | honest |
| ernst | serious |
| frech | cheeky |
| freundlich | friendly |
| gemein | mean / nasty |
| großartig | awesome |
| komisch | funny |
| lieb | likeable / nice |
| nervig | annoying |
| nett | nice |
| optimistisch | optimistic |
| schüchtern | shy |
| sympathisch | nice |
| vernünftig | reasonable |
| Ich bin humorlos. | I have no sense of humour. |

## The verb sein (to be)

| ich | bin | I am |
|---|---|---|
| du | bist | you are |
| er / sie / es | ist | he / she / it is |
| wir | sind | we are |
| ihr | seid | you are |
| Sie / sie | sind | you / they are |

## Imperfect tense

ich war (I was)   sie waren (they were)

You may well need to distinguish between past and present characteristics:

Obwohl er heute frech ist, war er als Kind sehr schüchtern. Although he is cheeky today, he was very shy as a child.

Sara ist intelligent, aber faul.
Sara is clever but lazy.

## Worked example

LISTENING TRACK 1

**Lauras Freunde**

Du hörst einen Bericht im Internet über Lauras Freunde in der Grundschule.

Wie waren sie? Trag entweder **faul**, **freundlich**, **laut** oder **lustig** ein.

Beispiel: Thomas war _lustig_.

— Thomas finde ich super, denn bei ihm konnte man immer gut lachen. Er war sehr humorvoll und das habe ich echt gut gefunden.

Listen to the recording

You don't hear the word lustig, but understand the whole extract and you will be able to identify the characteristic!

## Aiming higher

Give your work an edge by including one or two of these Higher level adjectives in your writing / speaking.

| | |
|---|---|
| angeberisch | pretentious |
| ausgeglichen | well-balanced |
| deprimiert | depressed |
| eingebildet | conceited |
| großzügig | generous |
| selbstbewusst | self-confident |
| verrückt | mad / crazy |
| zuverlässig | reliable |

## Now try this

Listen to the recording

LISTENING TRACK 2

Now complete the listening activity by writing the correct adjective to complete each sentence.

(a) Laura findet Nils ............... **(1 mark)**

(b) Yasmin war früher ............ **(1 mark)**

(c) Yasmin ist jetzt sehr ............ **(1 mark)**

(d) Claudia war früher nicht ............... **(1 mark)**

(e) Laura findet die Zeit mit Claudia...............  **(1 mark)**

# Family

Make sure you have a good supply of family-related vocabulary at your disposal!

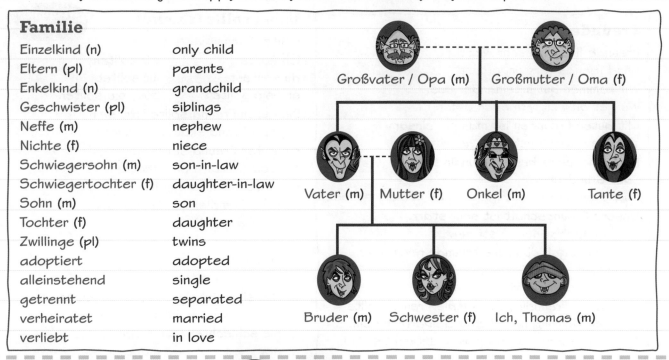

**Familie**

| | |
|---|---|
| Einzelkind (n) | only child |
| Eltern (pl) | parents |
| Enkelkind (n) | grandchild |
| Geschwister (pl) | siblings |
| Neffe (m) | nephew |
| Nichte (f) | niece |
| Schwiegersohn (m) | son-in-law |
| Schwiegertochter (f) | daughter-in-law |
| Sohn (m) | son |
| Tochter (f) | daughter |
| Zwillinge (pl) | twins |
| adoptiert | adopted |
| alleinstehend | single |
| getrennt | separated |
| verheiratet | married |
| verliebt | in love |

Großvater / Opa (m) — Großmutter / Oma (f)

Vater (m) — Mutter (f) — Onkel (m) — Tante (f)

Bruder (m) — Schwester (f) — Ich, Thomas (m)

## Worked example

**Deine Familie**

Beantworte diese Frage:
• Wie ist deine Familie?

In meiner Familie gibt es meine Mutter und meinen jüngeren Bruder.

**Aiming Higher**

Als wir jünger waren, musste meine Mutter ab und zu auf Dienstreise gehen, also hat meine Großmutter auf uns aufgepasst. Das hat Spaß gemacht, weil wir immer viel Zeit beim Keksebacken in der Küche verbracht haben. Nächstes Jahr werden wir nach Amerika fliegen, um unsere Tante dort zu besuchen. Sie ist <u>die Schwester meiner Mutter</u>, und sie ist sehr lustig, also wird es mich freuen, sie zu sehen. Ich persönlich würde gern in Kanada wohnen, aber ich würde meine Familie kaum sehen, und das wäre schlecht.

Improve your speaking by adding adverbs of time, such as **oft**, **ab und zu** and **immer**.

### Tenses

In the Speaking exam, include as many tenses as possible when discussing your family:
- ✓ who your family consists of – in the **present**
- ✓ description of an occasion with a family member – in the **past**
- ✓ your family plans – in the **future**
- ✓ something you would like to change about your family – in the **conditional**.

To show excellent knowledge of German, see if you can include the **pluperfect** tense!

Use a genitive to describe who's who in your family: **die Schwester meiner Mutter** – my mother's sister.

Pluperfect suggestion for this student: Als Kind hatte mein Vater Urlaub in Amerika gemacht, aber er konnte es dort nicht ausstehen!

## Now try this

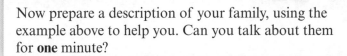

Now prepare a description of your family, using the example above to help you. Can you talk about them for **one** minute?

Use the advice above to help you include different tenses. Can you fit the pluperfect in too?

# Friends

Are friends more important to you than family? What should your best friend be like?

## Freunde

Freunde finde ich sehr wichtig.
I find friends very important.

Wir kommen gut miteinander aus.
We get on well with each other.

Mit guten Freunden ist man nie einsam.
You are never lonely with good friends.

Ich kenne meine beste Freundin seit
  der Grundschule.
I have known my best friend since primary school.

Unsere Freundschaft ist sehr stark.
Our friendship is very strong.

Es ist mir egal, ob meine Freunde reich oder
  arm sind.
I don't care if my friends are rich or poor.

Die ideale Freundin / Der ideale Freund sollte
  meiner Meinung nach lieb und sportlich sein.
The ideal friend, in my opinion, should be kind
  and sporty.

## Using sollte (should)

Grammar
page 98

sollte + infinitive

| ich sollte | wir sollten |
| du solltest | ihr solltet |
| er / sie sollte | Sie / sie sollten |

Ein guter Freund sollte treu sein.
A good friend should be loyal.

Ein guter Freund sollte ...
A good (male) friend should ...

Eine gute Freundin sollte ...
A good (female) friend should ...

... geduldig sein.
... be patient.

... immer Zeit für mich haben.
... always have time for me.

... dieselben Interessen wie ich haben.
... have the same interests as me.

... nie schlechter Laune sein.
... never be in a bad mood.

... immer guter Laune sein.
... always be in a good mood.

---

## Worked example

**Freunde**
Übersetze **ins Deutsche**.                    **(2 marks)**

My best friend, Max, is quite sporty and happy.

Mein bester Freund, Max, ist ziemlich
sportlich und glücklich.

In German you need to identify the gender of a
'friend': **der Freund** – male friend / boyfriend; **die**
**Freundin** – female friend / girlfriend.

## Translating into German

If you just can't think of the word for the
translation, don't panic, but try one of
these strategies:

☑ Do you know the German for
  the **opposite** word? If you have
  forgotten the German for 'happy',
  use the opposite, traurig (sad),
  instead, with the negative nie: nie
  traurig = never sad = happy.

☑ Can you **change** an adjective into a
  verbal phrase? For example, if your
  best friend is sporty and you can't
  remember the adjective, you could say
  er mag Sport or er treibt gern Sport.

☑ Can you perhaps use a word **similar** to
  English? Sporty could equally be aktiv,
  a very similar word to one in English,
  which conveys the same meaning.

---

## Now try this

Now translate these sentences **into German**.
(a) My friend Carol is clever and very funny.
                                    **(2 marks)**
(b) I often see my friends after school.    **(2 marks)**
(c) Last week my boyfriend had a party.    **(3 marks)**
(d) My best friend lived in Spain when she
    was eight years old.    **(3 marks)**

You need the German word for
'female friend' here, as it is a 'she'!
Remember that **als** (when) in the
past tense sends the verb to the
end of the clause.

# Role models

Do you have a role model? What can you say about him / her? Look at this page for some ideas.

## Vorbilder

| Mein Vorbild ... | My role model ... |
| --- | --- |
| ist ein Familienmitglied. | is a family member. |
| kommt aus meinem Freundschaftskreis. | |
| comes from my friendship group. | |
| ist ein/e Sportler/in. | is a sports person. |
| ist ein Star. | is a celebrity / star. |
| versucht, die Welt besser zu machen. | |
| tries to make the world better. | |
| hilft anderen Menschen. | helps other people. |

| Charakter (m) | character |
| --- | --- |
| Leben (n) | life |
| Persönlichkeit (f) | personality, character |
| abenteuerlich / unternehmungslustig | adventurous |
| selbstsicher | self-confident |
| sensibel / empfindlich | sensitive |
| Respekt haben (vor) | to respect |

## The verb haben (to have)

### Present tense

| ich | habe | I have |
| --- | --- | --- |
| du | hast | you have |
| er / sie / es | hat | he / she / it has |
| wir | haben | we have |
| ihr | habt | you have |
| Sie / sie | haben | you / they have |

Use the verb haben to add variety to your sentences:

Ich **habe** kein Vorbild, aber ich **hätte** gern eins.

I don't have a role model but I would like one.

**Imperfect tense**
ich hatte (I had)
wir hatten (we had)

**Perfect tense**
ich habe / er hat ... gehabt
(I have / he has had ...)

---

## Worked example

READING

**Role models**
Read this article from a German newspaper.

> Jugendliche brauchen Vorbilder. Sie sind oft Motivation und manchmal werden durch sie sogar die Träume ihrer Fans wahr. Sie können jungen Leuten helfen, ihre ganz speziellen Charaktereigenschaften zu entwickeln. Jeder hat ein anderes Vorbild, je nach individuellen Lieblingsbeschäftigungen.
>
> Vorbilder kommen aus verschiedenen Bereichen, manche kommen zum Beispiel aus der Film - oder Musikwelt. So hoffen Jugendliche, ihre eigenen Talente entwickeln zu können. Auch berühmte Sportler sind bei einigen Jugendlichen sehr beliebt, denn sie motivieren sie, ihre persönlichen Ziele in diesem Bereich zu verfolgen. Und zuletzt gibt es noch eine Gruppe von jungen Leuten, die zum Beispiel Lehrer, Naturschützer, Wissenschaftler oder Schriftsteller als Vorbilder wählen, denn diese haben unsere Welt verändert.

Answer the question **in English**.
Give one example of a positive effect role models have on people.
**(1 mark)**

Role models help people achieve their dreams.

## Exam alert

Don't be distracted by plurals of familiar words: **der Traum** = dream, **Träume** = dreams!

Break down long words to get to the meaning:
**Lieblings + Beschäftigungen = Lieblingsbeschäftigungen** (favourite pastimes).

Watch out for words like **manche** and **einige** which can both be translated as 'some'.

You need to say that role models 'help people achieve their dreams' – just 'achieve dreams' is not enough.

---

## Now try this

READING

Now answer these questions on the text **in English**.
You do not need to write in full sentences.

(a) Why do role models come from a variety of areas?    **(1 mark)**
(b) Give **one** effect of a celebrity role model on somebody.    **(1 mark)**
(c) Give **two** examples of role models who have changed something.    **(2 marks)**

# Relationships

Talking about different people requires not just a matching verb ending, but also a matching possessive pronoun. Make sure you can apply these in your writing and speaking tasks.

## Possessive adjectives

Possessive pronouns use the same endings as ein and kein.

Grammar page 88

| mein | my | unser | our |
| dein | your | euer | your (plural familiar) |
| sein | his | Ihr | your (polite) |
| ihr | her | ihr | their |

### Masculine
Ich liebe meinen Hund.    I love my dog.

### Feminine
Ihre Katze ist so süß.    Her cat is so sweet.

### Neuter
Er mag sein Meerschweinchen sehr.
He likes his guinea pig a lot.

### Plural
Wo sind eure Mäuse?    Where are your mice?

## Beziehungen

(Mein Bruder) nervt mich / geht mir auf die Nerven.
(My brother) annoys me.
Wir streiten uns ständig. We always argue.
Ich kann (meine Tante) nicht ausstehen.
I can't stand (my aunt).
Ich komme gut / schlecht mit (den Lehrern) aus.
I get on well / badly with (the teachers).
Ich verstehe mich gut mit (der Klasse).
I get on well with (the class).
Ich stehe / bleibe in Kontakt mit (meinen Cousinen).
I am / stay in contact with (my cousins).
Ich lerne gern neue Leute kennen.
I like getting to know new people.
Ich fühle mich (meinem Opa) sehr verbunden.
I feel very close to (my grandad).
(Meine Mutti) ist mir wichtig.
(My mum) is important to me.
Ich kann mich auf (meine Schwester) verlassen.
I can rely on (my sister).

## Worked example

LISTENING TRACK 3

Listen to the recording

### Wichtige Leute
Du hörst dieses Interview im Radio.

Füll die Lücke in jedem Satz mit einem Wort oder Wörtern aus dem Kasten. Es gibt mehr Wörter als Lücken.

Beispiel: Hakans ..Oma.. verbringt viele Stunden mit ihm.

> mag   dreimal   45   Lehrer   Schüler   54   Mutter
> Freunde   viermal   ~~Oma~~   hasst   Hobbys

— Meine Mutter arbeitet lange Stunden, also ist meine Oma mir besonders wichtig. Sie hat immer Zeit für mich.

## Exam alert

Before you listen, identify the two words from the box that work grammatically in each gap. Then listen to find out which of those two words is correct.

Don't jump to the wrong conclusion: just because Hakan mentions **Mutter** in the interview, it does not mean this must be the answer.

## Now try this

LISTENING TRACK 4

Now listen to the rest of the recording and complete the sentences.
(a) Im Moment hat Hakan ein Problem mit einem .......    **(1 mark)**
(b) Hakan ist gestern ...... Minuten extra in der Schule geblieben.    **(1 mark)**
(c) Hakan hat seine Hausaufgaben ...... nicht gemacht.    **(1 mark)**
(d) Hakan hat viele ...... .    **(1 mark)**
(e) Hakan ...... die Schule aufgrund seiner Freunde.    **(1 mark)**

Listen to the recording

# When I was younger

Use different pronouns with the matching verb ending to add variety to your work.

## Die Kindheit

Ich bin in (Wien) geboren.
I was born in (Vienna).
Er hatte oft Ärger in der Schule.
He was often in trouble at school.
Sie war ein stures Kind.
She was a stubborn child.
Wir durften nicht alleine zur Schule gehen.
We weren't allowed to go to school on our own.
Ich musste keine Hausaufgaben machen.
I didn't have to do any homework.
Mit acht Jahren konnte ich (schwimmen).
At eight years old I could (swim).
Er wollte (Feuerwehrmann) werden.
He wanted to be (a fireman).

## Pronouns

**Grammar page 91**

Pronouns = he, him, their, her, your, our

| nominative | accusative | dative |
|---|---|---|
| ich | mich | mir |
| du | dich | dir |
| er | ihn | ihm |
| sie | sie | ihr |
| es | es | ihm |
| wir | uns | uns |
| ihr | euch | euch |
| Sie / sie | Sie / sie | Ihnen / ihnen |

Sie war immer gut gelaunt.
She was always in a good mood.
Hast du mich gesehen?     Did you see me?

## Worked example

### Daily life

Schau dir das Foto an und sei bereit, über Folgendes zu sprechen:

• Deine Meinung dazu, ob die Kindheit eine gute Zeit ist

Die sechs Kinder im Foto sehen alle sehr glücklich aus, denn es gibt nichts, worüber sie sich Sorgen machen müssen! Sie stehen noch nicht unter Leistungsdruck in der Schule, denn der Schulalltag in der Grundschule ist entspannt und locker. Je älter man wird, desto stressiger wird das Leben und das finde ich schade. In der Klasse neun muss ich jeden Abend entweder Hausaufgaben machen oder für die Klassenarbeiten lernen, aber diese Kinder im Bild müssen das nicht. Sie spielen wahrscheinlich nach der Schule Fußball oder gehen ins Schwimmbad, stelle ich mir vor.

This student has slipped in the idiom je mehr ... desto ... (the more ... the more ...) to raise the level.
Try to include idioms in your work:
entweder ... oder = either ... or
weder ... noch = neither ... nor

Try to speak for at least 30 seconds on each point.

## Picture-based task (Higher)

In your preparation time for the picture task:

✓ Think about the sort of **unexpected** question you might be asked at the end. It won't be the same as one of the four bullet points on the sheet, so you need to think of further aspects you could be asked about.

✓ Make sure you can **describe** the photo to begin with, by recalling plenty of relevant adjectives as well as positional words: in der Mitte des Bildes, vor der Tafel, etc.

✓ Use the preparation time to consider the **four** known points, which you have to speak about (see page 57 in the Now try this for an example of these). Spend a few minutes on each point, noting the tenses you can use and any relevant vocabulary, but remember: you **must not** read out whole prepared sentences.

## Now try this

Now prepare answers to these unexpected questions you could be asked about the photo.
• Was für Probleme gibt es oft bei Kindern?
• Was war das beste Ereignis aus deiner Kindheit?
• Wie würdest du deine Grundschule verändern?
• Was werden die Kinder im Foto in Zukunft machen, meinst du?

7

# Peer group

Understanding question words is crucial to exam success – make sure you have the answers!

## Die Altersgenossen

| | |
|---|---|
| Alleinstehende (m/f) | single person |
| Bande / Gruppe (f) | gang / group |
| Bekannte (m/f) | acquaintance |
| Beziehung (f) | relationship |
| Diskriminierung (f) | discrimination |
| Feier / Party (f) | party |
| Freundschaft (f) | friendship |
| Jugend (f) | youth (i.e. time of life) |
| Jugendliche (m/f) | teenager / adolescent |
| Typ / Kerl (m) | guy |
| aussehen wie | to look like |
| gehören | to belong |
| mobben / schikanieren | to bully |
| minderjährig | underage |
| multikulturell (multikulti) | multicultural |
| rassistisch | racist |
| sexistisch | sexist |
| treu | loyal / faithful |
| unter Druck stehen | to be under pressure |

> Make sure you don't confuse **wer?** (who?) with **wo?** (where?).

## Question words

**Grammar page 106**

| | |
|---|---|
| Wann? | When? |
| Warum? | Why? |
| Was? | What? |
| Wer? | Who? |
| Wie? | How? |
| Wo? | Where? |
| Was für …? | What sort of…? |
| Wen? Wem? | Who(m)? |
| Wessen? | Whose? |
| Wie viele? | How many? |

## Justifying opinions

- ✓ Always **justify** your opinion by adding a weil or denn clause to give the reason for your opinion.
- ✓ You can also use an um … zu … clause to give a reason: Ich hänge gern mit meinen Freunden herum, um Spaß zu haben.
- ✓ Or start with a justification: Damit wir sicher sind, fahren wir im Bus zusammen zur Party.

## Worked example

> Question words are used here – but as statements.
> Remember to **justify** your ideas and opinions.

**Freundschaftsprobleme**

Du hast einen neuen Freundeskreis, aber es gibt ein Problem damit.

Schreib einen Brief an deine Freundin, der das Problem erklärt. Du **musst** über diese Punkte schreiben:

- was das Problem ist
- wann es begonnen hat
- die Vorteile einer festen Freundesgruppe
- wie du in Zukunft Probleme mit Freunden lösen könntest.

Rechtfertige deine Ideen und Meinungen.

Schreib ungefähr 130–150 Wörter **auf Deutsch**.

**(28 marks)**

Letztes Jahr musste ich an einer anderen Schule anfangen, wo ich glücklicherweise schnell neue Freunde in der Klasse kennengelernt habe. Ein Junge in der Gruppe ist aber rassistisch, und da meine Familie aus der Türkei kommt, hat er ein Problem mit mir.

## Now try this

Now prepare your own answers to the four points in the worked example and complete the writing activity.

> Aim to write a total of around 130–150 words. Divide the number of words required by the number of points you need to answer.

> This is the first part of a student answer, addressing the first bullet.
> A modal verb in the imperfect tense is an effective way of introducing the past tense into your work: **musste** = had to.
> The use of the conjunctions **wo** and **da** + verb at the end of the clause helps to raise the level of this answer.

# Customs

In German-speaking countries, a host parent and even your exchange partner might well shake your hand when they greet you, so be prepared!

## Guten Tag!

|  |  |
|---|---|
| Wie geht's dir / Ihnen? | How are you? |
| Entschuldigung | excuse me / sorry |
| Wie bitte? | Pardon? |
| bis später | see you later |
| bis bald | see you soon |
| guten Abend | good evening |
| auf Wiedersehen | goodbye |
| grüß Gott / servus | hello |
| guten Tag | hello, good day |
| guten Appetit | enjoy your meal |
| hallo | hello |
| Mahlzeit! | enjoy your meal |
| gute Reise | have a good trip |
| danke schön | thank you |
| bitte sehr / schön | you're welcome |
| Ich bin satt. | I am full. |
| Bedien dich. | Help yourself. |
| Es ärgert mich. | It annoys me. |
| Moment mal. | Wait a moment. |
| Was bedeutet das? | What does that mean? |
| Kann ich etwas ausrichten? | Can I take a message? |
| Ich verstehe eigentlich nicht. | I don't actually understand. |

## Qualifiers

If you don't want to appear over-enthusiastic, add a qualifier to your adjectives:

|  |  |
|---|---|
| gar nicht | not at all |
| nicht | not |
| ein bisschen | a bit |
| ganz | quite |
| ziemlich | quite |
| meistens | mostly |
| ein wenig | a bit |
| kaum | hardly |
| vielleicht | perhaps |

### Exam alert

Speak clearly during the role play and remember to use the correct register. It will say on the instruction card whether you have to use *Sie* (a formal role play) or *du* (an informal role play) when addressing your teacher. Use that register.

In the role play, remember:

- the teacher will speak first
- you will talk to the teacher using the five prompts provided
- where you see – ? – you must ask a question (do not simply repeat the words in the task)
- where you see – ! – you must respond to something you have not prepared.

## Worked example

**Instructions to candidate:** You have just arrived at your exchange family's home in Austria. Your teacher will play the role of your exchange partner and will speak first. You must address your exchange partner as *du*.

**Task**

Du bist gerade bei deiner Gastfamilie in Österreich angekommen. Du und dein(e) Austauschpartner(in) lernen einander kennen.

There are no wrong answers, as long as you respond fully to the bullet point and your answer makes sense. For example, in response to question 3, you could have anything in your suitcase: clothes, books, presents, shoes … Choose words you are confident with.

**1 Wie es dir geht – zwei Details**
– Hallo. Wie geht's?
– Sehr gut, danke, aber ich bin ein bisschen müde.

**2 Essen – zwei Details**
– Möchtest du etwas essen?
– Ja, einen Apfel und Kekse, bitte.

**3 ! – Was hast du im Koffer?**
– Ich habe meine Kleider.

### Now try this

Now practise the whole role play yourself, including the final two prompts. Listen to the audio file containing the teacher's part and fill in the pauses with your answers:
**4** Mittagessen – wann und wo
**5** ? Abends bei der Gastfamilie

Listen to the recording

# Home

Use your knowledge of tenses to write about when something **is** happening, **has** happened or **will** happen!

## Three key tenses

To aim for the top grades, you need to recognise and use different tenses.

## Present tense

- Make sure you know the present tense regular and irregular endings (page 95).

Ich esse zu Mittag.    I eat / am eating lunch.

Wir essen zu Mittag.    We eat / are eating lunch.

Watch out for the present tense implying future meaning.

Morgen esse ich Pizza zu Mittag.
Tomorrow I am going to have pizza for lunch.

### Das Zuhause

| | |
|---|---|
| Badezimmer (n) | bathroom |
| Dusche (f) | shower |
| Esszimmer (n) | dining room |
| Küche (f) | kitchen |
| Schlafzimmer (n) | bedroom |
| Wohnzimmer (n) | sitting room |
| Garage (f) | garage |
| Garten (m) | garden |
| Haustier (n) | pet |
| Doppelhaus (n) | semi-detached house |
| Reihenhaus (n) | terraced house |
| Wohnung (f) | flat |

## Past tenses

- Use the correct form of haben and sein + past participle to form the **perfect** tense.

Ich habe zu Mittag gegessen.
I ate lunch.

Er ist in die Küche gegangen.
He went into the kitchen.

- Use the **imperfect** tense war (was), hatte (had) and es gab (there was / were) for descriptions in the past.

- Use the correct form of haben and sein in the imperfect tense + past participle to form the **pluperfect** tense.

Ich hatte zu Mittag gegessen.
I had eaten lunch.

Er war in die Küche gegangen.
He had gone into the kitchen.

## Future tense

- Use the correct form of werden (to become) + infinitive verb to form the future tense.

Ich werde zu Mittag essen.
I will eat lunch.

Er wird in die Küche gehen.
He will go into the kitchen.

## Worked example

**Translation**
Translate this passage **into English**.

Zu Hause darf man nicht im Wohnzimmer essen, obwohl es dort so bequem ist.

At home you are not allowed to eat in the sitting room, although it is so comfortable there.

Remember that **darf** is part of the verb **dürfen** (to be allowed to).

Why is **ist** at the end of the sentence? It's because of **obwohl** (although) earlier on – read the entire sentence **before** you attempt to translate it.

## Now try this

Now complete the translation **into English**.

Meine Eltern sind altmodisch und wir müssen zu Mittag immer zusammen essen und plaudern, weil Handys am Tisch verboten sind. Mein Traum ist es, alleine in der Stadtmitte zu wohnen, sodass ich meine eigenen Regeln machen kann. Als Kind habe ich auf dem Land gewohnt, aber das war schrecklich langweilig.

# Everyday life

You will need to understand both 12- and 24-hour clock times.

## Der Alltag

Wir wohnen in einer Wohnung.  We live in a flat.
Ich stehe um sechs Uhr auf. I get up at six o'clock.
Ich fahre mit dem Rad zur Schule.
I go by bike to school.
Nachmittags habe ich (keine) Schule.
I (don't) have school in the afternoon.
Um vier Uhr gehe ich in den Sportverein.
I go to the sports club at four o'clock.
Abends bin ich oft online.
I am often online in the evenings.
Um zwei Uhr ist Ruhezeit im Wohnblock.
At two o'clock it is quiet time in the block of flats.
Man darf sonntags nicht Auto waschen.
You are not allowed to wash the car on a Sunday.
Die Geschäfte sind bis acht Uhr abends offen.
The shops are open until eight o'clock in the evening.

## 12-hour clock

zwei Uhr

fünf nach zwei

Viertel nach zwei

halb drei

Be careful! **Halb drei** is half past two (literally, half **to** three).

Viertel vor drei

zehn vor drei

## Worked example

 LISTENING TRACK 6

**Daily life**

You hear a radio report about the daily life of modern teenagers.

Listen to the report and answer the following question **in English**. You do not need to write in full sentences.

Listen to the recording

**(a)** What is the effect of modern life on teenagers?
**(1 mark)**

no longer able to concentrate

— Heute berichten wir über Jugendliche. Haben sie wirklich einen Alltag wie früher nur Manager?

— Na ja. Ständig neue Handys, neue Computer, neue Fächer, Nachrichten im Minutentakt und die ganze Welt im Internet: Kein Wunder, dass sich junge Leute nicht mehr konzentrieren können.

## Answering questions in English

✓ Use the rubric to guide you into the passage you are going to hear. How many clues can you already pick up from the introductory sentence here?

✓ Ignore the distractors! You may well be chuffed that you understand all the items mentioned, but that is **not** what the question is asking you about.

Make sure you learn time words such as **früher / vorher** (earlier), **später** (later) and **momentan** (at the moment) to help you answer questions precisely. Here, **nicht mehr** means 'no longer' or 'not any more', and that needs to be in your answer.

## Now try this

Listen to the recording

  LISTENING TRACK 7

Now listen to the rest of the report and answer the following questions **in English**.
**(b)** What has led to teenagers having to act like top managers, according to the report? **(1 mark)**
**(c)** Give **two** differences between managers and teenagers, according to the report. **(2 marks)**
**(d)** According to the report, what do teenagers now have to do? **(1 mark)**

# Meals at home

Learn a variety of food and drink words so you can talk about food, whatever the time of day!

## Mahlzeit!

| | |
|---|---|
| Abendessen / Abendbrot (n) | supper |
| Aufschnitt (m)  | cold meat |
| Bratwurst (f) | sausage |
| Brötchen (n) | bread roll |
| Ei (n) | egg |
| Frühstück (n) | breakfast |
| Gebäck (n) | biscuits / pastries |
| Hähnchen (n) | chicken |
| Mittagessen (n) | lunch |
| Obst (n) | fruit |
| Suppe (f) | soup |
| Teigwaren / Nudeln (pl) | pasta / noodles |

## Dative verb schmecken (to taste)

The dative verb schmecken works in the same way as gefallen (to like): es gefällt mir (I like it).

| | |
|---|---|
| Es schmeckt mir gut. | It tastes good. |
| Es hat mir nicht geschmeckt. | It didn't taste good. |
| bitter | bitter |
| lecker / köstlich | tasty / delicious |
| sauer | sour |
| scharf | highly seasoned / hot |
| süß | sweet |
| würzig | spicy |

## Expanding your vocabulary

✓ While you are revising, keep expanding your vocabulary. All the words in this activity are ones which may crop up in an exam, so use an online dictionary to check their meanings and add them to your wordlists.

✓ Use the audioscripts from this book as well as the reading passages to find new words to learn – make a note of ones you think are useful and revise them for your writing and speaking tasks.

## Worked example

READING

**Tagesablauf**
Lies Samiras Essensblog.

**Frühstück:** Gestern habe ich ein Brötchen mit Aufschnitt und ein Stück Obst dazu gegessen. Gestern war das ein Apfel, aber es kann auch eine Orange oder eine Birne sein.

**Mittagessen:** Das ist die Hauptmahlzeit, und ich esse immer einen Braten oder einen Hamburger mit Kartoffeln.

**Abendessen:** Das ist ein leichtes Essen und normalerweise esse ich eine Suppe oder ein Spiegelei. Ab und zu kommt auch ein Salat aufs Menü.

**Kaffee und Kuchen:** Während der Woche trinke ich meistens nur Mineralwasser, aber am Wochenende trinke ich gern eine heiße Schokolade oder eine Tasse Kräutertee und esse ein Stück Kuchen dazu.

Was hat Samira wann gegessen? Trag entweder **Frühstück**, **Mittagessen**, **Abendessen** oder **Kaffee und Kuchen** ein.

Beispiel: Samira hat gestern zum ‾Frühstück‾ einen Apfel gegessen.

## Now try this

Now read Samira's food blog again and complete the activity.
(a) Samira hat Obst zum …… gegessen.                    **(1 mark)**
(b) Samira hat zum …… etwas Süßes getrunken.            **(1 mark)**
(c) Manchmal isst Samira Tomaten und Gurke zum ……     **(1 mark)**
(d) Samira isst immer Fleisch zum ……                   **(1 mark)**
(e) Wochentags isst Samira nichts zum ……               **(1 mark)**

# Food and drink

What is your favourite dish (Lieblingsessen)? Make sure you know how to say it in German.
See page 115 for lots of Obst and Gemüse vocabulary!

## Essen

| | |
|---|---|
| Braten (m) | roast |
| Ente (f) | duck |
| Hackfleisch (n) | mince |
| Käse (m) | cheese |
| Lammfleisch (n) | lamb |
| Leberwurst (f) | liver sausage |
| Obsttorte (f) | fruit pie |
| Pizza (f) | pizza |
| Reis (m) | rice |
| Schweinefleisch (n) | pork |
| Soße (f) | sauce |
| Spiegelei (n) | fried egg |
| Steak (n) | steak |
| Thunfisch (m) | tuna |

## Trinken

| | |
|---|---|
| Bier (n) | beer |
| Fruchtsaft (m) | fruit juice |
| Limonade (f) | lemonade |
| Milch (f) | milk |
| Mineralwasser (n) | mineral water |
| Wein (m) | wine |

## Quantities

Be careful not to use von (of) with quantities:

 eine Dose +  Erbsen =

 a tin of peas

Here are a few more:

| | |
|---|---|
| ein Dutzend | a dozen |
| ein Glas | a jar / glass of |
| eine Packung | a packet of |
| eine Scheibe | a slice of |
| eine Tafel | a bar of |
| eine Tüte | a bag of |

Wir essen gern Kuchen!
We like eating cake!

## Developing a sentence

**Start** small: Ich esse gern Kekse.
**Expand** with und: Ich esse gern Kekse und Torten.
**Double** with a reason: Ich esse gern Kekse und Torten, weil sie mir so gut schmecken.

## Worked example

**Essen**
Dein Austauschpartner Eymen schickt dir Fragen über deine Essgewohnheiten.
Schreib eine Antwort an Eymen.
Du **musst** über diese Punkte schreiben:
- was du nicht gern isst und warum
- was du gestern gegessen hast
- was du gern zum Frühstück isst
- ob du bei ihm Fastfood essen wirst.
Schreib ungefähr 80–90 Wörter **auf Deutsch**.

**(20 marks)**

Ich esse nicht so gern Nudeln mit Tomatensoße, weil sie mir nicht schmeckt. Ich esse lieber eine Fleischsoße. Mein Lieblingsessen ist Schinkenpizza ohne Käse, aber ich esse nicht gern indisches Essen, weil das zu würzig und scharf ist.

Present, past and future are all in these bullet points, so make sure you use these tenses yourself as you work your way through each point.

Expand your writing using **weil**, **und** and **aber**, like this student has done in the answer to the first bullet point: three easy steps to developing a sentence!

## Now try this

Now write 80–90 words **in German** to answer the points above and complete the writing activity.

# Shopping for clothes

Learn clothes with their **gender**, so you can make sure your adjectives agree.

## Einkäufe

| | |
|---|---|
| Auswahl (f) | choice |
| Geld (n) | money |
| Größe (f) | size |
| Kunde (m) / Kundin (f) | customer |
| Marke (f) | brand |
| Quittung (f) | receipt |
| Umkleidekabine (f) | changing room |
| anprobieren | to try on |
| umtauschen | to exchange |
| das passt / | that fits / |
| steht dir | that suits you |

## Kleider / Klamotten

| | |
|---|---|
| Badeanzug (m) | swimming costume |
| Badehose (f) | trunks |
| Gürtel (m) | belt |
| Handschuh (m) | glove |
| Jeans (f) | jeans |
| Mütze (f) | cap |
| Schlafanzug (m) | pyjamas |
| Stiefel (m) | boot |
| altmodisch | old-fashioned |
| eng | tight |
| groß / weit | loose (i.e. too big) |
| mittelgroß | medium |
| schick / gepflegt / flott | smart |

## Adjective endings (der, die, das)

### Masculine nouns

| nom | acc | dat | |
|---|---|---|---|
| der blaue | den blauen | dem blauen | Mantel Pullover |

### Feminine nouns

| nom / acc | dat | |
|---|---|---|
| die blaue | der blauen | Hose Jacke |

### Neuter nouns

| nom / acc | dat | |
|---|---|---|
| das blaue | dem blauen | Hemd Kleid |

### Plural nouns

| nom / acc | dat |
|---|---|
| die blauen Schuhe Socken | den blauen Schuhen Socken |

Leder  leather    Baumwolle  cotton    Wolle  wool

gepunktet  spotted    gestreift  striped    gefärbt  dyed

---

## Worked example

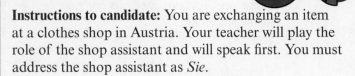

SPEAKING

**Instructions to candidate:** You are exchanging an item at a clothes shop in Austria. Your teacher will play the role of the shop assistant and will speak first. You must address the shop assistant as *Sie*.

**Task**

Sie sind im Kaufhaus in der Kleiderabteilung.
Sie wollen ein Kleidungsstück umtauschen.

**1 Kleidungsstück – Problem**

 – Wie kann ich Ihnen helfen?
– Ich möchte bitte dieses Hemd umtauschen, weil es zu eng ist.

**2 Feier – was**

 – Schade! Es ist so schön. Ist es für eine Party?
– Ja, für meinen Geburtstag.

**3 !**

 – Wann haben Sie das gekauft?
– Ich habe es gestern gekauft.

In the Higher task you have one unexpected question to respond to. Make sure you mirror the tense in your answer.

## Exam alert

When you read the instructions, decide what you are going to choose (in this case an item of clothing), check you know its gender and stick with that item. You do not have time to change your ideas once your preparation time is up.

This student has communicated both the item and the problem, just as was asked on the task card.

## Now try this

LISTENING TRACK 8

Now practise the whole role play yourself, including the final two prompts:

**4 ?** Anderes Kleidungsstück

**5 ?** Preis

Listen to the recording

# Social media

Be aware of separable verbs in listening and reading passages – the verb is not complete until you have heard / read the **whole** sentence to see if there is a missing prefix at the end!

## Soziale Netzwerke

| | |
|---|---|
| Blog (m/n) | blog |
| Chatraum (m) | chatroom |
| Homepage (f) | homepage |
| Internetseite / Webseite (f) | website |
| soziales Netzwerk (n) | social network |
| brennen | to burn |
| chatten | to chat (online) |
| hochladen | to upload |
| laden | to load |
| löschen | to delete |
| mailen | to email |
| sichern / speichern | to save |
| teilen | to share |
| tippen | to type |

## Separable verbs

> **Grammar page 96**

Separable verbs break into two parts:
- main verb = second in the sentence
- prefix = at the end.

Make sure you can use separable verbs in all tenses.

hochladen – to upload

| | |
|---|---|
| Present | Ich lade Fotos hoch. |
| Past | Ich habe Fotos hochgeladen. |
| Future | Ich werde Fotos hochladen. |
| Modals | Ich kann Fotos hochladen. |

## More separable verbs

| | |
|---|---|
| ausschalten | to turn off |
| einschalten | to turn on |
| herunterladen | to download |

---

## Worked example

LISTENING TRACK 9

**Technology**

You hear an interview on the school radio.

What does it say?

Listen to the recording and put a cross ✗ in the correct box.

Listen to the recording

> Hilfe! Die Katze hat mein Profil gelöscht!
> Help! The cat has deleted my profile!

- ☒ **A** The report is about social media.
- ☐ **B** 89% of teenagers had a profile.
- ☐ **C** All teenagers visit social media daily.
- ☐ **D** Gerd enjoys uploading content to his social media pages.
- ☐ **E** He finds commenting on other people's content fun.
- ☐ **F** Gerd never posts online.
- ☐ **G** Gerd shares digital material online.

> – Diese Woche diskutieren wir im Schulradio: Jugendliche und soziale Medien.

### Exam alert

Numbers are bound to come up somewhere in the exams, so make sure you are confident with them – see page 108 to brush up on them now.

⬅ Use the example answer to help you settle into the listening activity.

---

## Now try this

LISTENING TRACK 10

Listen to the recording

Now listen to the rest of the recording and put a cross ✗ next to the **three** remaining correct statements. **(3 marks)**

⬅ Listen carefully to **every** word – Gerd says **manche Jugendliche** (some teenagers). That is not statement **C** (all teenagers).

# Technology

In the Speaking exam, you could be asked about what technology you use and the effect it has on your life – be prepared with the vocabulary on this page!

## Technologie

| | |
|---|---|
| Anschluss (m) / Verbindung (f) | connection |
| E-Mail (f) | email |
| Handy (n) | mobile phone |
| Passwort (n) | password |
| Platte (f) | disk |
| Schrägstrich (m) | forward slash |
| Smartphone (n) | smartphone |
| Software (f) | software |
| Tablet-PC (m) | tablet computer |
| Telefon (n) | telephone |
| Webcam / Netzkamera (f) | webcam |
| (be)nutzen | to use |
| digital | digital |

## Pluperfect tense

Grammar page 105

Pluperfect tense = had done something.
It is formed by using the imperfect form of haben / sein + past participle.

Ich hatte es gedruckt.    I had printed it.
Sie war online gewesen.    She had been online.

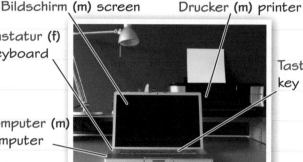

Bildschirm (m) screen
Drucker (m) printer
Tastatur (f) keyboard
Taste (f) key
Computer (m) computer

---

## Worked example

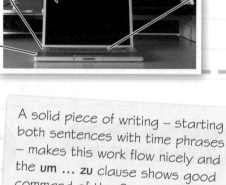

### Technology

Beantworte diese Frage:

• Wie benutzt du Technologie zu Hause?

> Abends sehe ich gern meine Lieblingsserien auf meinem Tablet-PC. Im Moment spare ich mein Taschengeld, um ein Smartphone zu kaufen, weil ich das echt super finde.

**Aiming Higher**

> Zu Hause werden wir in Zukunft immer mehr Technologie haben, denke ich. Abends sitzen wir im Wohnzimmer zusammen und jeder sieht schon seinen eigenen Bildschirm an. Das finde ich schade, weil wir uns nicht direkt miteinander unterhalten. Letzten Monat hat meine Mutter mir einen neuen Computer für die Schulaufgaben gekauft und ich finde ihn sehr nützlich.

A solid piece of writing – starting both sentences with time phrases – makes this work flow nicely and the **um ... zu** clause shows good command of the German language. Note also the opinion used.

### Adapting tenses

Prepare to speak in a variety of tenses by imagining that the question is in the past tense (Wie hast du letzte Woche Technologie zu Hause benutzt?) or in the future tense (Wie wirst du in Zukunft Technologie benutzen?).
You can use the same vocabulary, but you just need to change the tense each time to suit the question being asked.

This student uses:
• **wir** and **ich** parts of the verb
• **jeder** (everyone) + **sieht**
• an idiom: **schade** (pity)
• a reflexive verb: **sich unterhalten**
• present, past and future tenses.

---

## Now try this

The length of time you speak for is crucial. Don't try to squeeze too much content in – you might run out of time. It is important that your conversation flows and that you speak clearly.

Now prepare to speak for about 30 seconds on the same subject.
Wie benutzt du Technologie zu Hause?

# Online activities

Use time phrases – zu oft, fast täglich, kaum – to add interest when discussing your online life.

## Aktivitäten online

| | |
|---|---|
| Ich spiele online / Computerspiele. | I play online / computer games. |
| Ich lade Fotos hoch. | I upload photos. |
| Ich lade Musik herunter. | I download music. |
| Ich sehe mir Videoclips an. | I watch video clips. |
| Ich surfe im Internet. | I surf the internet. |
| Ich schreibe E-Mails / mein Blog. | I write emails / my blog. |
| Ich chatte online mit meinen Freunden. | I chat to my friends online. |
| Ich besuche Chatrooms. | I visit chatrooms. |
| Ich benutze soziale Netzwerke. | I use social networking sites. |
| Ich bleibe mit meinen Freunden in Kontakt. | I stay in contact with my friends. |
| Ich mache Einkäufe. | I do shopping. |
| Ich schicke eine Kurznachricht. / Ich simse. | I send a text. |
| Ich lese die Nachrichten am Computer. | I read the news on the computer. |

## Dürfen (to be allowed to)

> **Grammar page 98**

Dürfen is a modal verb so it needs an infinitive.
Ich darf nicht nach 22:00 Uhr auf Facebook surfen.
I am not allowed to be on Facebook after ten o'clock.
Ich darf keine Musik herunterladen.
I am not allowed to download music.

## Worked example

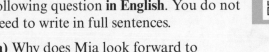

### Daily life

You hear this podcast about a teenager's life. Listen to the recording and answer the following question **in English**. You do not need to write in full sentences.

Listen to the recording

**(a)** Why does Mia look forward to the evening? **(1 mark)**

she can relax

> — Mia freut sich immer auf den Abend, weil sie sich dann endlich einmal ausruhen kann.

## Listening tips

✓ Don't worry about doing a simultaneous translation for yourself as you listen – read the questions in advance and then focus on the parts of the recording that are **relevant** to those questions.

✓ The more practice you have of **listening** to German, the easier you will find it. Make sure you listen to all the recorded material supplied with this Revision Guide to give your listening skills a boost.

## Now try this

Listen to the recording

Now listen to the rest of the recording and answer the following questions **in English**. You do not need to write in full sentences.

**(b)** Why does Mia have to watch the news? **(1 mark)**
**(c)** What does Mia do when she phones her friends? **(1 mark)**
**(d)** Give **two** actions Mia does after she has phoned her friends. **(2 marks)**
**(e)** Why does Mia feel nervous? **(1 mark)**

> There are several cognates (words similar to English words) in this recording – use them to help you understand.

17

# For and against technology

Be prepared to give positive and negative views on modern technology by using the phrases here.

## Technologie: für und gegen

Man kann in Kontakt mit Leuten aus der ganzen
Welt bleiben.
You can stay in contact with people from all over
the world.
Die Spiele sind lehrreich.
The games are educational.
Man muss sich der Gefahren bewusst sein.
You must be aware of the dangers.
Computerspiele sind eine Geld- und
Zeitverschwendung.
Computer games are a waste of money and time.
Bildschirme sind für die Augen schädlich.
Screens are damaging for the eyes.
Internet-Mobbing ist ein großes Problem
für Jugendliche.
Cyberbullying is a big problem for teenagers.
Es gibt immer ein Risiko mit Online-Aktivitäten.
There is always a risk with online activities.
Für junge Kinder ist das Internet zu gefährlich.
The internet is too dangerous for young children.

## Using ob (whether)

**Grammar page 93**

Ob sends the verb to the end:
Ich weiß nicht, ob er online ist.
I don't know whether he is online.

These conjunctions all send the verb to
the end of the clause too:

| | |
|---|---|
| als | when (in the past) |
| dass | that |
| obwohl | although |
| wenn | if |

Als ich ein Kind war, hat das Internet
mich fasziniert.
When I was a child, the internet
fascinated me.

### Aiming higher
- ✓ Use meiner Meinung nach +
  imperfect modal.
- ✓ A present tense modal reinforces
  knowledge of modal + infinitive.
- ✓ Use higher level structures such
  as etwas anderes and sich
  vorstellen + dative pronoun.

## Worked example

**Technologie: Vor- und Nachteile**

Schreib einen Artikel für eine Technologiewebseite.
Du **musst** über diesen Punkt schreiben:
• ob du Technologie eher positiv oder negativ findest.

**Aiming Higher**

Meiner Meinung nach sollten die Eltern dafür
verantwortlich sein, dass ihre Kinder sich
körperlich betätigen und nicht das Risiko
eingehen, computersüchtig zu werden.
Obwohl ich mir ein Leben ohne Computer nicht
vorstellen kann, weiß ich schon, wann die
Bildschirmzeit zu Ende sein sollte und wann ich
etwas anderes und Gesundes machen muss.

Once you have written your text,
check that:
- **word order is correct** (verb
  second or sent to the end by
  subordinating conjunction)
- **tenses are secure** and make
  sense (don't hop from past to
  present to future without time
  markers or sensible meaning)
- **spelling is accurate**, including
  adjective endings, genders and
  capital letters.

## Now try this

Now prepare answers to these points and complete the above writing activity:
• ob du Technologie eher positiv oder negativ findest
• wie dir Technologie besonders geholfen hat
• was du für junge Kinder im Bereich Technologie nicht empfehlen würdest
• ob du in Zukunft mit Technologie arbeiten wirst und warum (nicht).
Rechtfertige deine Ideen und Meinungen.
Schreib ungefähr 130–150 Wörter **auf Deutsch**.

Don't forget
to justify
(**rechtfertigen**)
your ideas – in
other words, give
a reason for the
ideas and opinions
you express!

# Hobbies

Make sure you can talk about your hobbies, as well as those of family and friends, by learning the different parts of present tense verbs.

## Hobbys

Ich sehe gern fern.

Ich spiele gern Computerspiele.

Ich höre gern Musik.

Ich koche gern.

Ich lese gern.

Ich spiele gern Schach.

Ich schicke gern SMS.

Ich gehe gern kegeln.

Ich treibe gern Sport.

## Present tense (regular)

Grammar page 95

machen – to do / to make

| ich | mache |
|---|---|
| du | machst |
| er / sie / es | macht |
| wir | machen |
| ihr | macht |
| Sie / sie | machen |

infinitive

Gehen (to go) follows the same pattern as machen in the present tense.

Ich trainiere.
I do training.

Ich gehe gern aus.
I like going out.

## Worked example

LISTENING TRACK 13

Listen to the recording

### Leisure time

You hear a recording about leisure time. What do you find out?

Listen to the recording and complete the sentence by putting a cross ✗ in the correct box.

In her free time, Anna enjoys …

- ☐ **A** shopping.
- ☒ **B** cooking.
- ☐ **C** going out.
- ☐ **D** watching TV.

— In meiner Freizeit bin ich oft in der Küche, weil ich sehr gern backe.

- You are not necessarily going to hear the **exact** activity you are familiar with, but you will hear enough to lead you to the words you know.
- Anna says she is mostly **in der Küche**. **Küche** means kitchen, so select the phrase which is related to this.
- There is only one suitable answer here, which is **B** cooking. Nothing else is vaguely related to 'kitchen' or 'baking'.

## Now try this

Listen to the recording

LISTENING TRACK 14

Now listen to three more people saying what they enjoy doing and put a cross ✗ in the correct box for each question.

**(i)** In the evenings, Oliver enjoys …

- ☐ **A** doing sport.
- ☐ **B** cooking.
- ☐ **C** going out.
- ☐ **D** watching TV.

**(1 mark)**

**(ii)** Petra is always …

- ☐ **A** listening to music.
- ☐ **B** meeting friends.
- ☐ **C** studying.
- ☐ **D** playing the piano.

**(1 mark)**

**(iii)** At the moment Bert is enjoying …

- ☐ **A** singing.
- ☐ **B** writing.
- ☐ **C** reading.
- ☐ **D** playing sport.

**(1 mark)**

# Interests

Make sure you can say what you **do** and do **not** enjoy doing in your leisure time.

### Interessen

| | |
|---|---|
| Bergsteigen finde ich toll. | I find mountaineering great. |
| Als Hobby bevorzuge ich Bogenschießen. | As a hobby I prefer archery. |
| Meine Lieblingsfreizeitbeschäftigung ist Chillen. | My favourite leisure activity is chilling. |
| Ich sammle gern Karten. | I like collecting cards. |
| Ich gehe nachmittags in den Sportverein. | I go to the sports club in the afternoons. |
| Diese Unterhaltung finde ich prima. | I find this entertainment great. |
| Ich gehe gern mit dem Hund spazieren. | I like going for a walk with the dog. |
| Ich gebe mein Taschengeld für Musik aus. | I spend my pocket money on music. |
| Ich gehe lieber ins Kino als ins Konzert. | I prefer going to the cinema than to a concert. |
| An Klettern habe ich wenig Interesse. | I have little interest in climbing. |
| Das macht mir keinen Spaß. | I don't enjoy that. |
| Ich interessiere mich nicht für Nachtklubs. | I am not interested in nightclubs. |

### Weil (because)

> **Grammar page 93**

Weil **always** sends the verb to the **end**.

Ich kann nicht kommen, weil ...
I can't come because ...
  ich dann Fußballtraining mache.
  I've got football training then.
  ich kein Geld habe.
  I haven't got any money.
  meine Eltern es nicht erlauben.
  my parents won't allow it.
  Verwandte zu Besuch sind.
  relatives are visiting.

> **Haben** and **sein** in the perfect tense go after the past participle.
> Modal verbs go after the infinitive.

Ich kann nicht kommen, weil ...
I can't come because ...
  ich den Film schon gesehen habe.
  I have already seen the film.
  ich Hausaufgaben machen muss.
  I've got to do homework.

---

## Worked example

### Translation

Translate this passage **into English**. **(3 marks)**

> Am Wochenende gehe ich immer in den Sportverein.
> Ich mache dort Fitnesstraining, oder ich spiele Federball.

At the weekend I always go to the sports club.
I do fitness training there or I play badminton.

Don't miss out any words in a translation, such as **dort** here – what does it tell you?

## Learning vocabulary

To be able to translate into English, you need to recognise lots of vocabulary, so learning plenty is crucial to success.

☑ **Look** at and learn the German words.

☑ **Cover** the English words.

☑ **Write** the English words.

☑ **Look** at all the words.

☑ **See** how many you have got right.

To help prepare for the translation into German, cover the **German** words and repeat the above stages.

---

## Now try this

Now complete the translation.

> Gestern bin ich mit meiner Familie ins Kino gegangen. Ich habe den Film langweilig gefunden, weil die Spezialeffekte altmodisch sind.

**(4 marks)**

# Music

Whether you love listening to music or prefer to play in an orchestra, it is important to know vocabulary about this topic.

**Musik**

Ich spiele ...

*ich spiele + instrument – no need for 'a'*

I play ...

Flöte (f)     Geige (f)

Gitarre (f)     Klarinette (n)

Klavier (n)     Schlagzeug (n)

Trompete (f)

Ich höre gern ...    I like listening to ...
Popmusik / Rockmusik (f)    pop / rock music

## Worked example

**Musik machen**

Du postest dieses Foto online für deine Freunde.

Beschreib das Foto und schreib deine Meinung über Musik.

Schreib ungefähr 20–30 Wörter **auf Deutsch**.

**(12 marks)**

In diesem Foto gibt es eine Band. Drei Jugendliche spielen Instrumente und ein Mädchen singt. Ich höre gern Musik und ich bin Mitglied im Schulorchester. Musik ist wichtig für mich.

*There are **two** parts to this writing task – a description of the photo **and** your opinion about music generally.*

### Favourite things

Use Lieblings + any noun (lower case) to talk about favourite things.

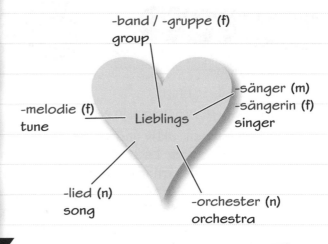

-band / -gruppe (f) group

-sänger (m) / -sängerin (f) singer

-melodie (f) tune

Lieblings

-lied (n) song

-orchester (n) orchestra

## Now try this

Now answer the photo question for yourself.

*Remember, half your writing must be description and half opinion.*

# Sport

You may want to refer to sports when talking about various topics. Make sure the **main verb** always comes in **second** position in a sentence.

## Sportarten

| ich … | I … |
|---|---|
| angle | go fishing |
| jogge | go jogging |
| reite | go riding |
| fahre Rad | go cycling |
| fahre Skateboard | go skateboarding |
| gehe schwimmen | go swimming |
| mache Gymnastik | do gymnastics |
| mache Leichtathletik | do athletics |
| laufe Rollschuh | go rollerskating |
| spiele Fußball | play football |
| spiele Tischtennis | play table tennis |
| treibe Sport | do sport |

Ich bin Mitglied einer Hockeymannschaft.
I am a member of a hockey team.
Letzte Saison haben wir die Meisterschaft gewonnen.
We won the championship last season.

## Verb in second place

> **Grammar page 92**

 ❶ Ich  ❷ spiele  ❸ Rugby.

 ❶ Im Winter  ❷ spiele  ❸ ich  ❹ Rugby.

In the perfect tense, the part of haben or sein goes in second place.

❶ Im Winter  ❷ habe  ❸ ich  ❹ Rugby  ❺ gespielt.

Im Sommer spiele ich Tennis.

---

## Worked example 🗣 SPEAKING

### Sports activities

Beantworte diese Frage:

• Welche Sportarten treibst du gern?

 Aiming Higher

> Ich bin sehr aktiv und treibe dreimal in der Woche Sport. Letztes Jahr war es ganz anders, weil ich mir das Bein gebrochen hatte und vier Monate lang keinen Sport treiben konnte. Das war eine Katastrophe für mich und ich musste dauernd Computerspiele spielen, die ich langweilig fand. Mein Traum ist es, eines Tages Profifußballer zu werden und ich würde am allerliebsten für Chelsea spielen.

## Aiming higher

Including three tenses in your work is as easy as 1, 2, 3, if you can say which sports you:
- ✓ **do** now
- ✓ **did** previously
- ✓ **would like to do** or **will do**.

Use past tense 'markers' such as **letztes Jahr** (last year), and conditional markers such as **eines Tages** (one day).

---

## Now try this 🗣 SPEAKING

Now prepare to answer these questions as fully as you can:
- Welche Sportarten treibst du gern?
- Wie viel Sport hast du letzte Woche gemacht?
- Was wäre dein sportlicher Traum?
- Soll Sport in der Schule Pflicht sein?

Try to speak for at least 30 seconds on each point.

Here's a useful Higher level phrase:

**Mein Traum ist es, mein Land bei den Olympischen Spielen zu vertreten.** It is my dream to represent my country at the Olympic Games.

# Reading

Reading is something exam boards enjoy promoting, so make sure you are not caught out by this topic!

## Lesen

Comic (m) / Comicheft (n)

Krimi (m)

Roman (m)

Schauspiel (n)

Zeitschrift (f)

Zeitung (f)

## Imperfect tense

Grammar page 102

| ist | ➡ | war | is / was |
| hat | ➡ | hatte | has / had |
| geht | ➡ | ging | goes / went |
| spielt | ➡ | spielte | plays / played |
| fährt | ➡ | fuhr | drives / drove |
| heißt | ➡ | hieß | is called / was called |
| liest | ➡ | las | reads / read |
| sieht | ➡ | sah | sees / saw |
| trägt | ➡ | trug | wears / wore |

Im Buch ging es um Freiheit / einen Mord / eine Beziehung.

The book was about freedom / a murder / a relationship.

---

## Worked example

***Paula die Leseratte* by Martin Ebbertz**

Read the extract from the text.

Paula is being introduced to the reader.

> Es war einmal eine Leseratte, die hieß Paula und die trug eine große Brille mit dicken Gläsern. Die Gläser waren so dick, dass es aussah, als hätte Paula winzige Augen. … Ohne Brille sah Paula überhaupt nichts, und mit Brille sah sie zwar ein bisschen, doch immer noch sehr wenig. Und das ist für eine Leseratte schlecht, denn zum Lesen braucht man gute Augen. Paula sah so wenig, und das Lesen war für sie so anstrengend, dass sie an jedem Tag nur einen Buchstaben las.

Answer the following question **in English**.

**(a)** How can you tell Paula was short-sighted? **(1 mark)**

She wore thick glasses / had thick lenses in her glasses.

## Exam alert

In literary extracts you may well come across the imperfect tense being used to tell the story. Make sure you recognise key verbs by learning the ones given above.

You might remember **dick**, meaning 'fat', from describing people, but as in English it can describe objects too. You never know where vocabulary from one topic might appear, so keep learning!

Learn your prepositions: **ohne** = without, **mit** = with, and **für** = for. These small words can be crucial to understanding a text correctly.

---

## Now try this

Now answer these three further questions on the extract **in English**.
You do not need to write in full sentences.

**(b)** What effect did Paula's glasses have on her eyes? **(1 mark)**

**(c)** What could Paula see without her glasses? **(1 mark)**

**(d)** Give **two** reasons why Paula made slow progress with her reading. **(2 marks)**

# Films

Films, books and television programmes all require the same kind of vocabulary, so make sure you are secure with the basics, and then transfer them across these topics.

## Kino

| | |
|---|---|
| fantastisch | fantastic |
| komisch | funny (strange) |
| spannend | exciting |
| toll | great |
| traurig | sad |

Ich habe ... im Kino / auf DVD gesehen.
I saw ... at the cinema / on DVD.
Es war ein Abenteuerfilm / Horrorfilm / Liebesfilm.
It was an adventure / horror / love film.
Das Hauptthema war Liebe / Familie.
The main theme was love / family.
Die Geschichte war kompliziert / romantisch.
The story was complicated / romantic.
Der Film spielte in Köln. The film was set in Cologne.

## Time expressions

Add time expressions wherever you can.

| | |
|---|---|
| ab und zu | now and again |
| dann und wann | now and then |
| immer | always |
| manchmal | sometimes |
| nie | never |
| oft | often |
| selten | seldom |

These sentences both mean the same thing, but have a different word order!
Ich gehe manchmal ins Kino.
Manchmal gehe ich ins Kino.
I sometimes go to the cinema.

## Worked example

**Ein Kinoabend**
Du organisierst einen Kinoabend für deine Freunde.

Schreib eine Einladung an deine Freunde, damit sie zum Kinoabend kommen.

Du **musst** über diese Punkte schreiben:

- Details zum Kinoabend
- warum deine Freunde den Abenteuerfilm sehen sollten
- wie der letzte Kinoabend gelaufen ist
- deine Pläne für das nächste Event.

Rechtfertige deine Ideen und Meinungen.

Schreib ungefähr 130–150 Wörter **auf Deutsch**.

**(28 marks)**

Hallo,

ich möchte euch heute zu einem Kinoabend einladen, den ich organisiere. Am 12. Mai werden wir hier in unserer Stadt einen spannenden Abenteuerfilm sehen.

## Writing tips

Read the rubric.
- ✓ **Who** are you addressing? Is your writing for a Sie or a du person?
- ✓ **What** are you writing? An invitation, a report or a blog?
- ✓ **Make notes** beside each bullet point to focus your mind before you start writing – do not go off task.
- ✓ Keep an eye on **tenses** – include a good variety across the bullet points.
- ✓ Be decisive – **plan** an answer and **stick** to it!

This paragraph is 24 words in length, so the student must move on to address the remaining three bullet points to complete the task. Look how the student has already worked in the present and future tenses!

## Now try this

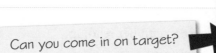 Can you come in on target?

Now prepare your own answers to the bullet points on the left and complete the writing activity.

# Television

When reading or listening to extracts, tense markers such as those below can all help you identify when the action is happening.

## Fernsehsendungen

| Ich sehe mir gern ... an. | I like watching ... |
| Dokumentarfilm (m) | documentary |
| Fernsehstar (m) | TV celebrity |
| Kabelfernsehen (n) | cable TV |
| Lieblingsprogramm (n) | favourite programme |
| die Nachrichten (pl) | the news |
| Quizsendung (f) | quiz programme |
| Seifenoper (f) | soap opera |
| Sendung (f) | (TV) programme |
| Serie (f) | series |
| Show (f) | show |
| Zeichentrickfilme (mpl) | cartoons |
| Zuschauer/in (m/f) | viewer |
| einschalten | to switch on |
| ausschalten | to switch off |

ZDF and ARD are TV broadcasters.

## Tense markers

### Past tense

| als kleines Kind | as a small child |
| früher | previously, in the past |
| gestern | yesterday |
| letzte Woche | last week |

### Present tense

| heute | today |
| heutzutage | these days |
| jetzt | now |
| momentan | at the moment |

### Future tense

| in Zukunft | in future |
| morgen (früh) | tomorrow (morning) |
| nächste Woche | next week |
| übermorgen | the day after tomorrow |

Ich sehe mir gern Zeichentrickfilme an.

## Worked example

LISTENING TRACK 15

### Podcast

Du hörst einen Podcast im Internet über Sophies Freizeit.

Listen to the recording

Was sagt sie? Trag entweder **entspannend, interessant, blöd** oder **lustig** ein. Du kannst jedes Wort mehr als einmal verwenden.

Beispiel: Sophie findet Musiksendungen <u>entspannend</u>

– Normalerweise schalte ich nach der Schule den Fernseher ein und sehe mir eine Musiksendung an, um mich auszuruhen.

- Read the **four** adjectives carefully and make sure you know what they mean.
- Don't mistake **entspannend** (relaxing) for **spannend** (exciting) here.
- A process of elimination can help you in this sort of activity – if you are not sure which is the correct adjective, it may be helpful to narrow down your options by ruling out some of the adjectives first.
- Copy the whole adjective into the space provided – abbreviations or translations are not what are asked for here!

## Now try this

LISTENING TRACK 16

Listen to the rest of the recording and complete the sentences.

Listen to the recording

(a) Als Kind hat Sophie Zeichentrickfilme ........................ gefunden.  **(1 mark)**
(b) Jetzt findet sie die Zeichentrickfilme ........................ .  **(1 mark)**
(c) Sophie hat Dokumentarfilme ........................ gefunden.  **(1 mark)**
(d) Sophie findet die Nachrichten gar nicht ........................ .  **(1 mark)**
(e) Sophie mag Filme, die ........................ sind.  **(1 mark)**

# Celebrations

Prepare yourself to talk about parties and celebrations with the vocabulary on this page.

**Feier**

| | |
|---|---|
| Ehe (f) | marriage |
| Feuerwerk (n) | fireworks |
| Herzlichen Glückwunsch zum Geburtstag! | Happy Birthday! |
| Hochzeit (f) | wedding |
| Hochzeitsfeier (f) | wedding celebration |
| Sekt (m) | sparkling wine |
| Spezialität (f) | speciality |
| Torte (f) | gateau |
| Verlobung (f) | engagement |
| feiern | to celebrate |
| sich verkleiden | to dress up (costume) |

**Dative prepositions**

> Grammar page 86

| | | | |
|---|---|---|---|
| aus | from | nach | after |
| außer | except | seit | since |
| bei | at (the home of) | von | from |
| mit | with | zu | to |

(m) der Freund ➡ bei dem Freund
at the friend's house

(f) die Party ➡ nach der Party
after the party

(n) das Zimmer ➡ aus dem Zimmer
out of the room

(pl) die Geschenke ➡ mit den Geschenken
with the gifts

Frohes Neues Jahr!
Happy New Year!

zu + dem = zum
zu + der = zur
von + dem = vom

## Worked example

**READING**

**Celebrations**
Read this blog post by Ömer.

> Wir feiern immer zum Geburtstag als Familie. Meine Schwester backt meine Lieblingsschokoladentorte. Mein Bruder kauft oft die Luftballons. Meine Oma schickt mir immer Geld in der Post und mein Opa trinkt ein Glas Sekt für mich!
>
> Ich gehe aber nie ins Büro, weil man das an so einem besonderen Tag nicht machen soll!

Complete the gap in each sentence using a word from the box below. There are more words than gaps.

Ömer is writing about a .....birthday......

> mobile phone   never   money   ~~birthday~~   cake   often
> wedding   eats   card   drinks   always   works

## Exam alert

In this style of activity, there are often **two** answers which could fit each gap grammatically, so use your knowledge and understanding of the text to lead you to the correct word.

You need a noun for this gap – so ignore the time expressions and the verbs.

## Now try this

**READING**

Now complete the above reading activity.

(a) His sister makes a ......... .   **(1 mark)**
(b) His brother ......... buys balloons.   **(1 mark)**
(c) He receives ......... in the post.   **(1 mark)**
(d) His grandad ......... something special.   **(1 mark)**
(e) Ömer never ......... on his special day.   **(1 mark)**

# Festivals

Festival vocabulary could come up in any part of your exams – make sure these words don't throw you!

## Feste

**Muttertag (m)**

**Ostern (n)**

**Silvester (n)**

**Weihnachten (n)**

**Fasching (m) / Karneval (m)**

**Dorffest (n)**

| | |
|---|---|
| Dreikönigsfest (n) | Epiphany (6 January) |
| Fastenzeit (f) | Lent |
| Heiligabend (m) | Christmas Eve |
| Karfreitag (m) | Good Friday |
| Ostermontag (m) | Easter Monday |
| Glühwein (m) | mulled wine |
| Imbissstube (f) | snack bar |
| Krapfen (m) | doughnut |
| Umzug (m) | procession |
| Volksmusik (f) | folk music |

## Accusative prepositions

**Grammar page 86**

The following prepositions are followed by the accusative case:

| | |
|---|---|
| durch | through |
| ohne | without |
| für | for |
| um | around |
| gegen | against / towards |

- (m) der Bruder ➡ für den Bruder (der ➡ den) for the brother
- (f) die Idee ➡ gegen die Idee against the idea
- (n) das Haus ➡ um das Haus around the house
- (pl) die Getränke ➡ ohne die Getränke without the drinks

zu Weihnachten – at Christmas
an Neujahr – at New Year
auf der Neujahrsparty – at the New Year's party

---

## Worked example

**WRITING**

**Feiern**
Übersetze **ins Deutsche**.

> At the carnival I will take part in the procession through the town, because I like to dress up.

Im Karneval/Fasching werde ich am Umzug durch die Stadt teilnehmen, weil ich mich gern verkleide.

## Aiming higher

- ✓ Get your word order right by reminding yourself of the rule: **time – manner – place**. Which is which in this first sentence?
- ✓ If you use a weil clause, make sure you send the following verb to the end: weil ich mich gern verkleide.

---

## Now try this

**WRITING**

Now complete the translation **into German**.

> When my boyfriend had a carnival party, I did not enjoy it at all and I went home early. Tonight I am going into the town centre for New Year's Eve, because there is a band on the market square and we can dance there. I like to celebrate with lots of people outside.

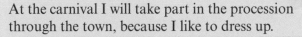

zu Hause sein
– to be at home
nach Hause gehen
– to go home

# Holiday preferences

What sort of holiday do you like – sporty, lazy, chilled? As well as saying what you **do** enjoy doing, make sure you can say what you **don't** enjoy.

## Thinking positively

Ich mache gern Urlaub in (Amerika).
I like going on holiday to (America).
Ich ziehe (Aktivurlaube) vor.
I prefer (active holidays).
Am liebsten (bleibe ich in einem Hotel).
Most of all I like (staying in a hotel).
Mein Lieblingsurlaub wäre (eine Woche in der Türkei).
My favourite holiday would be (a week in Turkey).

| Urlaub mit Freunden finde ich ... | I find holidays with friends ... |
|---|---|
| ausgezeichnet. | excellent. |
| entspannend. | relaxing. |
| locker. | relaxed / chilled. |
| super / prima. | super. |

## Thinking negatively

Ich fahre nicht gern (ins Ausland).
I don't like going (abroad).
(Sporturlaube) kann ich nicht ausstehen.
I can't stand (sports holidays).
Ich würde nie (Skiurlaub machen).
I would never (go on a skiing holiday).
(Eine Woche in der Sonne) interessiert mich nicht.
(A week in the sun) doesn't interest me.
Es gefällt mir gar nicht, (die Sehenswürdigkeiten zu besuchen).
I don't like (visiting the sights) at all.

| Familienurlaub finde ich ... | I find family holidays ... |
|---|---|
| ermüdend. | tiring. |
| schlecht. | bad. |
| schrecklich. | terrible. |
| stressig. | stressful. |

## Worked example

**Ein idealer Urlaub**

Deine Freundin schickt dir Fragen über deinen idealen Urlaub. Schreib eine Antwort.

Du **musst** über diesen Punkt schreiben:

• wohin du gern in den Urlaub fährst.

> Ich fahre in den Ferien sehr gern ans Meer. Ich bin Wassersportfan. Ich windsurfe gern. Ich liebe Segeln.

Skiurlaube interessieren mich nicht.

Although this is an accurate answer, it does little to show Higher skills because the sentences are very short and basic.

**Aiming Higher**

> In den Sommerferien fahre ich sehr gern ans Meer, da ich ein ziemlich großer Wassersportfan bin. Ich windsurfe äußerst gern, aber am liebsten segle ich. Segeln ist meine Leidenschaft.

To improve your writing:
• Add more detail, which this student does by using **Sommer** + **ferien**.
• Add an adjective.
• Include a **da** (because, since) or **weil** clause – with verb to the end!
• Add **am liebsten** to express preference.
• Combine your sentences with the connective **aber**.

## Now try this

Now include these points and complete the above writing activity:
• was du im letzten Urlaub gemacht hast
• wie du das gefunden hast
• warum ein Urlaub wichtig ist oder nicht
• Pläne für den nächsten Urlaub.

Schreib ungefähr 80–90 Wörter **auf Deutsch**.

# Hotels

Much of the hotel vocabulary on this page is also relevant for staying at a bed and breakfast or a youth hostel.

## Im Hotel wohnen

| | |
|---|---|
| Aufenthaltsraum (m) | games room |
| Aufzug / Fahrstuhl (m) | lift |
| Fenster (n) | window |
| Fitnessraum (m) | gym |
| Gast (m) | guest |
| Gepäck (n) | luggage |
| Klimaanlage (f) | air conditioning |
| Koffer (m) | suitcase |
| Reservierung (f) | reservation |
| Satellitenfernsehen (n) | satellite TV |
| Schwimmbad (n) | pool |
| auspacken | to unpack |
| funktionieren | to work |
| familienfreundlich | family friendly |
| mit Blick auf | with a view of |

## Compound words

Germans love long words! If you are joining words together in the Writing or Speaking exam to make a new word, the gender of the word is determined by the last word in the compound noun.

das Spiel + der Platz = **der** Spielplatz
(playground)

der Preis + die Liste = **die** Preisliste (price list)

die Stadt + das Zentrum = **das** Stadtzentrum
(town centre)

die Unterhaltung + die Möglichkeiten =
**die** Unterhaltungsmöglichkeiten (things to do)

If you come across a long word in a reading extract, take it apart, as above, to work out what each part means individually.

## Worked example

**Ein Hotelbesuch**

Lies Ninas Blogpost.

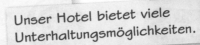
Unser Hotel bietet viele Unterhaltungsmöglichkeiten.

Die Familienreise im Frühling macht immer viel Spaß. Das ist ein absoluter Höhepunkt für mich! Wir wohnen in einem Drei-Sterne-Hotel. Das Hotel hat einen Fitnessraum, ein Schwimmbad und ein tolles Abendunterhaltungsprogramm. Glücklicherweise hat jedes Zimmer Internetanschluss. Mein jüngerer Bruder kann sich also gut selbst unterhalten. Am Ende des Aufenthalts versprechen wir, dieselben Zimmer für das folgende Jahr zu reservieren. Es ist immer ein einmaliger Urlaub!

### Exam alert

In this style of activity, you have to understand **both** the extract itself **and** the questions. Break down the long words to help you understand the extract **before** you tackle the questions, one by one.

Füll die Lücke in diesem Satz mit einem Wort aus dem Kasten.

**Beispiel:** Nina findet die Frühlingsreise ....wunderbar....

You won't find the exact sentences from the extract in the questions – you need to understand the meaning of the extract to choose the correct answer.

| | | | | | |
|---|---|---|---|---|---|
| Bett | schwimmen | viel | regelmäßig | plant | w̶u̶n̶d̶e̶r̶b̶a̶r̶ |
| reserviert | online | selten | Zelt | langweilig | nichts |

## Now try this

Now complete the above reading activity.

(a) Nina schläft in einem ............... **(1 mark)**
(b) Abends gibt es ............... zu tun. **(1 mark)**
(c) Ninas Bruder geht gern ............... **(1 mark)**
(d) Ninas Familie bleibt ............... hier. **(1 mark)**
(e) Sie ............... schon den nächsten Urlaub. **(1 mark)**

Es gibt mehr Wörter als Lücken.

You won't need to use all the words from the box.

29

# Campsites

Most of the vocabulary for this topic will also be useful for other types of holiday accommodation.

## Auf dem Campingplatz

| | |
|---|---|
| Badetuch (n) | towel |
| Bettwäsche (f) | bedlinen |
| Grill (m) | barbecue |
| Schlafsack (m) | sleeping bag |
| Wanderweg (m) | walk / trail |
| Zahnbürste (f) | toothbrush |
| Zahnpasta (f) | toothpaste |
| buchen | to book |
| reservieren | to reserve |
| wandern | to walk / hike |
| zelten | to camp |
| im Freien | in the open air |
| im Wohnwagen (m) | in a caravan |
| im Zelt (n) | in a tent |

## Giving location details

Here are some ways of letting someone know where you live or are staying.

| | |
|---|---|
| am | at / on |
| dort | there |
| entfernt | away from |
| hier | here |
| in der Nähe von | near to |
| neben | next to |

| Der Campingplatz ... | The campsite ... |
|---|---|
| liegt in der Nähe von Lindau. | is near to Lindau. |
| ist etwa 30 Gehminuten vom Stadtzentrum entfernt. | is about 30 minutes on foot from the town centre. |
| liegt am Bodensee. | is on Lake Constance. |
| befindet sich am Waldrand. | is situated on the edge of the wood. |

Unser Campingplatz befindet sich direkt am Meer.

## Worked example

LISTENING TRACK 17

### Campsite

You hear this campsite advertisement on local radio in Germany. What do you find out?

Listen to the recording and put a cross ✗ next to the correct statement.

Listen to the recording

- ☐ **A** The campsite is looking for a new manager.
- ☒ **B** You can hire a boat.
- ☐ **C** Caravans are allowed on site.
- ☐ **D** You cannot reserve a pitch.
- ☐ **E** The campsite is divided into four areas.
- ☐ **F** You have to bring your own drinking water.
- ☐ **G** There will be a new area for washing.

- Identify language which is not needed for the question. Here, the first couple of words are 'padding' and can be ignored. They don't offer any information about the campsite.
- Use all the clues provided. Don't be worried by **Bootsverleih** when you hear it mentioned. The cognates **Boot**, **Kajak** and **Kanu** along with the context of a campsite on Lake Constance should lead you to its meaning: boat hire.

— Herzlich willkommen auf dem Campingplatz Maria am Bodensee. Neu ist dieses Jahr unser Bootsverleih (Kajak und Kanu) vor Ort.

Bodensee – Lake Constance

## Now try this

LISTENING TRACK 18

Now listen to the rest of the recording and put a cross ✗ next to each of the other **three** correct statements.

Listen to the recording

**(3 marks)**

# Accommodation

Use this page to help you say what type of holiday accommodation you prefer.

## Die Ferienunterkunft

| | |
|---|---|
| Bauernhaus (n) | farmhouse |
| Bauernhof (m) | farm |
| Campingplatz (m) | campsite |
| Ferienwohnung (f) | holiday flat |
| Halbpension (f) | half board |
| Hotel (n) | hotel |
| Jugendherberge (f) | youth hostel |
| Mietwohnung (f) | rented flat |
| Pension (f) | bed and breakfast, B & B |
| Übernachtung (f) | overnight stay |
| Unterkunft (f) | accommodation |
| Wohnwagen (m) | caravan, mobile home |
| mieten | to hire, rent |
| übernachten | to stay the night |
| im Voraus | in advance |
| inbegriffen | included |

## Gern, lieber, am liebsten

A simple way of showing a preference is to use gern (like), lieber (prefer) and am liebsten (like most of all).

gern  ♥
lieber  ♥♥
am liebsten  ♥♥♥

- Put gern and lieber after the verb:
  Ich schlafe gern im Freien.
  I like sleeping outdoors.
  Ich bleibe lieber im Hotel.
  I prefer staying in a hotel.
- Use am liebsten to start your sentence:
  Am liebsten zelte ich.
  Most of all I like camping.

Ich schlafe lieber im Freien.

---

## Worked example

SPEAKING TRACK 19

### Holidays and travel

Beantworte diese Frage:

- Wo übernachtest du am liebsten im Urlaub?

Listen to the recording

**Aiming Higher**

Letzten Sommer haben wir in einer Pension übernachtet, aber das war schrecklich, weil wir abends um neun Uhr ins Bett gehen mussten. Diesen Sommer werden wir eine Ferienwohnung mieten und ich freue mich darauf. Ich finde es ungemütlich, im Zelt zu schlafen, weil es oft so kalt und unbequem ist. Am liebsten übernachte ich in einem Hotel.

Listen to this student's response.

## Aiming higher

Include the following in your speaking and writing, to aim for a higher grade.

✓ **Adjectives** make your speaking and writing much more … fascinating, exciting, amusing.

✓ Think PPF (past, present, future) **tenses** before you say anything and then figure out a way to include all three in your answer.

✓ **Conjunctions** give lots of scope for great sentences, so make sure you are confident with weil, wenn and dass, and can also have a go with obwohl, bevor and wo.

✓ Be prepared for prompts from your teacher such as noch etwas? (anything else?) or warum (nicht)? (why (not)?) to encourage you to add extra detail.

---

## Now try this

SPEAKING

Now prepare to answer these questions as fully as you can:
- Übernachtest du gern weg von zu Hause? Warum (nicht)?
- Was war deine beste Übernachtung?
- Wo würdest du gern in Zukunft übernachten?

Try to speak for at least 30 seconds on each point.

Think:
- connectives
- adjectives
- tenses
- conjunctions.
Throw each of these into the mix and you are well on the way to a very good answer.

# Holiday destinations

Always check your translation carefully – does your English flow well and does your text really make sense?

### Ferienziele

| | |
|---|---|
| Am liebsten übernachte ich ... | Most of all I like staying ... |
| auf dem Land | in the countryside |
| an der Küste | on the coast |
| in den Bergen | in the mountains |
| in einer Stadt | in a town |
| in einem Dorf | in a village |
| zu Hause | at home |
| bei Freunden | with friends |

weil man im See schwimmen kann
because you can swim in the lake

weil es dort viel wärmer als in England ist
because it is much warmer there than in England

weil meine Eltern gern in den Bergen wandern gehen
because my parents like walking in the mountains

### Dative and accusative prepositions

> **Grammar page 87**

| | |
|---|---|
| an | on, to, at |
| auf | on, to |
| in | in, into |

These use the **dative** case when there is **no movement** involved.

Ich wohne im Ausland. I live abroad.

Das Haus liegt am See.
The house is on the lake.

**But** if there is **movement towards** something, this signals the **accusative** case.

Ich fahre ins Ausland.
I am going abroad.

Ich fahre an die Küste.
I am going to the coast.

Am liebsten übernachte ich **an der Küste**.

---

## Worked example

**Translation**
Translate this passage **into English**.   **(1 mark)**

> Am liebsten übernachte ich am Meer, vor allem wenn das Wetter dort schön ist.

Most of all I like to stay at the seaside, especially when the weather is lovely there.

If you can't remember what **Meer** means, carry on reading for further clues. It is somewhere this person likes to go when the weather is good. Where might it be?

There is often more than one word you can use to translate a word – here, **schön** can be translated as 'lovely', 'fine' or even 'very good'.

---

## Now try this

Now complete the translation.

> Als Familie fahren wir jedes Jahr nach Teneriffa, wo der größte Wasserpark Europas ist. Ich würde auch einen Tagesausflug zur Hauptstadt empfehlen, um die wunderbaren Märkte zu besuchen und Andenken zu kaufen. Wir fahren seit vier Jahren dorthin und sind früher im Sommerurlaub an die windige Nordsee gefahren.

**(6 marks)**

# Holiday experiences

Make sure you can use the perfect tense when talking about holidays in the past.

## Vergangene Ferien

| | |
|---|---|
| letzten Sommer | last summer |
| in den Winterferien | in the winter holidays |
| letztes Jahr | last year |
| vor zwei Jahren | two years ago |
| Ich habe eine Tour gemacht. | I went on a tour. |
| Er ist nach Rom geflogen. | He flew to Rome. |
| Wir haben gefaulenzt. | We lazed. |

Ich bin Ski gefahren.
I went skiing.

Er ist Bergsteigen gegangen.
He went mountain climbing.

Sie ist schwimmen gegangen.
She went swimming.

Ich bin zelten gegangen.
I went camping.

## The perfect tense

Grammar
page 100

If you did something in the past, use the perfect tense!

| | |
|---|---|
| ich habe | |
| du hast | gekauft (bought) |
| er / sie / man hat | gemacht (did) |
| | besucht (visited) |
| ihr habt | gesehen (saw) |
| wir / Sie / sie haben | |
| ich bin | |
| du bist | gegangen (went) |
| er / sie / man ist | geflogen (flew) |
| ihr seid | gefahren (went / drove) |
| wir / Sie / sie sind | |

To give your opinion in the past, use Es war + adjective:

Es war ...

spektakulär / schön   stinklangweilig / furchtbar

Ich bin nach Berlin gefahren. Es war prima!
I went to Berlin. It was great!

## Worked example

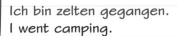

**Urlaubserlebnisse**

Du hörst einen Bericht im Internet über Katjas Urlaub letztes Jahr. Wie war es? Trag entweder **fantastisch**, **enttäuschend**, **langweilig** oder **interessant** ein.

Listen to the recording

Beispiel: Die Übernachtung war <u>enttäuschend</u>

> Letzten Sommer bin ich in den Schwarzwald gefahren. Der Campingplatz sah in der Broschüre wunderbar aus, aber er war in Wirklichkeit dreckig und sehr laut.

## Be prepared

✓ **Read the rubric** first: this is about 'last year', so you are going to hear past tense sentences.

✓ **Look at the four adjectives** to choose from and think about what words you might expect to hear for each one.

✓ Remember – you will hear the extract **twice**, so don't panic if you don't get the answer first time round.

## Now try this

Now complete the listening activity by selecting the correct adjective for each of these **three** reports. Some words can occur more than once.  **(3 marks)**

Listen to the recording

(a) ..............     (b) ..............     (c) ..............

# Holiday activities

For more things you might do on holiday, look at the leisure activities on page 19.

## Urlaubsaktivitäten

Man kann ...

 Bergsteigen gehen

 segeln

 eislaufen gehen

Ski fahren

faulenzen

spazieren gehen

Rad fahren

Tennis spielen

schwimmen gehen

## Saying what you can do

The verbs on the left are in the infinitive form – you need to use this form after the expression Man kann ... (You can ...).

| Man kann ... You can ... | ins Schwimmbad gehen. go to the pool. sich sonnen. sunbathe. |
|---|---|

If you start your sentence with a time or place expression, kann and man swap places.

In den Alpen kann man ...
In the Alps you can ...
In den Ferien kann man reiten.
In the holidays you can go horse riding.

Im Schwarzwald kann man auch reiten.

## Dealing with unknown words

✓ Break words down to decode them.
  – schwarz (black) + Wald (wood) = Black Forest
  – frei (free) + Zeit (time) + Park (park) = leisure / theme park
  – Bogen (bow) + schießen (shoot) = archery
  – wild (wild) + Wasser (water) + rutschen (slide) = white-water slides / flumes

✓ Use any other clues in the text. For example, Bogenschießen is listed as a sport and Wildwasserrutschen can be found in a theme park.

**Worked example** READING

### Holidays
Read the advert for holiday activities.

> **Verbringen Sie bei uns mitten im Schwarzwald entspannende Tage!**
>
> Hier kann man:
> - viele Sportarten ausprobieren (Bogenschießen, Klettern, Wasserski)
> - herrliche Spaziergänge im Wald machen
> - Tagesausflüge nach Freiburg machen
> - den Freizeitpark mit Wildwasserrutschen besuchen.
>
> „Letzten Sommer haben wir zum ersten Mal eine Woche im Urlaubszentrum verbracht. Wir werden sicher wieder zurückkommen!"

Answer the following question **in English**. You do not need to write in full sentences.

**(a)** Where is the place advertised? **(1 mark)**

Black Forest

 You won't get a mark if you write **Schwarzwald** – German place names need translating if they are different in English.

## Now try this
READING

Now answer these questions on the advert on the left **in English**. You do not need to write in full sentences.

**(b)** Name **one** sport you can try at the holiday centre. **(1 mark)**
**(c)** What can you do in the woods? **(1 mark)**
**(d)** What is offered to Freiburg? **(1 mark)**
**(e)** What tells you the visitor had a great time at the centre? **(1 mark)**

# Holiday plans

Talking about plans in any topic **will** require the use of the future tense.

## Ferienpläne

|  |  |
|---|---|
| Ich werde … | I will … |
| In den Ferien wird er … | In the holidays he will … |
| Hoffentlich werden sie … | Hopefully they will … |
| Eines Tages werden wir … | One day we will … |
|   nach Australien fahren. |   go to Australia. |
|   zu einem Musikfest gehen. |   go to a music festival. |
|   meine Cousine besuchen. |   visit my (female) cousin. |
| nächsten Sommer | next summer |
| nächsten Winter | next winter |
| nächstes Jahr | next year |
| in Zukunft | in future |
| in zwei Jahren | in two years |
| Ich freue mich (sehr) darauf. | I am (really) looking forward to it. |
| Wenn ich älter bin, werde ich einen Ferienjob machen. | When I am older, I will get a holiday job. |

## Future tense

Grammar
page 103

The future tense is formed using a part of werden (to become) + infinitive.

| | |
|---|---|
| ich | werde |
| du | wirst |
| er / sie / man | wird |
| ihr | werdet |
| wir / Sie / sie | werden |

Ich werde nach Ungarn fahren.
I will go to Hungary.
Sie wird Wasserski fahren.
She will go waterskiing.

If you start your sentence with a time expression, werde and ich swap places.
Nächstes Jahr werde ich zu Hause bleiben.
Next year I will stay at home.

You can also use **hoffen + zu** (to hope to) and **möchten** (would like) to indicate future plans.

Ich hoffe, nächstes Jahr nach Amerika zu fahren.
Next year I hope to go to America.

## Worked example

**Urlaub**
Übersetze **ins Deutsche**.

> Next year I will fly to Switzerland to visit my girlfriend in Zurich.

Nächstes Jahr werde ich in die Schweiz fliegen, um meine Freundin in Zürich zu besuchen.

## Aiming higher

- ✓ Tense markers such as 'next year', 'next week' and 'in future' all scream **future**. Don't translate these using any other tense.
- ✓ Genders – 'girlfriend' is a feminine noun, so make sure the article or adjective with it is also feminine.
- ✓ Translate **accurately** – the verb here is 'fly' – don't use fahren!
- ✓ Zurich is the English spelling – make sure you use the German spelling.

## Now try this

Now complete the translation **into German**.

> When I was there last time, I got to know some really nice people. We will meet again in May, and will all go on a day trip to the lake. I prefer holidays with friends rather than my family, because that suits me better.

# Holiday problems

Watch out for verbs in the present tense that change their vowels!

## Urlaubsprobleme

Ich habe ...
  meinen Reisepass verloren.
  einen Unfall gehabt.
Jemand hat meine Brieftasche genommen / gestohlen.
Das Hotelzimmer ...
  ist schmutzig / laut.
  hat keinen Internetanschluss.
Der Fernseher ist kaputt.
Der Kühlschrank funktioniert nicht.
Es sind Haare im Waschbecken.
Es gibt keine Seife.

I have ...
  lost my passport.
  had an accident.
Somebody has taken / stolen my wallet.

The hotel room ...
  is dirty / loud.
  has no internet connection.
The television is broken.
The fridge does not work.
There is hair in the basin.
There is no soap.

## Present tense irregular verbs

Grammar page 95

| geben | nehmen |
|---|---|
| – to give | – to take |
| ich gebe | ich nehme |
| du gibst | du nimmst |
| er / sie / es gibt | er / sie / es nimmt |
| ihr gebt | ihr nehmt |
| wir / Sie / sie geben | wir / Sie / sie nehmen |

## Negative words

Signs with these words on are warnings **not** to do something!

not | not a / no | forbidden

Attention! | Bitte hier nicht rauchen | Schwimmen verboten

---

## Worked example

SPEAKING

**Instructions to candidate:**
You are staying in a hotel in Switzerland. You are at the reception desk to report a problem. Your teacher will play the part of the hotel manager and will speak first. You must address the hotel manager as *Sie*.

**Task**
An der Hotelrezeption. Sie beschweren sich über ein Problem.

**1 Problem – zwei Details**
  – Guten Tag. Wie kann ich Ihnen helfen?
– Der Fernseher im Zimmer funktioniert nicht.

**2 Zimmer – Nummer und Stock**
  – Das tut mir leid. Was ist Ihre Zimmernummer?
– Nummer dreihundertacht im dritten Stock.

**3 !**
  – Woher kommen Sie?
– Aus England.

> This tells you the context of the conversation: here you are reporting a **problem**, so think of **one** problem you might report at a hotel reception desk. It can be anything – within reason!

> This student keeps things simple – and completes the task by giving **two** details about a problem.

> Again, this student completes the mission: a room number and floor details.

> If you don't catch this unexpected question first time, just ask politely: Wie bitte?

## Now try this

LISTENING TRACK 22

Now practise the whole role play yourself, including the final two prompts. Listen to the audio file containing the teacher's part and fill in the pauses with your answers:
**4 Urlaubsaktivitäten – zwei Details**
**5 ? Abendprogramm**

Listen to the recording

# Asking for help

Being able to ask for help when you have a problem and suggesting a Lösung (solution) might come up in your Speaking exam as well as being a useful life skill!

## Hilfe!

Ich habe eine Panne.
I have broken down.

Haben Sie das Ersatzteil?
Have you got the replacement part?

Wo finde ich den Kundendienst?
Where do I find customer services?

Könnten Sie die Rechnung nachprüfen?
Could you check the bill?

Wo kann ich das Auto reparieren lassen?
Where can I get the car fixed?

Ich habe schreckliche Magenschmerzen.
I have a dreadful stomach ache.

Gibt es hier in der Nähe eine Apotheke?
Is there a pharmacy nearby?

Wo ist die Polizeiwache?
Where is the police station?

Ist diese Urlaubsversicherung noch gültig?
Is this holiday insurance still valid?

Könnten Sie bitte einen Krankenwagen rufen?
Could you please ring for an ambulance?

## Saying something hurts

Mein(e) … tut weh. My … hurts.
Use tut (one thing) or tun (more than one thing) + weh.

Mein Fuß tut weh. My foot hurts.

Meine Füße tun weh. My feet hurt.

You can also talk about past pain:
Meine Hand tat weh. My hand hurt.

Meine Arme taten weh. My arms hurt.

| | | | |
|---|---|---|---|
| Bein (n) | leg | Knie (n) | knee |
| Finger (m) | finger | Schulter (f) | shoulder |

Naming a body part and adding -schmerzen (pain) is an easy way to express what part of your body needs help! Ich habe Kopfschmerzen (I have a headache).

## Worked example

**Instructions to candidate:**
You have an accident on a skiing holiday in Austria. Your teacher will play the part of a ski instructor and will speak first. You must address the ski instructor as *Sie*.

**Task**
Sie sind im Skiurlaub in Österreich. Sie haben einen Unfall auf der Piste und sprechen mit dem Skilehrer / der Skilehrerin.

**1 Problem – zwei Details**
– Kann ich Ihnen helfen?
– Mein linkes Bein tut schrecklich weh.

**2 Wo – Familie**
– Oje! Wo kann ich Ihre Eltern finden?
– Sie sind unten im Dorf in einem großen Hotel.

**3 !**
– Was ist passiert?
– Ich bin auf der Piste gefallen.

This unexpected question is in the past tense, and the student replies in the past tense too.

## Exam alert

Don't be over-ambitious in your role play. Communication is the key, so concentrate on getting the message across from your task sheet.

The two details given here are 'leg' and 'hurts'. Message communicated, along with a nice addition of the adjective 'left'.

## Now try this

 TRACK 23

Now practise the whole role play yourself, including the final two prompts:
4 ? Hilfe – wann
5 ? Holen – was

**Listen to the recording**

# Transport

Don't forget the **time – manner – place** rule when you are writing and translating in German.

## Verkehrsmittel

mit dem Auto / Wagen

mit der Bahn / mit dem Zug

mit dem Boot / Schiff

mit dem Bus

mit dem Rad (Fahrrad)

mit dem Flugzeug

mit dem Lastwagen

mit dem Mofa

mit dem Motorrad

mit der Straßenbahn

zu Fuß

> DB = Deutsche Bahn
> ICE = Inter City-Express

## Time – Manner – Place

> **Grammar page 92**

A detail of transport counts as Manner, so put it **after** a Time expression, but **before** a Place.

 **T**    gestern / heute / letzte Woche / in Zukunft

 **M**    mit dem Zug / zu Fuß / mit meiner Familie

 **P**    nach London / in die Stadt / über die Brücke

> Heute fahre ich mit der U-Bahn in die Stadtmitte. Ich bin letzte Woche mit der Straßenbahn gefahren.

## Worked example

**Die Verkehrsmittel in deiner Stadt**
Deine Austauschpartnerin schickt dir Fragen über die Verkehrsmittel in deiner Stadt. Schreib eine Antwort.

Du **musst** über diesen Punkt schreiben:

• wie du in die Stadt fährst.

> Wenn ich samstags mit meinen Freunden in die Stadt fahre, nehmen wir immer die U-Bahn. Ich finde, dass die U-Bahn praktisch ist.

**Aiming Higher**

> Ich muss nie länger als fünf Minuten warten, jeder Zug kommt pünktlich an.

> Great use of singular **ich fahre** and plural **wir nehmen** structures.

> Giving an opinion with **Ich denke / finde, dass** ... raises the level of your writing.

> This student has added a modal verb and used a comparative adjective, which raises the level more.

## Now try this

Now include the following points and complete the above writing activity:
• wie du zur Schule fährst und warum
• wie du letztes Jahr in den Urlaub gefahren bist und warum
• ob du als Erwachsene/r lieber mit dem Auto oder mit dem Bus fahren wirst und warum.

Schreib ungefähr 80–90 Wörter **auf Deutsch**.

# Travel

Whether it is by car, train or plane, travelling is part of life, so make sure you are secure with the vocabulary on this page.

## Unterwegs

| | |
|---|---|
| Autobahn (f) | motorway |
| Benzin (n) | petrol |
| Fahrt (f) | journey |
| Hubschrauber (m) | helicopter |
| Motor (m) | engine |
| Passagier (m) | passenger |
| Raststätte (f) | motorway services |
| Stau (m) | traffic jam |
| Stoßzeit (f) | rush hour |
| Tankstelle (f) | petrol station |
| Umleitung (f) | diversion |
| öffentliche Verkehrsmittel (npl) | public transport |
| Verspätung haben | to be delayed |

## Opinions

Use Ich glaube, dass (I believe that) or Ich finde, dass (I think that) as handy ways to add an opinion. Dass sends the verb to the end of the clause.

Fahrradwege sind ausgezeichnet.
Cycle paths are excellent.

↓

Ich finde, dass Fahrradwege ausgezeichnet sind.
I think that cycle paths are excellent.

Here are some other adjectives you could use when talking about transport:

| | |
|---|---|
| bequem | comfortable |
| praktisch | practical |
| pünktlich | punctual |
| schädlich | harmful |
| umweltfreundlich | environmentally friendly |

## Worked example

**Travelling**
Read the opinions about travelling.

**Fatma:** Meiner Meinung nach sollte jeder versuchen, öfter mit der Bahn oder mit dem Rad zu fahren, weil die immer steigenden Benzinpreise und die Umweltverschmutzung das Autofahren immer unakzeptabler machen.

**Jake:** Ich finde, es ist erstaunlich, wie viel besser die öffentlichen Verkehrsmittel hier in Berlin sind als bei mir zu Hause in England. Wenn man bei uns mehr Geld in Züge investieren würde, könnten wir vielleicht auch stolz auf unser Verkehrsnetz sein!

Answer the following **in English**.

**(a)** Give **two** reasons why Fatma thinks people should travel by train or bike more. **(2 marks)**

Rising petrol prices and environmental pollution are both reasons why people should use trains or bikes more.

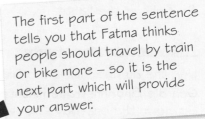

The first part of the sentence tells you that Fatma thinks people should travel by train or bike more – so it is the next part which will provide your answer.

erstaunlich – incredible
stolz auf – proud of

## Exam alert

When you are asked a question in English you have to **answer** in English. You will not score if you answer in German. Also, if the question asks for **two** reasons, make sure you don't write one or three. If you write three, the third one will be ignored.

## Now try this

Now answer these questions on Jake's opinion. You do not need to answer in full sentences.
**(b)** What does Jake think of the public transport in Berlin? **(1 mark)**
**(c)** What would make transport better in England? **(1 mark)**

# Directions

Practise your directions in German by giving yourself a running commentary in your head while you are out and about!

## Richtungen

Gehen Sie ...    Go ... (on foot)
Fahren Sie ...    Drive

links   left      rechts   right

geradeaus    straight on

links um die Ecke
left at the corner

über die Brücke
over the bridge

über den Fluss
over the river

zur Ampel
to the traffic lights

an der Kreuzung links
left at the crossroads

zum Kreisverkehr
to the roundabout

auf der linken Seite
on the left

---

## Instructions using Sie

 **Grammar page 97**

Use the Sie form (-en) of the verb + Sie:
Überqueren Sie die Straße.    Cross the road.
Gehen Sie an der Ampel rechts.
Go right at the lights.

## Instructions using du

Use the du form minus the final -st:
Geh die Einbahnstraße hinunter.
Go down the one-way street.

## Learning vocabulary

✓ Make your own learning cards – German on one side, English on the other; or a picture on one side, German on the other.

✓ Use learning cards to help you revise. Write key words on them as well as structures you find tricky.

an der Kreuzung links

---

## Worked example

 **LISTENING TRACK 24**

### Giving directions

You hear people being given directions.

Listen to the recording and put a cross ✗ in the correct box.

**Listen to the recording**

To get to the market square, go ...

☐ **A** right first of all

☒ **B** over the footbridge

☐ **C** past the lights

☐ **D** left after 100 metres

> – Zum Marktplatz gehen Sie hier gleich links und dann 100 Meter geradeaus. Sie kommen dann zum Fluss, wo es eine Fußgängerbrücke gibt. Gehen Sie hinüber und Sie sehen den Marktplatz auf der rechten Seite.

## Exam alert

In multiple-choice questions, prepare yourself before you listen by trying to say the options to yourself in German. You will be better prepared when you listen!

## Now try this

 **LISTENING TRACK 25**

Now complete the listening activity by selecting the correct option from the worked example for each of these **three** further directions.    **(3 marks)**

**Listen to the recording**

(i) ☐    (ii) ☐    (iii) ☐

# Eating in a café

Lots of these food words look very similar to English, so you should recognise them in a reading or listening passage.

## Im Café essen

| | |
|---|---|
| Bratwurst (f) | fried sausage |
| Erfrischungen (pl) | refreshments |
| Frikadelle (f) | meatball |
| Fruchtsaft (m) | fruit juice |
| Hamburger (m) | hamburger |
| heiße Schokolade (f) | hot chocolate |
| Imbiss (m) | snack |
| Mineralwasser (n) | mineral water |
| Omelett (n) | omelette |
| Pommes (frites) (pl) | chips |
| Salat (m) | salad |
| Schinkenbrot (n) | ham sandwich |
| Schnellimbiss (m) | snack bar |
| Selbstbedienung (f) | self-service |
| Spiegelei (n) | fried egg |
| Einmal / Zweimal ... bitte. | One / Two portion(s) of ... please. |

## Indefinite article (a, an)

Grammar page 86

**Masculine nouns**

- nominative – ein
  Ein Kaffee kostet 3 Euro.
  A coffee costs 3 euros.

- accusative – einen
  Ich hätte gern einen Kaffee.
  I'd like a coffee.

**Feminine nouns**

- nominative and accusative – eine
  Eine Limonade kostet 2,50 Euro.
  A lemonade costs 2.50 euros.
  Ich hätte gern eine Limonade.
  I'd like a lemonade.

**Neuter nouns**

- nominative and accusative – ein
  Ein Käsebrot kostet 4 Euro.
  A cheese sandwich costs 4 euros.
  Ich hätte gern ein Käsebrötchen.
  I'd like a cheese roll.

## Worked example

There is no need for 'of' in German when talking about quantities!
eine Tasse Tee – a cup **of** tea
ein Stück Torte – a piece **of** gateau

**Translation**

Translate this passage **into English**.　(3 marks)

> Samstags gehe ich oft mit meiner Mutter ins Café. Ich bestelle gern eine Limonade und eine Portion Pommes.

Don't miss out **gern** here – what does it tell you?

On Saturdays I often go with my mum to the café. I like to order a lemonade and a portion of chips.

## Identifying tenses

✓ Use **key words** to help identify the tense of each sentence in a translation:
- jetzt (now) and im Moment (at the moment) tell you something is happening now, i.e. in the present tense
- früher (earlier) and gestern (yesterday) indicate the past tense
- nächste Woche (next week) is a future tense time marker.

✓ Use **grammar** to help identify tenses:
- verbs ending in -e, -t, -st, etc. indicate the present tense: ich gehe, sie schläft
- part of haben or sein and a participle starting with ge- at the end of a clause indicates the past tense
- part of werden plus an infinitive at the end indicates the future tense.

## Now try this

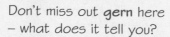  

Now complete the translation.

> Das letzte Mal hat meine Mutter ein Spiegelei bestellt. Dieses Mal bestellt sie etwas anderes.

　　　　　　　　　　　　　　　(4 marks)

# Eating in a restaurant

A restaurant setting might be the focus for an activity, so prepare with this page.

## Im Restaurant

| | |
|---|---|
| Speisekarte (f) | menu |
| Speisesaal (m) | dining room |
| Tagesgericht (n) | dish of the day |
| Menü (n) | set meal |
| Getränk (n) | drink |
| Vorspeise (f) | starter |
| Hauptgericht (n) | main course |
| Nachspeise (f) | dessert |
| Gabel (f) | fork |
| Geschirr (n) | crockery |
| Löffel (m) | spoon |
| Messer (n) | knife |
| Teller (m) | plate |
| gebraten | roast |
| gekocht | cooked |

## Using wenn

**Grammar page 93**

Try to include a complex sentence using wenn to improve your work.

Wenn ich Hunger hätte, würde ich Frikadellen mit Pommes bestellen.

If I were hungry, I would order meatballs and chips.

Wenn ich Vegetarier wäre, würde ich meistens italienisch essen.

If I were a vegetarian, I would eat mostly Italian food.

### Listening strategies

✓ Cognates are easy to spot when you see them, but they can sound slightly different – here, Blog sounds more like 'block', so ask yourself which is more likely in this context?

✓ Listening extracts will have a selection of vocabulary from across all the topics – just because this is titled 'Restaurants in Germany', it does not mean that what you hear will be exclusively restaurant-themed vocabulary.

---

## Worked example

LISTENING TRACK 26

**Restaurants in Germany**

You hear an interview about local restaurants.

Listen to the recording and complete the sentence by putting a cross ✗ in the correct box.

This diner chose the restaurant because ...

☐ **A** of the menu.

☐ **B** of the location.

☒ **C** of a recommendation.

☐ **D** it is new.

Listen to the recording

— Welches Restaurant hast du besucht?

— Das neue gegenüber dem Dom. Das ist eine gute Strecke weg, aber ein Freund hatte es auf seinem Blog beschrieben, also wollte ich es selbst ausprobieren. Er war sehr begeistert davon, aber ich habe die Speisen ziemlich enttäuschend gefunden, muss ich sagen.

## Now try this

LISTENING TRACK 27

Now complete the listening activity by selecting the correct option for these **three** recordings. **(3 marks)**

This diner chose the restaurant because ...

**(i)** ☐ **A** of the view.

☐ **B** of the location.

☐ **C** of the prices.

☐ **D** of the chef.

Listen to the recording

**(ii)** ☐ **A** it is cheap.

☐ **B** it is easy to get to.

☐ **C** it was good last time.

☐ **D** it is new.

**(iii)** ☐ **A** of the menu.

☐ **B** friends own it.

☐ **C** of a recommendation.

☐ **D** it is fashionable.

This speaker says the restaurant is **neu** (option **D**), but that is not **why** she chose it.

# Shopping for food

To buy fruit and vegetables, add a quantity first: ein Kilo (Äpfel) or 400 Gramm (Pilze), bitte! Note that there is no word for 'of' in this context in German.

## Auf dem Markt

| Obst | Fruit | Gemüse | Vegetables |
|---|---|---|---|
| Ananas (f) | pineapple | Blumenkohl(-e) (m) | cauliflower |
| Apfel(¨) (m) | apple | Bohne(-n) (f) | bean |
| Apfelsine(-n) (f) / | orange | Erbse(-n) (f) | pea |
| Orange(-n) (f) | | Gurke(-n) (f) | cucumber |
| Aprikose(-n) (f) | apricot | Karotte(-n) (f) | carrot |
| Banane(-n) (f) | banana | Kartoffel(-n) (f) | potato |
| Birne(-n) (f) | pear | Knoblauch (m) | garlic |
| Erdbeere(-n) (f) | strawberry | Kohl(-e) (m) | cabbage |
| Himbeere(-n) (f) | raspberry | Kopfsalat(-e) (m) | lettuce |
| Kirsche(-n) (f) | cherry | Pilz(-e) (m) | mushroom |
| Pfirsich(-e) (m) | peach | Rosenkohl (m) | Brussels sprout |
| Pflaume(-n) (f) | plum | Spinat (m) | spinach |
| Tomate(-n) (f) | tomato | Zwiebel(-n) (f) | onion |
| Traube(-n) (f) | grape | | |

## Plurals

German nouns all have different plurals. You can look in a dictionary if you are unsure.

An online search for 'Kartoffel plural' gives you the answer instantly:

> Kartoffel (f) (genitive der Kartoffel, plural die Kartoffeln) – potato

The nominative plural word for 'the' is always **die**.

## Reading tips

☑ Go through the text and underline the nouns that are fruit and vegetables – they start with a **capital letter**.

☑ Use cognates, such as Karotten (carrots), and words with a link to an English word, such as Gurke (cucumber), which is similar to 'gherkin'.

## Worked example

**Shopping for food**
Read what these people are buying.

> **Alex** Ich kaufe immer Karotten und manchmal kaufe ich auch eine Gurke.
> **Kai** Im Sommer kaufe ich gern Erdbeeren und Himbeeren, aber im Winter kaufe ich kein Obst.
> **Petra** Ich kaufe oft online, und ich klicke immer Erbsen und Bohnen an, denn sie sind lecker.
> **Edi** Ich kaufe jede Woche ein Kilo Kartoffeln, denn ich liebe Pommes. Ich kaufe auch immer Kirschen, denn das ist mein Lieblingsobst.

Who says what about fruit and vegetables?
Enter either **Alex**, **Kai**, **Petra** or **Edi**.

*Edi* buys potatoes.

## Exam alert

Just because one person has already been the answer to a question, it does not mean they can't still be the answer to another question. Always read the rubric carefully.

## Now try this

Now complete the reading activity. You can use each person more than once.

(a) ........ finds peas tasty. **(1 mark)**
(b) ........ sometimes buys a cucumber. **(1 mark)**
(c) ........ doesn't always buy fruit. **(1 mark)**
(d) ........ loves chips. **(1 mark)**
(e) ........ buys vegetables on the computer. **(1 mark)**

# Opinions about food

If you are giving an opinion on food (or anything else), always justify it: 'I would recommend the restaurant **because** the staff are so friendly.'

## Meinungen über das Essen

mein Lieblingsessen — my favourite food

lecker / schmackhaft — tasty

(un)gesund — (un)healthy

ekelhaft / eklig — disgusting

salzig — salty

Es hat mir (nicht) geschmeckt.

I liked (didn't like) it.

Ich würde das Restaurant (nicht) empfehlen.

I would (not) recommend the restaurant.

Es gab eine große / kleine Auswahl an Gerichten.

There was a big / small selection of dishes.

Meiner Meinung nach war es teuer / billig.

In my opinion it was expensive / cheap.

Ich fand die Vorspeise zu scharf.

I found the starter too spicy.

Das Hähnchen hat besonders gut geschmeckt.

The chicken was particularly tasty.

Ich kann Fastfood nicht ausstehen / leiden.

I can't stand fast food.

## Imperfect tense

Es ist teuer. — It is expensive.

Es war teuer. — It was expensive.

Ich habe Hunger. — I'm hungry.

Ich hatte Hunger. — I was hungry.

Es gibt kein Besteck. — There's no cutlery.

Es gab kein Besteck. — There wasn't any cutlery.

Note the **plural** forms:

Die Tischtücher waren schmutzig.

The tablecloths were dirty.

Meine Freunde hatten Hunger.

My friends were hungry.

Es gab viele Gläser.

There were a lot of glasses.

## Worked example

LISTENING TRACK 28

**Restaurants**

You hear an interview on local radio about a restaurant visit.

Listen to the interview and answer the following question **in English**. You do not need to write in full sentences.

**(a)** Why was Stefan's sister disappointed?  **(1 mark)**

soup was very salty

> — Hat das Essen geschmeckt?
>
> — Mir ja, aber meine Schwester fand die Suppe sehr salzig.

**Listen to the recording**

### Exam alert

You must be precise in your answers to gain the marks. Here, it is specifically the **soup** that was **very salty** so that needs to be written down. You must avoid giving vague answers.

If you don't understand **unhöflich** (rude), it is still worth thinking of an answer after the second hearing rather than leaving a blank. The speaker's **tone of voice** indicates it is something negative, so guess a negative characteristic that a waiter might have.

## Now try this

LISTENING TRACK 29

Now listen to the rest of the interview and answer the following questions **in English**.

**(b)** How did Stefan describe the waiter?  **(1 mark)**

**(c)** Why would Stefan recommend the restaurant to friends? Give **two** reasons.  **(2 marks)**

**Listen to the recording**

Alarm bells should be ringing here – you must write down **two** reasons to answer the question completely.

# Buying gifts

Practise German numbers (see page 108) so you can deal with euro prices on purchases.

## Geschenke kaufen

| | |
|---|---|
| Abteilung (f) | department |
| Andenken (n) | souvenir |
| Auswahl / Wahl (f) | choice |
| Bedienung (f) | service |
| Einkaufszentrum (n) | shopping centre |
| Ermäßigung (f) | reduction |
| Laden (m) / Geschäft (n) | shop |
| Notausgang (m) | emergency exit |
| Quittung (f) | receipt |
| Schaufenster (n) | shop window |
| kaufen | to buy |
| verkaufen | to sell |
| billig | cheap |
| preiswert | good value for money |
| an der Kasse zahlen | to pay at the till |

## Money

100 Cents = 1 Euro

 ein 10-Euro-Schein

 ein 2-Euro-Stück

Be careful with -zehn and -zig numbers in prices.

fünfzehn = 15          fünfzig = 50

siebzehn = 17          siebzig = 70

If you are noting down a price you hear, make sure you get the numbers the right way round:

vierunddreißig = 4 + 30 = 34

---

## Worked example

**READING**

***Emil und die Detektive*** by Erich Kästner
Read the extract from the text.

Emil has arrived in Berlin from his village to visit his grandmother.

> So ein Krach! Und die vielen Menschen auf den Fußsteigen! Und von allen Seiten Straßenbahnen, Fuhrwerke, zweistöckige Autobusse! Zeitungsverkäufer an allen Ecken.
>
> Wunderbare Schaufenster mit Blumen, Früchten, Büchern, goldenen Uhren, Kleidern und seidener Wäsche. Und hohe, hohe Häuser.
>
> Das war alles Berlin.

Answer the following question **in English**. You do not need to write in full sentences.

**(a)** What is Emil's first impression of Berlin?  **(1 mark)**

noisy

## Dealing with a literary text

☑ Don't be afraid of literary texts. They are no different from any other text in the Reading exam – and they give you an interesting insight into German culture.

☑ Use the same strategies as you would with any extract – cognates, context and reading the questions to see which words you really do need to focus on.

☑ The answers in English have to be precise, but there is often more than one way of relaying each answer. For example, the answer to the example question could be 'busy' or 'hectic', as well as 'noisy'.

☑ You will need to use your own words to answer these questions – read the extract through to get the gist first, so you can create a picture of the action in your head.

---

## Now try this

**READING**

Now answer these **three** further questions on the extract **in English**. You do not need to write in full sentences.

**(b)** What is Emil's impression of the shops?  **(1 mark)**

**(c)** Why do you think the shops might have looked expensive to Emil?  **(1 mark)**

**(d)** What strikes Emil about Berlin, apart from the shops and the transport?  **(1 mark)**

# Weather

There are lots of cognates in weather vocabulary, so it shouldn't take you long to master these.

## Das Wetter

 Es ist sonnig.   Es ist kalt.   Es ist neblig.

 Es ist windig.  Es ist heiß.   Es schneit.

 Es ist bewölkt / wolkig.   Es regnet.   Es donnert und blitzt.

Es friert.    It's freezing.
Es hagelt.    It's hailing.
Jahreszeit (f) season
im Frühling   in spring    im Herbst   in autumn
im Sommer     in summer    im Winter   in winter

## Weather in different tenses

Add value to these weather expressions by adapting them to different tenses.

**Present:** Es regnet. It is raining.
**Imperfect:** Es war regnerisch / Es regnete. It was rainy / raining.
**Perfect:** Es hat geregnet. It rained.
**Pluperfect:** Es hatte geregnet. It had rained.
**Future:** Es wird regnen. It will rain.

More weather words in different tenses:

| Es ist / war … | | It is / was … |
| Es wird … sein. | | It will be … |
| bedeckt | overcast | nass | wet |
| frostig | frosty | schlecht | bad |
| heiter | bright | trocken | dry |

## Exam alert

Look out for the **detail**: 'strong winds' is option **D**, but weaker winds are the only type mentioned in the text, so **D** can't be right.

## Worked example

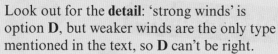

**Weather**
Read the weather forecast.

> Nach Osten hin wird der Wind am Dienstag immer schwächer werden. Höchstwerte liegen bei −14 Grad am Alpenrand und bis −1 Grad an der Ostseeküste. Die Nacht über wird es stark schneien. Es bleibt weiterhin bedeckt.

Put a cross ✗ in the correct box.

What sort of weather is heading for this area?

- ☐ **A** sunshine
- ☐ **B** hail
- ☒ **C** snow
- ☐ **D** strong winds

- Read to the very end of the report to find the word **bedeckt** (cloudy), so you can rule out A 'sunshine'.
- Can you find any reference to hail or hailing in the report? If not, the answer can't be **B** either.
- The minus temperatures and the verb **schneien** (to snow) in the future tense tell you that snow is on the way – answer **C**.

## Now try this

Read the report again and put a cross ✗ in the correct box for these two further questions.

**(i)** What is the wind report?

- ☐ **A** It will be stronger.
- ☐ **B** It is weaker than on Tuesday.
- ☐ **C** It is blowing from the north.
- ☐ **D** It will be weaker.  **(1 mark)**

**(ii)** What is the report for the Alps?

- ☐ **A** It will be colder than the coast.
- ☐ **B** It will be as cold as the coast.
- ☐ **C** It will have rain.
- ☐ **D** It will have a mild night.  **(1 mark)**

# Places to see

When you talk or write about sights you have visited, try to include some comparatives or superlatives to improve your answer.

## Sehenswürdigkeiten

| | |
|---|---|
| Brücke (f) | bridge |
| Brunnen (m) | fountain |
| Denkmal (n) | monument |
| Dom (m) | cathedral |
| Fluss (m) | river |
| Hafen (m) | port |
| Kirche (f) | church |
| Kunstgalerie (f) | art gallery |
| Markt(platz) (m) | market (square) |
| Museum (n) | museum |
| Palast (m) | palace |
| Rathaus (n) | town hall |
| Schloss (n) / Burg (f) | castle |
| Stadion (n) | stadium |
| Theater (n) | theatre |
| Tiergarten (m) / Zoo (m) | zoo |
| Turm (m) | tower |
| | |
| historisch | historic |
| malerisch | picturesque |
| sehenswert | worth seeing |

## Comparisons

**Grammar page 90**

Make your writing more interesting by using **comparatives** and **superlatives**.

| Meine Stadt ist ... My town is ... | interessant. interesting. |
|---|---|
| | interessanter als Hamburg. more interesting than Hamburg. |
| | am interessantesten. the most interesting. |
| | eine der interessantesten Städte in Deutschland. one of the most interesting towns in Germany. |

Florenz ist die schönste Stadt, die ich je besucht habe.

---

## Worked example

### Tourism

Read this tourist information. Answer the following question **in English**. You do not need to write in full sentences.

Stadtzentrum → hin – to

Stadtzentrum ← her – from

---

**Entdecken Sie Rothenburg – die schönste Stadt Deutschlands**

Rothenburg ist eines der beliebtesten Touristenziele in Deutschland. Die kleine Stadt hat viele historische Gebäude wie das Burgtor und das Rathaus, das zu den ältesten Gebäuden der Stadt zählt. Weitere Informationen findet man beim Verkehrsamt in der Innenstadt. Gehen Sie dorthin, um die günstigsten Theaterkarten zu reservieren.

**(a)** Where can you book theatre tickets? **(1 mark)**

You can book tickets at the tourist office.

## Now try this

Now answer these **four** further questions on the text **in English**. You do not need to write in full sentences.

**(b)** How do you know Rothenburg receives lots of visitors? **(1 mark)**

**(c)** Why do you think not many people live there? **(1 mark)**

**(d)** Why might tourists be especially interested in the town hall? **(1 mark)**

**(e)** Where exactly is the tourist office? **(1 mark)**

# At the tourist office

Make sure you are familiar with the places in town vocabulary from page 47 in case you have a role play situation at the tourist office.

## Beim Verkehrsamt

| | |
|---|---|
| Ausflug (m) | trip, outing |
| Ausstellung (f) | exhibition |
| Broschüre (f) | brochure |
| Eintrittsgeld (n) | entry fee |
| Eintrittskarte (f) | entry ticket |
| Ermäßigung (f) | reduction |
| Fahrradverleih (m) | bicycle hire |
| Hotelverzeichnis (n) | hotel list |
| Öffnungszeiten (pl) | opening hours |
| Reservierung (f) | reservation |
| Rundgang (m) | tour (on foot) |
| Rundfahrt (f) | tour (by transport) |
| Veranstaltung (f) | event |
| geschlossen | closed |
| geöffnet | open |
| Guten Aufenthalt! | Enjoy your stay! |
| im Voraus | in advance |

## Using weil, dass, wo (because, that, where)

**Grammar page 93**

Don't be worried by conjunctions that send the verb to the end of the sentence. Learn a few key phrases and it will become natural.

Ich möchte ein Fahrrad mieten, weil die Fahrradwege hier sehr gut sind.
I would like to hire a bike, because the cycle paths are very good here.
Möchten Sie, dass ich die Eintrittskarten reserviere?
Would you like me to reserve the entry tickets?
Ist das die Ausstellung, wo es moderne Kunst gibt?
Is that the exhibition where there is modern art?

Wir möchten wissen, wo es hier einen Fahrradverleih gibt.

## Worked example

**Instructions to candidate:**
You are asking for information in the tourist office in Austria. Your teacher will play the role of the tourist information employee and will speak first. You must address the information employee as *Sie*.

**Task**
Sie suchen Informationen beim Verkehrsamt in einer deutschen Stadt.

**1 Stadt – Meinung und Grund**
– Willkommen! Wie finden Sie unsere Stadt?
– Danke. Die Stadt gefällt mir besonders gut, weil die alten Gebäude so schön sind.

**2 Ausflug – wann und wohin**
– Sehr gut. Wie kann ich Ihnen helfen?
– Ich möchte am Mittwoch an die Küste fahren.

**3 !**
– Toll. Hier ist eine Broschüre. Was haben Sie gestern gemacht?
– Ich habe das Stadtmuseum besucht.
– Sehr schön.

## Aiming higher

✓ Don't lose sight of the question you are being asked or the statement you are responding to. First and foremost in the role play, you need to provide the answer to your prompts.

✓ Make sure you pronounce the German words accurately, and aim to use the correct articles and adjective endings, as this will make your work stand out. In a good way!

An opinion and a reason are needed here. Stay focused to ensure you don't miss either of them out! Here, the use of **weil** + verb to the end shows a competent command of German.

## Now try this

**LISTENING TRACK 30**

Now practise the whole role play yourself, including the final two prompts:
4   ? Einkaufen – wo
5   ? Geschäft – Zeiten

Listen to the recording

# Describing a town

Learn these words so you can write or speak about towns you have visited.

## In der Stadt

| | |
|---|---|
| Bäckerei (f) | baker's |
| Bahnhof (m) | station |
| Bank (f) | bank |
| Bowling (n) | tenpin bowling |
| Buchhandlung (f) | bookshop |
| Eishalle (f) | ice rink |
| Freizeitpark (m) | theme park |
| Freizeitzentrum (n) | leisure centre |
| Hallenbad (n) | indoor swimming pool |
| Kaufhaus (n) | department store |
| Kino (n) | cinema |
| Kneipe (f) / Lokal (n) | pub |
| Lebensmittelgeschäft (n) | grocer's |
| Markt (m) | market |
| Polizeiwache (f) | police station |
| Tankstelle (f) | service station |
| Waschsalon (m) | launderette |
| Zeitungskiosk (m) | newspaper stall |

## Es gibt ... (there is / are ...)

Use es gibt + accusative (einen, eine, ein) in different tenses to help improve your speaking and writing.

**Present:** Es gibt ... There is ...

**Imperfect:** Als ich klein war, gab es ... When I was young, there was ...

**Pluperfect:** Vorher hatte es ... gegeben. Earlier there had been ...

**Future:** In Zukunft wird es ... geben. In future there will be ...

**Conditional:** In meiner idealen Stadt gäbe es ... In my ideal town there would be ...

... eine Eishalle

---

## Adjectives

Make sure you have a good supply of adjectives to express your opinion.

| 😊 | | | | 😞 | | | 😐 | |
|---|---|---|---|---|---|---|---|---|
| großartig | magnificent | sauber | clean | dreckig / schmutzig | dirty | | flach | flat |
| hübsch | pretty | malerisch | picturesque | industriell | | industrial | ruhig | quiet |

---

## Worked example

**Freizeit**
Übersetze **ins Deutsche**.

There is a leisure centre in my town. **(2 marks)**

In meiner Stadt gibt es ein Freizeitzentrum.

## Translating into German

✓ Read the English sentence carefully and check you understand it properly: who or what is it talking about?

✓ It doesn't matter if you start with In meiner Stadt or Es, but you **must** put the verb gibt next so it is in **second** position.

---

## Now try this

Now translate these sentences **into German**.
- **(a)** The department store is very old and expensive. **(2 marks)**
- **(b)** I prefer to shop at the market. **(2 marks)**
- **(c)** Yesterday I went to the cinema. **(2 marks)**
- **(d)** My brother stayed at home because he was tired. **(2 marks)**

Two ways of saying 'because':
**denn** – no change to word order
**weil** – verb to end of clause.
Can't remember 'tired' in German?
How about **hatte keine Energie**?

# Describing a region

Make sure you know the points of the compass, so you can be specific when describing where places are located.

## Eine Gegend

| | | | |
|---|---|---|---|
| Autobahn (f) | motorway | Landschaft (f) | landscape |
| Badeort (m) | seaside resort | Natur (f) | nature |
| Berg (m) | mountain | Ort (m) | place |
| Bundesstraße (f) | main road | See (f) / Meer (n) | sea |
| Bürgersteig (m) | pavement | See (m) | lake |
| Dorf (n) | village | Stadtrand (m) | outskirts (of town) |
| Einwohner (m) | inhabitant | Stadtviertel (n) / | area of town |
| Feld (n) | field | Stadtteil (m) | |
| Gebiet (n) | area | Strand (m) | beach |
| Großstadt (f) | big city | Umgebung (f) | surrounding area |
| Hügel (m) | hill | Vorort (m) | suburb |
| Insel (f) | island | Wald (m) | forest, wood |
| Küste (f) | coast | sich befinden | to be situated |
| Land (n) | (German) state | | |

## North, South, East, West

im Norden

im Westen　im Osten

im Süden

To say NE, NW, SE, SW:
**in Südwestengland** – in south-west England
**in Nordostschottland** – in north-east Scotland

## Describing a region

- When saying where a region is, offer plenty of information and include adjectives (malerisch, einmalig) and interesting verbs (zählt, liegt, umgeben).
- Here is a top-level piece of writing: Der Schwarzwald ist ein malerisches Gebiet, das sich im Südwesten von Deutschland befindet. Die hübschen Städte in dieser Gegend sind von zahlreichen Wäldern und einer großartigen Landschaft umgeben.

Köln – Cologne
München – Munich
Wien – Vienna
Bayern – Bavaria
der Bodensee – Lake Constance
die Donau – the Danube
der Ärmelkanal – the English Channel

## Worked example

**LISTENING TRACK 31**

**Listen to the recording**

**Travel and tourism**
You hear this radio advertisement for the Black Forest.

What do you find out about it?

Look at the example and listen to the recording.

☒ **A** It is an area in south-west Germany.

☐ **B** You can swim in its lakes.

☐ **C** It has good weather.

☐ **D** It has lovely mountains.

☐ **E** The Danube has its origins here.

☐ **F** It is never sunny.

☐ **G** Its river is not well known.

— Der Schwarzwald ist ein wunderbares Gebiet in Südwestdeutschland.

## Now try this

**LISTENING TRACK 32**

Now listen to the rest of the recording and put a cross ✗ by **three** more correct statements.

**(3 marks)**

Listen to the recording

# Tourism

Look at page 47 for places in your town which might be popular with tourists.

## Die Touristik

| | |
|---|---|
| Alpen (pl) | Alps |
| Anmeldung (f) | registration, booking in |
| Aufenthalt (m) | stay |
| im Ausland | abroad |
| Ausländer/in (m/f) | foreigner |
| Besuch (m) | visit |
| Flughafen (m) | airport |
| Gastfreundschaft (f) | hospitality |
| Grünanlage (f) / Park (m) | park |
| Informationsbüro (n) | information office |
| Parkplatz (m) | car park |
| Pauschalreise (f) | package holiday |
| Postkarte (f) | postcard |
| Reisebus (m) | coach |
| Tour (f) | tour |
| Tourist/in (m/f) | tourist |
| Verkehr (m) | traffic |
| Verkehrsamt (n) | tourist office |

## Definite article (the)

Grammar page 85

Three genders and a plural make up the German words for 'the'.

| der – masculine | |
|---|---|
| die – feminine | die – all plurals |
| das – neuter | |

**masculine** – Der Besuch war erfolgreich.
The visit was successful.
**feminine** – Die Grünanlage hat auch einen Spielplatz.
The park also has a playground.
**neuter** – Das Verkehrsamt ist montags geschlossen.
The tourist office is closed on Mondays.
**plural** – Die Alpen sind großartig.
The Alps are magnificent.

## Picture-based task (Foundation)

In your preparation time:

✓ make sure you can **describe** the picture by recalling plenty of relevant adjectives, such as rot, groß, schön, as well as positional words: in, auf der linken Seite, hier im Zentrum and so on.

✓ consider the **four** points that you will have to speak about. Spend a few minutes on each one, noting the tenses you can use and any useful phrases, but remember: you **must not** read out whole prepared sentences.

## Worked example

**Tourist activities**

Schau dir das Foto an und sei bereit, über Folgendes zu sprechen:
• Beschreibung des Fotos.

Das Foto hat man in den Alpen gemacht, denke ich. Die Landschaft ist schön und ruhig, und hier gibt es viele Touristen draußen vor einem Café. Sie sitzen alle in der Sonne, um zu chillen. Meiner Meinung nach sind sie vorher Ski gefahren, und jetzt wollen sie sich ausruhen. Skifahren muss anstrengend sein!

## Now try this

Now prepare to talk on the subject of these bullet points as fully as you can:
• Ob Skifahren umweltfreundlich ist.
• Erzählung von einem Besuch in einer touristischen Stadt.
• Was du gern im Urlaub machst.
• Wo du nächstes Jahr Urlaub machen willst.
Try to speak for at least 30 seconds on each point.

# Countries

Learn countries and nationalities together. Many of them sound like English!

**Länder**
Countries

upper case / lower case → Adjective

| | Länder (Countries) | der / ein (m) | die / eine (f) | Adjective |
|---|---|---|---|---|
| | Spanien | der / ein Spanier | die / eine Spanierin | spanisch |
| | Deutschland | Deutsche / Deutscher | Deutsche | deutsch |
| | England | Engländer | Engländerin | englisch |
| | Frankreich | Franzose | Französin | französisch |
| | Großbritannien | Brite | Britin | britisch |
| | Irland | Ire | Irin | irisch |
| | Italien | Italiener | Italienerin | italienisch |
| | Indien | Inder | Inderin | indisch |
| | Österreich | Österreicher | Österreicherin | österreichisch |
| | Schottland | Schotte | Schottin | schottisch |
| | Wales | Waliser | Waliserin | walisisch |
| | die Schweiz | Schweizer | Schweizerin | schweizerisch |
| | die Türkei | Türke | Türkin | türkisch |
| | die Vereinigten Staaten | Amerikaner | Amerikanerin | amerikanisch |

## Worked example

**Dein letzter Urlaub**

Du nimmst an einem Urlaubswettbewerb teil.

Schreib einen Artikel über deinen letzten Urlaub.

Du **musst** über diesen Punkt schreiben:

• Details über den Urlaub

Obwohl ich letzten Sommer zwei Wochen Urlaub in Italien gemacht habe, hat es mir nicht besonders gut gefallen, weil das Wetter sehr schlecht war.

This is the first part of this student's answer.

## Exam alert

• In the Higher Writing paper you have to choose **one** topic from a choice of **two** to write about. Make sure you spend enough time selecting the topic you will be able to write best about – you will not have time to change your mind halfway through the task.

• Keep a count of the bullet points and your words: here, there are four bullet points, so divide the essay length (130–150 words) by four to remind yourself to write about 35 words for each bullet point.

### Aiming higher

For a higher grade, try to include:

✓ a subordinating conjunction, such as obwohl (although)

✓ dative expressions, such as es hat mir gefallen.

## Now try this

Now include the following points and complete the writing activity:

• was du gemacht hast
• warum andere Leute diesen Urlaub (nicht) genießen würden
• was du im nächsten Urlaub unternehmen wirst.

Rechtfertige deine Ideen und Meinungen.

Schreib ungefähr 130–150 Wörter **auf Deutsch**.

# School subjects

Knowledge of school subject vocabulary is essential for Listening and Reading exams.

## Schulfächer

 Mathe    Biologie    Chemie

 Physik    Deutsch    Englisch

 Französisch    Spanisch    Erdkunde

 Geschichte    Religion    Informatik

 Kunst    Sport    Turnen

## Seit + present tense

To talk about how long you have been doing something, use seit + present tense.

Ich lerne seit vier Jahren Deutsch.
I have been learning German for four years.

Seit (since) is followed by the dative case.

seit vier Monaten
for four months ← **Dative plurals add -n!**

seit diesem Trimester    for this term
seit letztem Jahr        since last year
seit letzter Woche       since last week

Other useful vocabulary:
Pflichtfach (n) – compulsory subject
Theater (n) – drama
Wahlfach (n) – optional subject
Werken (n) – DT

## Worked example

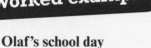 TRACK 33

**Olaf's school day**

**Listen to the recording**

You hear Olaf talking about his day at school. What do you find out?

**(i)** Listen to the recording and complete the sentence by putting a cross ✗ in the correct box.

On Tuesday Olaf arrived at school …

☐ **A** by bike.

☐ **B** on time.

☒ **C** late.

☐ **D** early.

– Am Dienstag habe ich den Bus verpasst und ich bin leider zu spät in der Schule angekommen. ←

spät – late
zu spät – too late
die Verspätung – delay

## Exam alert

Knowledge of vocabulary is essential for Listening exams. Olaf says **ich bin leider zu spät in der Schule angekommen**. If you didn't know that **spät** means 'late', did you pick up on the word **leider** to give you a further clue?

## Now try this

TRACK 34

Now listen to the rest of the recording and put a cross ✗ in the correct box for each sentence.

**Listen to the recording**

**(ii)** At breaktime Olaf …

☐ **A** had a detention.

☐ **B** had fun.

☐ **C** was with friends.

☐ **D** played.          **(1 mark)**

**(iii)** In the first lesson Olaf …

☐ **A** had his favourite subject.

☐ **B** was in a science room.

☐ **C** got on well with his partner.

☐ **D** annoyed his partner.          **(1 mark)**

# Opinions about school

You may be asked to express your opinion about school in at least one part of the Speaking exam – the role play, talking about a photo or in general conversation.

## Meinungen über die Schule

Meiner Meinung nach ist Chemie viel einfacher als Biologie.
In my opinion chemistry is much easier than biology.

Ich finde, dass Mathe sehr schwierig ist.
I think that maths is very difficult.

Ich bin stark / schwach in Deutsch.
I am good / weak in German.

Es ist gut, dass ich in der Schule oft erfolgreich bin.
It's good that I am often successful at school.

Die Lehrer sind echt streng / sympathisch.
The teachers are really strict / nice.

Es gefällt mir (nicht), in die Schule zu gehen.
I (don't) like going to school.

Ich mag es (nicht), wenn Stunden ausfallen.
I (don't) like it when lessons are cancelled.

Ich finde den Schultag sehr anstrengend / abwechslungsreich.
I find the school day very tiring / varied.

## Intensifiers

Use intensifiers to reinforce your opinion.

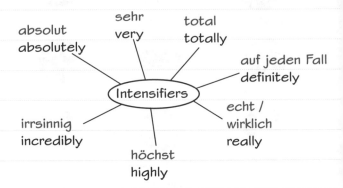

absolut absolutely   sehr very   total totally   auf jeden Fall definitely   echt / wirklich really   höchst highly   irrsinnig incredibly

Intensifiers

Ich finde Deutsch echt super.
I find German really great.

Spanisch ist sehr schwierig.
Spanish is very difficult.

Mein Lieblingsfach ist auf jeden Fall Werken.
My favourite subject is definitely DT.

In Geschichte habe ich absolut keine Probleme.
In history I have absolutely no problems.

---

## Worked example

**School**

Beantworte diese Frage:

• Wie findest du deine Schule?

> Meiner Meinung nach ist Mathe sehr schwierig, besonders wenn man kein fleißiger Schüler ist. Ich finde Sport viel besser, weil wir nie Klassenarbeiten schreiben müssen.

> **Aiming Higher**
> Es ist absolut fair, dass Rauchen auf dem Schulgelände streng verboten ist, weil Rauchen sowieso schlecht für die Gesundheit ist. Die Schule kann sehr stressig sein. Wenn ich schlechte Noten bekomme, werde ich auch ein schlechtes Zeugnis bekommen, und dann werden meine Eltern sehr böse sein. In der Grundschule hatte man keine Prüfungen, keinen Stress.

This student offers a couple of opinions and uses a **modal** with a conjunction, but it is all in the **present** tense.

Look at how this student uses a **variety** of elements and structures to give opinions about school:
• intensifiers
• present, future and past tenses
• modal verb
• **dass**, **weil** and **wenn** clauses.

## Now try this

Now prepare to answer these questions as fully as you can.
• Wie findest du deine Schulfächer?
• Was war der beste Tag in der Schule letztes Jahr?
• Ist die Schule stressig für dich?
Try to speak for at least 30 seconds on each point.

Use the tips above to make sure you include plenty of variety in your Speaking answers.

# School day

To understand and talk about a typical school day, you need a secure knowledge of times and days of the week which you'll find in the Grammar section on page 113.

## Der Schultag

Die erste Stunde beginnt um zehn vor neun.
The first lesson starts at ten to nine.
Wir haben sechs Stunden pro Tag.
We have six lessons each day.
In der Pause gehen wir auf den Schulhof.
At break we go to the playground.
Wir essen zu Mittag in der Kantine.
We eat lunch in the canteen.
Man kann in der Bibliothek Hausaufgaben machen.
You can do homework in the library.
Nach der Schule gibt es ein gutes Angebot an AGs.
After school there is a good selection of clubs.
Sport haben wir immer als Doppelstunde.
We always have a double lesson for PE.

## Linking words

These make your sentences longer and they **don't** change the word order!

| aber | but | oder | or |
| denn | because | und | and |

Man muss viel lernen und der Leistungsdruck ist enorm.
You have to learn a lot and the pressure to achieve is huge.

In der Pause plaudern wir **oder** wir machen Hausaufgaben.
At break we chat or we do homework.

## Worked example

*Stundenplan* by Christine Nöstlinger
Read the extract from the text. It describes a girl's day at school.

Anika geht aus der Klasse. Sie geht zum Waschraum, der am weitesten von der 4a entfernt ist. Sie geht an Türen vorbei, hinter denen es still ist, an Türen, hinter denen eine Stimme zu hören ist. Eine Stimme mag sie. Die erste Stimme sagt: »… trat in die Dienste des Prinzen Karl August von Sachsen-Weimar …«

Es ist eine langsame Mitschreibestimme. »Sachsen-Weimar«, sagt die Stimme noch einmal, »Sachsen-Weimar«. Vorne sind Schritte. Schnelle Schritte, Lehrerschritte. Schüler, die während der Unterrichtsstunde auf den Gängen sind, gehen nie so schnell.

Anika verschwindet im Waschraum.

Look at the example and read the text again.

☐ **A** She goes to a class nearby.
☐ **B** The school is completely silent.
☒ **C** Anika hears different people.
☐ **D** One voice is teaching about a prince.
☐ **E** Pupils should be copying details down.
☐ **F** Pupils are walking in the corridors.
☐ **G** Anika is not to be seen at the end.

## Reading tips

✓ Don't ignore the example answer – it is there to help you get into the text.

✓ Anika hears something, so even if you don't know exactly what she heard (Stimme = voice), you still know statement **B** must be wrong.

✓ If you change your mind about your three answers, make sure you clearly **cross out** any answer you don't want.

✓ Put crosses in only **three** of the boxes.

Sometimes you have to **infer** meaning. The text says that pupils who walk in the corridors never go that quickly, so statement **F** cannot be correct.

## Now try this

Now complete the activity on the left by putting a cross **X** next to **three** more correct statements.

# Types of schools

Make sure you are familiar with the German school system and types of schools, so you recognise a school if you hear or read about it!

## Deutsche Schulen

| | |
|---|---|
| Direktor (m) / Direktorin (f) | head teacher |
| Schulleiter (m) / Schulleiterin (f) | head teacher |
| Berufsschule (f) | vocational school |
| Gesamtschule (f) | comprehensive school |
| Grundschule (f) | primary school |
| Gymnasium (n) | grammar school |
| Hauptschule (f) | type of secondary school |
| Internat (n) | boarding school |
| Kindergarten (m) | pre-school |
| Privatschule (f) | private school |
| Realschule (f) | type of secondary school |
| Trimester / Semester (n) | term / semester |
| lernen | to learn |
| lehren / unterrichten | to teach |
| staatlich | state |
| gemischt | mixed |

## sich freuen auf + accusative

To talk about something you are looking forward to, use the verb sich freuen auf + the accusative case. So, if talking about school-related topics, you might say:

Ich freue mich (nicht) auf ...
I am (not) looking forward to ...

| | |
|---|---|
| den Druck (m) | the pressure |
| die Klassenfahrt (f) | the school trip |
| das Schuljahr (n) | the school year |
| die Prüfungen (fpl) | the exams |

Ich freue mich auf die Klassenfahrt.

---

## Worked example

**Deine Schule**

Dein Freund schickt dir Fragen über deine Schule. Schreib eine Antwort an ihn.
Du **musst** über diesen Punkt schreiben:

• Beschreibung von deiner Schule

> Ich gehe auf eine Gesamtschule mit etwa tausend Schülern und Schülerinnen. Als ich in die siebte Klasse kam, war ich sehr nervös, weil das Schulgebäude einfach so groß und imposant war.

**Aiming Higher**

> In der elften Klasse bin ich jetzt viel selbstbewusster und ich fange an, mich richtig auf die Oberstufe zu freuen. Hoffentlich werde ich bei den Prüfungen nicht durchfallen, damit ich nächstes Jahr das Abitur machen kann.

This extract is a good piece of writing, as it includes:
• present and past tenses
• als + opinion + weil clause
• an interesting adjective (imposant).

Add some additional features to achieve the best possible response:
• inverted sentences
• a comparative
• anfangen + zu + infinitive construction
• an idiom: sich freuen auf
• hoffentlich + future tense.

---

## Now try this

Now include the following points and complete the above writing activity:
• worauf du dich in der Schule am meisten freust
• wie du in der siebten Klasse warst
• deine Pläne für das nächste Trimester.
Schreib ungefähr 80–90 Wörter **auf Deutsch**.

# School facilities

Familiarise yourself with the rooms in a school so you can be specific in a description.

## Das Schulgelände

| | |
|---|---|
| Aula (f) | school hall |
| Bibliothek (f) | library |
| Computerraum (m) | computer room |
| Gang (m) | corridor |
| Kantine (f) | canteen |
| Klassenzimmer (n) | classroom |
| Labor (n) | laboratory |
| Lehrerzimmer (n) | staffroom |
| Schulhof (m) | playground |
| Sekretariat (n) | office |
| Sporthalle (f) | sports hall |
| Toiletten (fpl) | toilets |
| gut / schlecht ausgestattet | well / badly equipped |
| modern / altmodisch | modern / old-fashioned |
| neu gebaut | newly built |

## Relative pronouns

Relative pronouns translate as 'who', 'that', 'which'. They agree with the noun they are referring to and send the verb to the end of the clause.

Hier ist ein Schüler, der (m) auf den Bildschirm starrt.
Here is a pupil who is staring at the screen.
Hier ist eine Schülerin, die (f) einen Schal trägt.
Here is a pupil who is wearing a scarf.
Hier ist ein Klassenzimmer, das (n) altmodisch ist.
Here is a classroom that is old-fashioned.
Dort sind die Toiletten, die (pl) immer sauber sind.
There are the toilets, which are always clean.

## Describing a photo

- ✓ Give your opinion of the photo, saying what you think of the room pictured. Don't just identify it as a computer room.
- ✓ Compare the room to your school, saying whether you have lessons in a computer room and, if so, which ones and when.
- ✓ Try to use a different verb in each sentence to add variety to your work.

## Worked example

**SPEAKING**

### In the classroom

Schau dir das Foto an und sei bereit, über Folgendes zu sprechen:

- Beschreibung des Fotos

> **Aiming Higher**
>
> Hier ist ein Foto von einer Schulklasse beim Unterricht im Computerraum. In dieser Reihe sitzen drei Schüler am Computer und zwei schauen auf den Bildschirm. Im Hintergrund sehe ich eine Schülerin, die mit der Lehrerin sprechen will. Die Lehrerin lächelt. Vorne rechts gibt es einen Jungen, der ein buntes Hemd trägt, und neben ihm sehe ich ein Mädchen, das eine Brille trägt und die Lehrerin anschaut.

Describing a photo is a great opportunity to use relative pronouns to help your work flow better.

## Now try this

**SPEAKING**

Now prepare to talk on the subject of these bullet points as fully as you can:
- Ob deine Schule gut ausgestattet ist.
- Die beste Schulstunde, die du je gehabt hast.
- Was du an deiner Schule ändern möchtest.
- !

Try to speak for at least 30 seconds on each point.

At Higher level, you need to answer an unexpected question at the end of your description. Be ready to listen to the question and answer it accordingly!

# School rules

Use modal verbs müssen (to have to) and dürfen (to be allowed to) with an infinitive verb when talking about rules at school – or at home.

## Die Schulordnung

Die Regeln sind total ...
The rules are totally ...

| | |
|---|---|
| (un)fair / (un)gerecht. | (un)fair. |
| dumm / blöd. | stupid. |
| nervig / ärgerlich. | annoying. |
| Strafarbeit (f) | lines, written punishment |
| nachsitzen | to have a detention |
| Man muss ... | You have to ... |
| die Hausaufgaben machen. | do the homework. |
| im Klassenzimmer ruhig sein. | be quiet in class. |
| den Müll trennen. | sort the rubbish. |

Man darf nicht rauchen.
You are not allowed to smoke.
Man darf die Stunden nicht schwänzen.
You are not allowed to skip lessons.
Man darf keine ...   You are not allowed to ...
  Kopfhörer im Unterricht tragen.
  wear headphones in lessons.
  Sportschuhe in der Schule tragen.
  wear trainers to school.

## Using müssen (to have to)

Grammar page 98

Müssen is a modal verb, so it needs an infinitive:
Man muss Hausaufgaben machen.
You have to do homework.

| Man muss ... You have to ... | höflich sein.   be polite. |
|---|---|
| | viel üben, um ein Instrument zu spielen. practise a lot to play an instrument. |
| | sich ordentlich anziehen. dress smartly. |
| | sitzen bleiben. repeat a school year. |

## Translating into English

- ✓ Make sure you have learned plenty of vocabulary across all the topics before the exam – that way translations like this will be much easier.
- ✓ Don't ignore qualifiers and words such as mindestens – they all need to be translated.
- ✓ Look for word families to help you understand unfamiliar vocabulary: mindestens is linked to Minderheit (minority).
- ✓ Use common sense – the two pencil case items are the basic equipment needed, so they are unlikely to be a fountain pen and a protractor.
- ✓ If you come across a conjunction, such as wo or weil, look to the end of the clause to find the accompanying verb(s).

## Worked example

### Translation

Translate this passage **into English**.        (2 marks)

> Ich besuche eine Schule, wo die Schulordnung total dumm ist, weil man mindestens einen Bleistift und ein Lineal im Etui haben muss.

I go to a school where the rules are really stupid, because you have to have at least a pencil and a ruler in your pencil case.

Note how the English translation of **die Schulordnung ... ist** becomes 'the rules are'. Translating means using English terms, and not just doing a word-for-word translation: 'the school order ... is' does not make sense.

## Now try this

Now complete the translation.        (5 marks)

> Letztes Trimester hat ein Schüler auf dem Schulhof geraucht, weil er das cool gefunden hat. Der Direktor war aber sehr böse und hat den Jungen sofort nach Hause geschickt. Ich würde in der Schule nie rauchen oder Alkohol trinken, weil ich keine Strafarbeit bekommen möchte.

# Pressures at school

Learn a few key phrases to talk about problems and pressures at school.

## Der Schulstress

| | |
|---|---|
| Elternsprechabend (m) | parents' evening |
| Note (f) | grade |
| Zeugnis (n) | report |
| Angst vor den Noten haben | |
| to be anxious about the grades | |
| das Jahr wiederholen | to repeat the year |
| sitzenbleiben | to repeat a year |
| durchfallen | to fail (an exam) |

Die Prüfungen finde ich stressig.
I find exams stressful.

Wir stehen unter großem Leistungsdruck.
We are under a lot of pressure to achieve.

Viele Schüler leiden unter Schulstress.
Many pupils suffer from stress at school.

Ich bin oft abwesend, weil es mir schlecht
  geht. I am often absent because I feel ill.

Die Lehrer fehlen oft, weil sie gestresst
  sind. The teachers are often absent
  because they are stressed.

## Obwohl

Grammar page 93

Obwohl (although) is a subordinating conjunction which sends the verb to the end of the clause, like weil.

Obwohl es eine kleine Schule ist, gibt
  es hier viele AGs.
Although it is a small school, there are
  lots of clubs here.

Er ist zur Schule gegangen, obwohl er
  schreckliche Kopfschmerzen hatte.
He went to school, although he had a
  terrible headache.

Wir müssen viel arbeiten.
We have to work hard.

## Worked example

WRITING

**Schule**
Übersetze **ins Deutsche**.

> Today there is great pressure to achieve at school.
> In the past you could go to school to enjoy lessons
> and play with friends.

Aiming Higher

Heute gibt es großen Leistungsdruck in
der Schule. In der Vergangenheit konnte
man zur Schule gehen, um den Unterricht zu
genießen und mit Freunden zu spielen.

## Translating into German

✓ Grammar is the key to translations
  into German, so make sure you are
  confident with verbs and pronouns
  in the main tenses: present, past,
  future and conditional.

✓ Get your word order right –
  unless there is a subordinating
  conjunction (e.g. dass), the verb
  has to come in second place.

For the highest marks, you have to
show you can use subordinating
conjunctions, such as **weil, um ... zu**
and **obwohl** with a variety of tenses.

## Exam alert

Although the first sentence in a translation might appear 'easy', make sure you don't slip up with a silly mistake: check the tense, word order and any adjective agreements before you move on to the more challenging second sentence.

## Now try this

WRITING

Now complete the translation **into German**.

> Although pupils have to do tests frequently these days, we can still really look forward to class trips.
> If I study hard to get good grades, I will also perhaps get a present from my parents – and that
> would be great!

# Primary school

Talking about your primary school offers a great opportunity to use the imperfect tense.

## School equipment

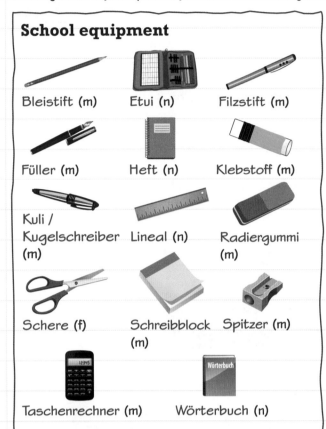

Bleistift (m)  Etui (n)  Filzstift (m)

Füller (m)  Heft (n)  Klebstoff (m)

Kuli / Kugelschreiber (m)  Lineal (n)  Radiergummi (m)

Schere (f)  Schreibblock (m)  Spitzer (m)

Taschenrechner (m)  Wörterbuch (n)

## Modals – imperfect tense

Grammar page 99

kann – can  ➡ konnte – could
muss – have to  ➡ musste – had to
darf – am allowed  ➡ durfte – was allowed
will – want  ➡ wollte – wanted
soll – am supposed to  ➡ sollte – should
mag – like  ➡ mochte – liked

| In der Grundschule ... At primary school ... | konnte ich kein Französisch sprechen. I couldn't speak French. musste ich mit meiner Mutter zur Schule gehen. I had to go to school with my mum. durfte ich kein Handy haben. I wasn't allowed a mobile. |
|---|---|

Using an imperfect modal is a good indicator that you are aiming high.

## Worked example

 READING

**At primary school**

Read the text.
The writer remembers childhood family life.

> In der Grundschule habe ich mich immer gut benommen, aber Tim wollte nie machen, was von ihm verlangt wurde. Meine Eltern sagten Tim, dass er mehr wie ich sein sollte. Wenn ich etwas Dummes machte, lachte mein Vater immer, aber mit Tim war er immer böse.

## Exam alert

For this task, good comprehension skills are needed, as well as an ability to draw conclusions from the text. The questions are not phrased in exactly the same way as they appear in the text, so be careful!

Put a cross ✗ in the correct box.
When Tim was younger, he ...

☒ **A** was not very obedient at school.

☐ **B** was a well-behaved pupil.

☐ **C** did not go to primary school.

☐ **D** was just like his brother.

## Now try this

 READING

Read the text again and put a cross ✗ in the correct box.

Their dad reacted to Tim and his brother ...

☐ **A** proudly.

☐ **B** in the same way.

☐ **C** in different ways.

☐ **D** negatively.

# Success at school

Talking about success at school can cover other topic areas – look at sport and volunteering for ideas of success at school.

## Wir feiern!

| | |
|---|---|
| Erfolg (m) | success |
| Leistung (f) | achievement |
| Erfolg feiern | to celebrate success |
| gratulieren | to congratulate |
| begabt | gifted, talented |
| erfolgreich | successful |
| gut in der Klasse aufpassen | to pay attention in class |
| ein gutes Zeugnis bekommen | to get a good report |
| Fortschritte machen | to make progress |
| die Prüfung bestehen | to pass the exam |
| einen Preis gewinnen | to win a prize |
| den zweiten Platz erreichen | to achieve second place |

## Dative verb gelingen (to succeed)

The dative verb gelingen works in the same way as gefallen (to like): es gefällt mir (I like it).

Es gelingt mir, die beste Note in der Klasse zu bekommen. I succeed in getting the best grade in the class.
Gestern ist es mir gelungen, einen Preis zu gewinnen.
Yesterday I succeeded in winning a prize.
Es gelingt ...

| | | | |
|---|---|---|---|
| mir | (me) | uns | (us) |
| dir | (you) | euch | (you – pl) |
| ihm | (him) | ihnen / Ihnen | (them / you – |
| ihr | (her) | | polite) |

Es ist mir gelungen, das Abitur zu bestehen! I succeeded in passing my A levels!

---

## Worked example

**Prize day interview**

Your penfriend Sonja has sent you a podcast of her interview as a school prize winner.

**Listen to the recording**

**(i)** Listen to the interview and put a cross ✗ in the correct box.

Sonja ...

☐ **A** finds her prize really unimportant.
☒ **B** wants to achieve more.
☐ **C** is satisfied with her level of achievement.
☐ **D** can't concentrate on her exams.

Recycle useful expressions you come across in audioscripts in your speaking and writing tasks:
der Höhepunkt – highlight
ohne Zweifel – without doubt
ehrlich gesagt – to be honest

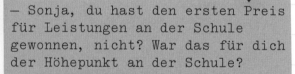

– Sonja, du hast den ersten Preis für Leistungen an der Schule gewonnen, nicht? War das für dich der Höhepunkt an der Schule?

– Ein Höhepunkt war das ohne Zweifel, aber ehrlich gesagt ist es mir wichtiger, jetzt noch fleißiger zu arbeiten, um noch bessere Leistungen zu erreichen. Nächstes Jahr hoffe ich, in die Oberstufe zu kommen, also muss ich mich auf die Prüfungen konzentrieren.

---

## Now try this

Now listen to the next part of the interview and put a cross ✗ in the correct box.

**Listen to the recording**

**(ii)** Sonja ...
☐ **A** met the mayor at primary school.
☐ **B** had her photo taken with the mayor.
☐ **C** took part in a competition at secondary school.
☐ **D** is unhappy that her photo can be found online.

**(1 mark)**

You need to infer the answer here – it isn't going to be spelled out for you!

# Class trips

German, Swiss and Austrian schools all organise annual class trips, so you may come across one in your exams!

## Die Klassenfahrt

einmal im Schuljahr   once in a school year
mit der Klasse wegfahren
to go away with the class
einander besser kennenlernen
to get to know each other better
miteinander gut / schlecht auskommen
to get on well / badly with each other
neue Sportarten ausprobieren
to try new sports

| | |
|---|---|
| Erfahrungen sammeln | to collect experiences |
| Wanderwoche (f) | walking week |
| Wochenprogramm (n) | week's agenda |
| im Wald | in the forest |
| in den Bergen | in the mountains |
| im Freien | in the outdoors |
| Heimweh haben | to be homesick |

ein positives / negatives Erlebnis
a positive / negative experience

## Giving your opinion

Make it clear when you are giving an opinion rather than stating a fact.

| | | |
|---|---|---|
| Ich | finde, denke, meine, glaube, | Klassenfahrten sind super. das Wochenprogramm ist interessant. das wird eine positive Erfahrung sein. |

For a reminder of how to use Ich finde, dass + verb to the end, see 'Opinions' on page 39.

Wir lieben die Klassenfahrt!
We love the class trip!

---

## Worked example

SPEAKING

### School trip

Sei bereit, über Folgendes zu sprechen:

• Ob eine Klassenfahrt immer positiv ist?

> Meiner Meinung nach machen Klassenfahrten immer viel Spaß, weil man eine Woche weg von der Schule und den Eltern verbringt.
> Letztes Jahr bin ich auf Klassenfahrt nach Leipzig gefahren und das war ein wunderbares Erlebnis.

**Aiming Higher**

> Das Wochenprogramm war besonders interessant, weil wir jeden Tag etwas Neues unternommen haben. Am Ende des Tages waren wir so erschöpft, dass wir sofort eingeschlafen sind. Ich stelle mir vor, die Lehrer waren darüber besonders zufrieden.

This student has included the conjunctions **weil** and **so ... dass**, as well as an infinitive verb construction: **ich stelle mir vor, ...**

## Exam alert

Read every word on the exam card – words like **immer** (always) are important.

If there is an **ob** at the start of a question, it is asking you 'whether' the statement is true: here, whether a class trip is always positive, or not.

Give your opinion using a phrase such as **meiner Meinung nach** + verb next. A great way to start!

Don't hang around in the present tense for too long, but move your conversation along by talking about a related experience you **had** in the past.

## Now try this

SPEAKING

Now prepare to answer the question in the worked example as fully as you can. Try to speak for at least 30 seconds.

# School exchange

You will have to ask one (Foundation) or two (Higher) questions in the role play section of the Speaking exam – make sure you are confident with doing just that.

## Asking questions in two ways

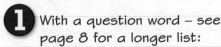 With a question word – see page 8 for a longer list:

| Wo? | Where? |
|---|---|
| Wer? | Who? |
| Was? | What? |

**2** By inverting a sentence:

Wir treffen uns. ➡ Treffen wir uns?

Du fährst auf Austausch. ➡ Fährst du auf Austausch?

### Auf Austausch

| | |
|---|---|
| Austauschpartner (m) / Austauschpartnerin (f) | exchange partner |
| Austauschschule (f) | exchange school |
| Besuch (m) | visit |
| Brieffreund (m) / Brieffreundin (f) | penfriend |
| Gastfamilie (f) | host family |
| zu Besuch sein | to be visiting |
| gut / schlecht miteinander auskommen | to get on well / badly with each other |
| Tagesausflüge machen | to go on day trips |
| die Sehenswürdigkeiten besichtigen | to go sightseeing |
| Die Tagesroutine hat mir (nicht) gefallen. | I liked (didn't like) the daily routine. |
| Das Essen hat mir (nicht) geschmeckt. | I liked (didn't like) the food. |
| Die Woche war ein großer Erfolg. | The week was a big success. |
| Ich möchte wieder dorthin fahren. | I would like to go there again. |

## Worked example

**Instructions to candidate:** You are on the German school exchange. You meet up with your exchange partner. Your teacher will play the part of your exchange partner and will speak first. You must address the exchange partner as *du*.

**Task**

Ich bin dein Austauschpartner / deine Austauschpartnerin und wir treffen uns in der Mittagspause an der Schule in Deutschland.

**1 Schule – Meinung und Grund**

– Hallo, wie findest du es hier in der Schule?
– Es gefällt mir hier gut, weil man keine Uniform tragen muss.

**2 Meinung zum Schultag**

– Wie findest du den Schultag bei uns?
– Die Schule beginnt zu früh, denke ich, aber es freut mich, dass man nachmittags nicht in der Schule ist.

**3 !**

– Wie hast du die letzte Stunde gefunden?
– Englisch war sehr einfach, habe ich gedacht.

### Exam alert

Get the register right – here, you are talking to somebody the same age as you, so use **du**.

Two pieces of information required here (opinion + reason) = two pieces communicated. Job done!

The student has prepared this answer in the preparation time – this makes the prompt easier to tackle.

A straightforward reply is required here – no need to embellish it but just ensure you respond accurately, using the correct tense: here, past.

## Now try this

Now practise the whole role play yourself, including the final two prompts. Listen to the audio file containing the teacher's part and fill in the pauses with your answers:

Listen to the recording
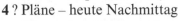

4 ? Pläne – heute Nachmittag

5 ? Schlafen – wann

# School events

Make sure you know about lots of different activities that go on at school – competitions, productions, concerts, sport, festivals and so on.

## Schulveranstaltungen

in der Theatergruppe sein
to be in the drama club
die Schülerzeitung produzieren
to produce the school newspaper
an einem Wettbewerb teilnehmen
to take part in a competition
beim Lesefest mitmachen
to take part in the reading festival
im Orchester mitspielen
to play in the orchestra
an einer Debatte teilnehmen
to take part in a debate
Mitglied der Mannschaft sein
to be a member of the team
Die Veranstaltung wird in der Bibliothek stattfinden.
The event will take place in the library.
Interessierst du dich für den Kuchenverkauf?
Are you interested in the cake sale?

## Verbs with prepositions

Some verbs are always followed by a preposition, so learn the parts together.

- Some take the accusative case:
  sich konzentrieren auf    to concentrate on
  sich interessieren für    to be interested in
  Ich muss mich auf die Kunstausstellung konzentrieren.
  I must concentrate on the art exhibition.

- And some take the dative case:
  Angst vor ... haben    to be anxious about
  teilnehmen an    to take part in

Ich habe Angst vor dem Schulfußballspiel.
I am anxious about the school football match.

## Worked example

**School competition**
You hear an interview on school radio about a competition. What is said?
**(a)** Choose the **two** correct answers.

Listen to the recording

☒ A The competition was a great success.
☐ B The competition was a disaster.
☐ C The competition is new.
☐ D The first play was unusual.
☐ E The cast were not very good.
☐ F The productions were fantastic.

**(2 marks)**

– Gestern Abend hat der Theaterwettbewerb unter großem Applaus in der Aula stattgefunden. Seit fünf Jahren läuft jetzt diese beliebte Veranstaltung und dieses Jahr waren die Theaterproduktionen besser als je zuvor!

Parts of words can lead you to the meaning – here, **je zuvor** is related to **vor** (before) and means 'ever before'.

## Now try this

Now listen to the rest of the recording so that you can complete activity **(a)** on the left and do activity **(b)** below.

Listen to the recording

**(b)** Choose the **two** correct answers.

☐ A Class 8 performed an old-fashioned piece.
☐ B Their outfits were impressive.
☐ C The play was a bit ordinary.
☐ D The play was well received.
☐ E The audience were not very impressed.
☐ F The audience were mainly parents.

**(2 marks)**

The fact that the competition happened **unter großem Applaus** indicates that it was a success. The recording is not going to spell out to you 'it was a success' – you have to glean this from the context of the piece.

# Future study

Talking about future plans enables you to say what you **want** to do over the next few years.

## Sich weiterbilden

| | |
|---|---|
| Ich möchte / werde … | I would like to / will … |
| in die Oberstufe gehen. | go into the sixth form. |
| einen Studienplatz bekommen. | get a university place. |
| auf die Uni(versität) gehen. | go to uni(versity). |
| die Prüfungen wiederholen. | retake the exams. |
| in die Weiterbildung gehen. | do further education. |
| (Wirtschaftslehre) studieren. | study (economics). |
| Mittlere Reife (f) | GCSE equivalent |
| Abitur (Abi) (n) | A level equivalent |
| Abiturient (m) / Abiturientin (f) | person doing the 'Abitur' |
| Student (m) / Studentin (f) | student (uni) |
| Abschlussprüfung (f) | school leaving exam |
| Schulabschluss (m) | school leaving certificate |
| Hochschulabschluss (m) | degree |
| Hochschulbildung (f) | higher education |
| Berufsberater/in (m/f) | careers adviser |
| Kurs (m) | course |
| Resultat / Ergebnis (n) | result |
| Qualifikation (f) | qualification |

## Using wollen (to want to)

> **Grammar page 98**

Wollen is a modal verb, so it needs an infinitive.

Ich will in die Oberstufe gehen.
I want to go into the sixth form.

> Don't confuse the German will (meaning 'want to') with the English 'will' (future intent).

| Ich will … I want to … | weiterbilden. carry on studying. |
|---|---|
| | auf die Universität gehen. go to university. |
| | eine Lehre machen. do an apprenticeship. |
| | an der Uni Englisch und Geschichte studieren. study English and history at university. |

## Worked example

🗣 SPEAKING

### Nächstes Jahr

Beantworte diese Frage:

• Was möchtest du nächstes Jahr machen?

*Aiming higher*

Gleich nach den Prüfungen will ich ein Wochenende mit meiner Clique an der Küste verbringen. Ich freue mich irrsinnig darauf, obwohl meine Eltern nicht so begeistert darüber sind. Nächstes Trimester werde ich hoffentlich in die Oberstufe kommen, wenn ich die notwendigen Noten bekomme. Ich will Fremdsprachen und Mathe lernen, weil ich eines Tages gern im Ausland arbeiten möchte.

## Exam alert

You will need to speak on both your prepared and unprepared conversation topics for an equal amount of time, so have plenty of practice conversations in advance to prepare.

Avoid long pauses by using fillers such as **Moment mal, Tja, Wie ich (schon) gesagt habe, Zum Beispiel.**

### Aiming higher

✓ Go for **quality** not quantity. Allow plenty of time for interaction to show that you can understand and respond to what the teacher says.

✓ You will get no credit for repeating language from other parts of your Speaking exam, so make sure you have a solid supply of **language** across **all topic areas**.

## Now try this

LISTENING TRACK 40

Now prepare to answer the following questions and speak for one minute without **hesitating** or **repeating** yourself!

• Warum sind Pläne dir wichtig oder nicht wichtig?
• Welche Pläne hattest du in der Grundschule?
• Warum können sich Pläne oft ändern?

> Record yourself and listen back to hear how German you sound.

# Jobs

Make sure you know both the male and female versions of the jobs listed below.

### Arbeit

| | |
|---|---|
| Angestellter (m) / Angestellte (f) | employee |
| Arbeitgeber/in | employer |
| Bäcker/in | baker |
| Bauarbeiter/in | builder |
| Bauer (m) / Bäuerin (f) | farmer |
| Elektriker/in | electrician |
| Fahrer/in | driver |
| Fleischer/in / Metzger/in | butcher |
| Flugbegleiter/in | cabin crew |
| Kassierer/in | cashier |
| Kellner/in | waiter / waitress |
| Klempner/in | plumber |
| Mechaniker/in | mechanic |
| Modeschöpfer/in | fashion designer |
| Techniker/in | technician |
| Tischler/in | carpenter / joiner |
| Vertreter/in | sales rep |

Mein Bruder arbeitet in der Schneiderei.
My brother works in tailoring.

| | |
|---|---|
| gut / schlecht bezahlt | well / badly paid |

### Saying 'somebody' and 'nobody'

jemand – somebody
Jemand arbeitet in der Bäckerei.
Somebody is working in the baker's.

niemand – nobody
Niemand arbeitet auf dem Bauernhof.
Nobody is working at the farm.

accusative = für jemanden / niemanden
dative = mit jemandem / niemandem

---

**Worked example**    LISTENING TRACK 41

### Listening tips
- ☑ Read the questions **before** you listen.
- ☑ Watch out for questions requiring **two** pieces of information.
- ☑ If the answers are supposed to be **in English**, jotting down words in German won't help you!

**Social media**

Listen to the recording

Your German penfriend, Leon, has sent you a podcast.

Listen to his podcast and answer the following question **in English**.

**(a)** How many sisters does Leon have? **(1 mark)**
..2 sisters..

> — Ich stelle dir meine Familie vor. Meine ältere Schwester arbeitet als Vertreterin bei einer Techno-Firma und spielt gern Tennis in ihrer Freizeit. Meine andere Schwester heißt Carmen und sie ist nervig.

You have to wait some time to get the answer to the first question. Don't jump to the conclusion that Leon only has one sister. Carry on listening and you will hear him mention **meine andere Schwester** (my other sister).

Question **(d)** asks for two pieces of information – make sure you give both of them.

---

**Now try this**    LISTENING TRACK 42

Now listen to the rest of the recording and answer the following questions **in English**.

**(b)** What are Carmen's job plans? Give **one** detail. **(1 mark)**
**(c)** How do we know that Leon's mother works hard? **(1 mark)**
**(d)** What is unusual about his father? Give **two** details. **(2 marks)**

Listen to the recording

# Professions

Use strategies to help you when translating into English – does the German word look like an English word?

## Berufe

| | |
|---|---|
| Apotheker/in | pharmacist |
| Architekt/in | architect |
| Arzt (m) / Ärztin (f) | doctor |
| Beamter (m) / Beamtin (f) | civil servant |
| Dichter/in | poet |
| Feuerwehrmann (m) / Feuerwehrfrau (f) | firefighter |
| Informatiker/in | computer scientist |
| Ingenieur/in | engineer |
| Journalist/in | journalist |
| Krankenpfleger (m) / Krankenschwester (f) | nurse |
| Künstler/in | artist |
| Lehrer/in | teacher |
| Manager/in | manager |
| Mechaniker/in | mechanic |
| Polizist/in | police officer |
| Schauspieler/in | actor |
| Zahnarzt (m) / Zahnärztin (f) | dentist |

Ich habe viel Ehrgeiz. / Ich bin ehrgeizig.
I am ambitious.

Man muss oft in Besprechungen sitzen.
You have to sit in meetings a lot.

## Imperfect subjunctive modals

Impress with these expressions in the Speaking exam. They are no more complicated than modals in the present tense, but they will improve your speaking and writing!

Ich möchte Tierärztin werden.
I would like to become a vet.

Note that in German the word for 'a' is not needed before the job.

Du könntest viel Geld verdienen.
You could earn lots of money.

Du solltest versuchen, Arzt zu werden.
You should try to become a doctor.

## Translating into English

- ☑ Use words that look like their English equivalent to help with translations.
- ☑ Don't switch tenses when you are translating – arbeitet is present tense: 'works'.
- ☑ Krankenhaus is linked to krank (ill), so what do you think an 'ill house' is?
- ☑ Connect words – if you can't remember what Ärztin is, can you recall the male term Arzt? Think logically about where this person works, the Krankenhaus. Who works there?

## Worked example

**Translation**

Translate this passage **into English**.

> Meine Mutter arbeitet als Ärztin. Um sechs Uhr fährt sie immer zum Krankenhaus.

My mother works as a doctor. At six o'clock she always drives to the hospital.

**(3 marks)**

## Now try this

Now complete the translation.

> Letztes Wochenende hat sie hart gearbeitet. Diese Woche bewerbt sie sich um einen neuen Job.

**(4 marks)**

# Job wishes

Use this page to learn some high level language about your wishes for a future job.

## Berufswünsche

Ich hoffe, ...                    I hope ...

bei einer globalen Firma zu arbeiten.
to work for a global company.
ein hohes Gehalt zu verdienen.
to earn a high wage.
Chef/in zu werden.
to become the boss.
meine eigene Firma zu gründen.
to found my own company.
(nicht) in einer Fabrik zu arbeiten.
(not) to work in a factory.
(nicht) draußen / im Freien zu arbeiten.
(not) to work outside.
von zu Hause aus zu arbeiten.
to work from home.
gute Aufstiegsmöglichkeiten zu haben.
to have good chances of promotion.
im Ausland zu arbeiten.    to work abroad.
Teilzeit zu arbeiten.          to work part-time.
in der Sportabteilung / Musikindustrie zu arbeiten.
to work in the sports sector / music industry.

## Infinitive expressions

Grammar page 94

| Ich | hoffe, ... (hope) versuche, ... (try) habe vor, ... (intend) | + zu + infinitive. |

Ich habe vor, ins Ausland zu reisen.
I intend to travel abroad.

Ich hoffe, viel Geld zu verdienen.
I hope to earn lots of money.
Ich fange an / beginne, an die Zukunft zu denken.
I am beginning to think about the future.
Ich versuche, einen Teilzeitjob zu finden.
I am trying to find a part-time job.

## Selecting correct words

✓ The question here gives you an idea of the content and helps you to be ready for the dialogue.
✓ Make sure you read through the gapped sentences before you listen – the recording is short and every word counts, so really concentrate once the audio starts.
✓ You only need to use **four** of the words from the box, so watch out for distractors.

## Worked example

LISTENING TRACK 43

**Job wishes**
Lothar and Markus are talking about their job wishes.
What are they looking for?
Complete the sentences. Use the correct words from the box.

Listen to the recording

**(a)** Lothar is looking for ...excitement... and ............ .
(1 mark)

**(b)** Markus is looking for ............ and ............ .
(2 marks)

| travel | routine |
| excitement | courses |
| variety | promotion |
| salary | accommodation |

— Was findest du wichtig für deinen Beruf, Lothar?

— Routine ist nichts für mich. Ich suche etwas Spannendes. Am liebsten würde ich Feuerwehrmann werden, weil man jeden Tag etwas anderes macht.

## Exam alert

Don't be put off by extra letters at the end of familiar words: **spannend** = exciting, **etwas Spannendes** = something exciting.

## Now try this

LISTENING TRACK 44

Now listen to the rest of the recording and complete the activity on the left.

Listen to the recording

Make sure you are aware of words that go together, such as **Geld** (money) and **das Gehalt** (salary).

# Opinions about jobs

The opinions on this page can equally well be applied to other topic areas – holidays, school, visits.

## Meinungen über die Arbeit

| Arbeitsbedingungen (pl) | work conditions |
|---|---|

| | |
|---|---|
| Ich habe ein sehr positives Gefühl. | I have a very positive feeling. |
| Es war mein Traum, diesen Job zu bekommen. | It was my dream to get this job. |
| Ich fühle mich auf der Arbeit wohl. | I feel comfortable at work. |
| Der Job ist ein großer Erfolg. | The job is a big success. |
| Es ist das Beste für mich. | It is the best for me. |
| Das ist ein ausgezeichnetes Erlebnis. | That is an excellent experience. |
| Ich wäre gern noch länger geblieben. | I would have liked to stay longer. |

| | |
|---|---|
| Dieser Job würde mich ärgern. | This job would annoy me. |
| Das ist so ein Pech, kein Gehalt zu bekommen. | That is such bad luck not to get a salary. |
| Ich wünsche mir keine schlecht bezahlte Stelle. | I don't wish for a badly paid position. |
| Es wäre eine große Enttäuschung. | It would be a big disappointment. |
| Ich würde es niemandem empfehlen. | I would not recommend it to anyone. |
| Ich würde das vermeiden. | I would avoid that. |

## Giving opinions

Use the following to express an opinion:

Meiner Meinung nach sind die Arbeitsbedingungen prima.
In my opinion the terms and conditions are excellent.

Other words for 'to think':

finden    denken

meinen    glauben

Remember that after **dass** the verb goes to the end of the clause, as with wo and weil:

Ich finde, **dass** manche Arbeitgeber gemein sind. I think that some employers are mean.

Es gefällt mir, dass es eine Kantine für die Mittagspause gibt.
I am pleased that there is a canteen for the lunch break.

---

## Opinions practice

You may need to identify whether an opinion is **positive**, **negative** or both **positive and negative**, so practise with this activity.

 LISTENING TRACK **45**

Listen to the recording

|   | ☺ | ☹ | ☺ ☹ |
|---|---|---|---|
| 1 | X |   |   |

— Ich finde, die neue Stelle ist ein großer Erfolg und macht mir besonders Spaß.

## Understanding opinions

✓ Listening activities often rely on you understanding the **opinion** given, so always listen for clues, such as the speaker's **intonation**, to help you identify whether they are being **positive** or **negative**.

✓ Also listen out for the opinion words above to alert you to the fact it is an **opinion** and not a **fact**.

✓ You will also come across **opinions** in the Writing, Speaking and Reading papers, so make sure you are full of opinion knowledge!

Lots of positive words here plus a happy-sounding speaker point you to the answer: positive.

### Now try this

 LISTENING TRACK **46**

Now listen to the remaining **nine** opinions. Decide whether they are **positive**, **negative** or both **positive and negative**.

Listen to the recording

Watch out for the word **Probleme** in no. 4. Here, it is linked with **trotz** (despite), so maybe it is a positive opinion after all?

# Job adverts

Make sure you're prepared with this vocabulary connected with job seeking.

## Stellenangebote

| | |
|---|---|
| Arbeitsbedingungen (pl) | work conditions |
| Arbeitsstunden (pl) | hours of work |
| Aufstiegsmöglichkeiten (pl) | chances of promotion |
| Euro pro Stunde | euros per hour |
| Kollege (m) / Kollegin (f) | colleague |
| Mitarbeiter (m) / Mitarbeiterin (f) | co-worker |
| Stelle (f) / Job (m) | job |
| Stellenangebote (pl) | job vacancies |
| Stellenanzeige (f) | job advert |
| Termin (m) | appointment |
| ausgebildet | qualified, educated |
| erfahren | experienced |
| qualifiziert | qualified |
| teamfähig | good team worker |
| verantwortlich | responsible |

## Genitive prepositions

The following all take the genitive case:

| | |
|---|---|
| außerhalb | outside, beyond |
| statt | instead of |
| trotz | despite |
| während | during |
| wegen | due to, because of |

(m) der Anruf – statt des Anrufs
(der ➡ des + -s) instead of the call
(f) die Pause – während der Pause
(die ➡ der) during the break
(n) das Gehalt – trotz des niedrigen Gehalts
(das ➡ des + -s) despite the low salary
(pl) die Arbeitsstunden – wegen der Arbeitsstunden
(die ➡ der) due to the working hours

To show possession, use the following:
der Job meines Vaters – my father's job
der Chef der Firma – the firm's boss
der Bruder meiner Tante – my aunt's brother
das Ziel der Kinder – the children's aim

Der Job eines Arbeitsuchenden ist schwierig!
The work of a job seeker is hard!

## Worked example

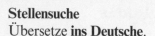  WRITING

**Stellensuche**
Übersetze **ins Deutsche**.

(a) I am looking for a job.          (2 marks)
<u>Ich suche eine Stelle.</u>

You do not need a word for 'for' in this translation, as **suchen** means 'to look for'.

eine Stelle = ein Job / eine Arbeit
ein Freund / eine Freundin = ein Bekannter / eine Bekannte

## Translating into German

✓ German nouns need **capital** letters!
✓ Look at **who** you are writing about in each sentence – yourself? Another person? More than one person? You need to have the correct part of the verb to match.
✓ Look at **when** you are writing about – is it something happening now (present tense) or a past action (past tense)?

You need to make sure your translated sentences flow and make sense. Leave yourself time to read them through to double check.

## Now try this

 WRITING

Now translate these sentences **into German**.
(b) My friend earns ten euros per hour.    (2 marks)
(c) He works in an office in the town centre.    (2 marks)
(d) Last year I worked as a waiter.    (3 marks)
(e) I need a job because I have no money.    (3 marks)

If you can't recall a specific German word, work around it, making sure you convey the same meaning; for example, 'I worked' could equally well be expressed as 'I had a job'.

# Applying for a job

Make sure you are familiar with letter-writing conventions.

## Sich um einen Job bewerben

einen Bewerbungsbrief schreiben
to write a letter of application
das Bewerbungsformular ausfüllen
to fill in the application form
Ich interessiere mich für den Job ...
I am interested in the job ...

  als Küchenhilfe.    as kitchen staff.
  als Kellner/in.    as a waiter / waitress.
  im Schwimmbad.    at the swimming pool.

Ich habe ausgezeichnete Sprachkenntnisse.
I have excellent language skills.
Ich möchte vom Juli bis September arbeiten.
I would like to work from July to September.
Anbei finden Sie meinen Lebenslauf.
Please find my CV enclosed.

## Writing a formal letter

| | |
|---|---|
| Sehr geehrter Herr X | Dear Mr X |
| Sehr geehrte Frau Y | Dear Mrs / Ms Y |
| zu Händen von Z | for the attention of Z |
| in Bezug auf | further to / following |
| Rufen Sie mich an. | Call me. |
| Vielen Dank im Voraus | Many thanks in advance |
| Mit bestem Gruß | With best wishes |
| Mit freundlichen Grüßen | Yours sincerely |
| Alles Gute | All the best |

### Exam alert

Tasks like these can be deceptively tricky. If you didn't know the meaning of **wieder einmal** (once again), this question would trip you up! Knowing key vocabulary is essential.

## Worked example

*Wieder keine Arbeit* by Wilfried Ernst

Read the extract from the text.
Wilfried is on his way to the job centre.
Put a cross ✗ in the correct box.

Why is Wilfried going to the job centre?

☐ **A** looking for his first job
☒ **B** had to leave his previous job
☐ **C** wants a long-term job
☐ **D** meeting friends there

Jetzt habe ich wieder einmal meinen Job verloren. Nun muss ich zum Arbeitsamt und eine neue Stelle finden. Ich verliere oft meinen Job, es ist immer dasselbe: Ich suche Arbeit, die mir gefällt. Ich finde etwas, das in Ordnung ist. Aber ich möchte eine Stelle, die interessanter ist, und ich arbeite nur so lange, bis ich etwas Besseres finde. Letztes Mal arbeitete ich in der Damenabteilung eines Kaufhauses. Da musste ich stundenlang herumstehen, die Kunden begrüßen und den ganzen Tag Kleider richtig aufhängen. Das wurde so langweilig, dass ich manchen Kunden Spitznamen gab. Jeder Kunde bekam je nach Charakter den Namen einer Figur aus dem Fix und Foxi Comicheft.

## Reading tips

✓ Don't expect to understand everything word for word and be prepared for vocabulary from a variety of topics: jobs, clothes, shopping and personality all come up here.

## Now try this

Now read the extract again and complete the reading activity.

**(a)** What sort of job has Wilfried always looked for?     **(1 mark)**
  ☐ **A** temporary     ☐ **B** more interesting     ☐ **C** full-time     ☐ **D** permanent

**(b)** Which word best describes Wilfried's job?     **(1 mark)**
  ☐ **A** outside     ☐ **B** exciting     ☐ **C** varied     ☐ **D** stationary

# Job interview

Here you can prepare for a Higher role play task in the Speaking exam.

## Vorstellungsgespräch

Ich bin höflich und freundlich.
I am polite and friendly.

Ich habe keine Erfahrung, aber ich lerne schnell.
I don't have any experience, but I learn fast.

Ich babysitte / mache Babysitting. I babysit.

Ich komme gut mit anderen Menschen aus.
I get on well with other people.

Ich arbeite gern in einem Team.
I like working in a team.

Ich habe einen Erste-Hilfe-Kurs besucht.
I have done a first aid course.

Letztes Jahr habe ich zwei Wochen bei einer
  Firma gearbeitet.
Last year I worked at a company for two weeks.

Möchten Sie meinen Lebenslauf sehen?
Would you like to see my CV?

## Different words for 'you'

### Familiar

du = 'you' to another young person, family member, friend or animal

ihr = 'you' plural of du

### Formal

Sie = 'you' to adult(s), teacher(s), official(s)

Sie = singular and plural

## Questions in a job interview

Wie sind die Arbeitsstunden?
What are the hours?

Gibt es gute Aufstiegsmöglichkeiten?
Are there good promotion prospects?

Wie viel Urlaub werde ich pro Jahr bekommen?
How much holiday will I get each year?

---

## Worked example

**Instructions to candidate:** You are having a telephone interview for a job as a waiter in a Swiss hotel. Your teacher will play the role of the hotel manager and will speak first. You must address the hotel manager as *Sie*.

**Task**
Sie möchten als Kellner/in in der Schweiz arbeiten.
Sie haben ein Vorstellungsgespräch am Telefon mit dem Manager / der Managerin.

**1 Job**
  – Guten Tag. Was für einen Job suchen Sie?
– Ich interessiere mich für den Job als Kellner/in in Ihrem Restaurant.

**2 Der Job – Gründe**
  – Warum möchten Sie in einem Restaurant arbeiten?
– Ich habe schon Erfahrung und ich arbeite gern mit Leuten zusammen.

**3 !**
  – Welche Arbeitserfahrung haben Sie schon gehabt?
– Letztes Jahr habe ich in einem Eiscafé in meiner Stadt gearbeitet.

• See page 9 for role play advice.
• See page 106 for question words.

Grund = one reason, Gründe = reasons. Make sure you give two pieces of information to score full marks.

### Role play strategy

Don't try to show off complex language in the role play – your aim is to communicate, so use constructions you are secure with. You can use the other Speaking parts of the exam to impress with more complex language!

---

## Now try this

Listen to the recording

Now practise the whole role play yourself, including the final two prompts. Listen to the audio file containing the teacher's part and fill in the pauses with your answers:

4 ? Arbeitsstunden     5 ? Kleidung

# Languages beyond the classroom

Collect a good stock of verbs for the Writing and Speaking exams, to add variety to your work.

## Sprachen für überall

| | |
|---|---|
| Traum (m) | dream |
| Fremdsprache (f) | foreign language |
| Fremdsprachenassistent/in (m/f) | |
| foreign language assistant | |
| Dolmetscher/in (m/f) | interpreter |
| Übersetzer/in (m/f) | translator |
| im Ausland leben | to live abroad |
| Leute kennenlernen | to get to know people |
| neue Freundschaften aufbauen | |
| to build new friendships | |
| um die Welt reisen | to travel the world |
| nach neuen Erfahrungen suchen | |
| to look for new experiences | |
| in ein neues Land ziehen | |
| to move to a new country | |
| an internationalen Konferenzen teilnehmen | |
| to take part in international conferences | |

## Verbs

| | |
|---|---|
| befehlen | to order / command |
| beschließen | to decide |
| erlauben | to allow |
| erreichen | to reach |
| erwarten | to expect |
| forschen | to research |
| helfen | to help |
| nennen | to call |
| raten | to advise |
| reden | to talk |
| schauen | to look |
| scheinen | to seem |
| stecken | to place |
| vermeiden | to avoid |
| versprechen | to promise |
| wechseln | to change |
| zeigen | to show |

## Worked example

### Arbeiten mit Sprachen

Lies diesen Artikel über Dolmetscherjobs.

> Ohne Fremdsprachen geht es heute weniger denn je – gleich ob auf Reisen, im Studium oder im Beruf. Es gibt also gute Gründe, möglichst früh Fremdsprachen zu lernen und diese Sprachkenntnisse ein Leben lang zu pflegen.
>
> Georg: „Ich habe Portugiesisch und Finnisch in der Schule gelernt, also kann ich auch in diese beiden Sprachen dolmetschen."
>
> Diese Aussage ist leider falsch. Man kann nur in eine Sprache dolmetschen, die man ausgezeichnet beherrscht. Die Zielsprache ist im Idealfall die Muttersprache. Dolmetscher müssen sofort reagieren, Informationen schnell verarbeiten und das Gesagte klar und flüssig – ohne allzu viele Ähs und Ähms – in der anderen Sprache wiedergeben können.

Beantworte die Frage **auf Deutsch**. Vollständige Sätze sind nicht nötig.

**(a)** Nenne **einen** Grund, warum Fremdsprachen wichtig sind. **(1 mark)**

sie helfen auf Reisen

## Answering questions in German

- ✓ Do **not** just copy extracts from the text as your answer – you will not get a mark for it.
- ✓ You can repeat individual words, but your answers must be in your own words to gain full marks.
- ✓ Although vollständige Sätze (complete sentences) are not necessary, you will need to supply your own verbs to answer.

## Now try this

Now read the above extract on the left again and complete the reading activity.

**(b)** Warum kann Georg nicht als Dolmetscher arbeiten? **(1 mark)**

**(c)** Was muss man als Dolmetscher vermeiden? **(1 mark)**

- Answer **in German**.
- Question **(a)** asks for **one** reason for **one** mark. Other reasons that would also score a mark are: sie helfen bei der Arbeit / beim Lernen.

# Volunteering

When talking about volunteering experiences, include time expressions with past tense modals: Zuerst musste ich ... (First I had to ...) or Danach sollte ich ... (Afterwards I was supposed to ...).

## Freiwillig arbeiten

Ich habe ...                          I ...
  freiwillige Arbeit geleistet.
  did voluntary work.
  eine Woche bei einem
   Wohltätigkeitsverein verbracht.
  spent a week at a charity.
  Aufgaben / Textverarbeitung gemacht.
  did tasks / word-processing.
  Akten abgeheftet.          ... did filing.
  viele Anrufe gemacht.
  made lots of phone calls.
  neue Fähigkeiten gelernt.
  learned new skills.
  eine Spendeaktion organisiert.
  organised a charity event.
Das hat großen Eindruck gemacht.
That made a big impression.
Die Erfahrung war sehr lehrreich.
The experience was very educational.

## Adverbs of time

Usually, the verb must come second:
Dann habe ich in der Klinik geholfen.
Then I helped in the clinic.

danach    afterwards      vorher   beforehand
dann      then            zuerst   first of all

With bevor and nachdem, the verb goes to the end:
Nachdem ich mit den Kindern gespielt hatte, war
 ich erschöpft.
After I'd played with the children, I was exhausted.

Ich habe Geld zu Gunsten einer Kindergruppe gesammelt.
I raised money in aid of a children's group.

## Worked example

*Hunger an der Tür*

You hear a radio interview with Frau Kahn from the charity „Hunger an der Tür". What does she say?

Listen to the recording

**(i)** Choose the **two** correct answers.

☐ **A** The charity is campaigning against homelessness.

☐ **B** The charity has over a million volunteers.

☒ **C** The charity is campaigning against child poverty.

☐ **D** 1.6 million children don't have a home.

☒ **E** The problem is increasing.

**(2 marks)**

— Morgen werden wir mit tausenden unserer freiwilligen Helfer zum Reichstag fahren, um gegen die Kinderarmut in Deutschland zu protestieren. Mehr als 1,6 Millionen Kinder leben in einem Haushalt, wo es nicht genug zu essen gibt. Und die Zahl nimmt ständig zu.

## Exam alert

Read the answer options and the rubric to get yourself 'in the zone' of the topic. Then listen to the whole passage to get the gist. Do any of the options strike you straight away as being wrong? If so, cross them out with a pencil. On the second listening, double check the audio against the remaining options. Only **two** are correct.

## Now try this

Now complete the activity below.

Listen to the recording

**(ii)** Choose the **two** correct answers.

☐ **A** The charity is targeting parents.

☐ **B** The charity is targeting the children directly.

☐ **C** Volunteers are often at risk.

☐ **D** Volunteers buy families new clothes.

☐ **E** Volunteers help parents with job seeking.

**(2 marks)**

# Training

Make sure you can refer to the different locations on a photo so that you can give a precise description in the exam.

## Lehrlinge

| | |
|---|---|
| Arbeitspraktikum (n) | work experience |
| Ausbildungszentrum (n) | training centre |
| Betriebspraktikum (n) | work experience |
| Lehrling (m) | apprentice |
| Praktikum (n) | internship |
| in die Berufsschule gehen | to go to vocational college |
| eine Ausbildung machen | to do training |
| eine Lehre machen | to do an apprenticeship |
| Man muss … | You have to … |
| Aufgaben ausführen. | do tasks. |
| Kaffee kochen. | make coffee. |
| Akten abheften. | do filing. |
| Telefonanrufe beantworten. | answer phone calls. |
| Kunden anrufen. | phone customers. |
| abends lernen. | study in the evenings. |
| einen Kurs besuchen. | do a course. |

Man hat viel / wenig / keinen Kontakt mit Kunden.
You have a lot / little / no contact with customers.
Man ist sehr / nicht beschäftigt.
You are very / not busy.

## Positions on a photo

When describing a photo, don't forget about your word order:
Man sieht eine Frau links. ➔ Links sieht man eine Frau.

im Hintergrund    oben
links — rechts
unten    im Vordergrund

## Describing a photo

- ✓ Don't worry if you don't know all the words for the items you can see – concentrate on those you **do** know how to say.
- ✓ German is great for inventing your own words. In the worked example you could use ein blauer Arbeitsanzug (work suit) to describe the outfit this apprentice is wearing. Be **creative** with language!

## Worked example

**SPEAKING**

**Work**

Schau dir das Foto an und sei bereit, über Folgendes zu sprechen:

• Beschreibung des Fotos

Im Vordergrund sieht man ein Mädchen. Ich denke, sie ist ein Lehrling und sie arbeitet heute in einer Werkstatt. Ein älterer Mann erklärt, wie die Maschine funktioniert. Das Mädchen trägt einen blauen Arbeitsanzug, weil die Arbeit manchmal schmutzig ist. Vielleicht muss sie manchmal eine Brille tragen, weil die Arbeit gefährlich für die Augen sein kann.

Have a go at adapting this sample answer for the description part of the task: Beschreibung des Fotos.

## Exam alert

The 'picture-based' conversation should be around two-and-a-half to three minutes in length. This includes all **five** of the teacher's questions. Here, you are only dealing with the first of those five questions, so go for an answer that will be around 30 seconds in length.

## Now try this

**SPEAKING**

Now prepare to talk on the subject of these bullet points as fully as you can:

• deine Meinung zum Arbeitspraktikum
• eine Arbeit, die du gemacht hast
• was du bei einem Arbeitspraktikum machen willst
• deine Meinung, ob eine Ausbildung oder studieren besser ist.

Try to speak for at least 30 seconds on each point.

Record yourself and play it back to see if you hesitated!

# Part-time jobs

When talking about part-time jobs, always use a range of vocabulary and structures, including weil, bevor and obwohl.

## Der Teilzeitjob

| | |
|---|---|
| Ich arbeite samstags als ... | I work on Saturdays as a ... |
| Kassierer/in | cashier |
| Kellner/in | waiter / waitress |
| Tellerwäscher/in | washer-upper |
| Verkäufer/in | sales assistant |

Ich trage Zeitungen aus.
I deliver newspapers.

Ich habe einen Ferienjob in einem Restaurant.
I've got a holiday job in a restaurant.

Ich habe einen Teilzeitjob in einer Autowerkstatt.
I've got a part-time job at a garage.

Ich verdiene 10 Euro pro Stunde.
I earn 10 euros an hour.

Mein Ziel ist es, einen Sommerjob zu finden.
It's my aim to find a summer job.

Ich bin ein erfahrener Babysitter / eine erfahrene Babysitterin.
I am an experienced babysitter.

Ich hefte gern Sachen ab.   I enjoy filing.

## This / that, these / those, every, which

**Grammar page 88**

These follow the pattern of der, die, das, which you will find on page 85 of the Grammar section.

| | |
|---|---|
| dieser | this / these |
| jener | that / those |
| jeder | every |
| welcher? | which? |

| | nom | acc | dat |
|---|---|---|---|
| masc | dieser | diesen | diesem |
| fem | diese | diese | dieser |
| neut | dieses | dieses | diesem |
| plural | diese | diese | diesen |

(m acc) Welchen Job würdest du lieber machen?
Which job would you prefer to do?

(f acc) Ich finde jede Arbeit ermüdend.
I find every job tiring.

(n dat) Ich möchte in diesem Restaurant arbeiten.
I would like to work in this restaurant.

---

## Worked example

**Ein Teilzeitjob**

Beschreib deinen Teilzeitjob.

> Jeden Samstag arbeite ich von neun bis dreizehn Uhr im Tanzstudio. Ich helfe beim Unterricht und verdiene dafür sechs Euro pro Stunde. Der Job gefällt mir sehr, weil Tanzen mein Lieblingshobby ist.

**Aiming Higher**

> In den Sommerferien habe ich als Kellner in einer sehr beliebten Bar im Stadtzentrum gearbeitet. Am Anfang war ich sehr nervös, weil ich vorher noch nie in einem Restaurant gearbeitet hatte. Zwar war es sehr anstrengend, den Gästen den ganzen Tag die Getränke und Mahlzeiten zu servieren, aber es hat auch riesigen Spaß gemacht, besonders wenn die Gäste sympathisch waren.

Remember to include opinions.

## Exam alert

Make sure you include some of these points in a piece of writing to help achieve a higher grade:

- excellent linking of the piece into a whole
- coherent and pleasant to read
- well-manipulated language which produces longer and more fluent sentences.

This uses lots of exciting structures: imperfect, pluperfect, zwar + inversion, both positive and negative opinions.

## Now try this

Describe your (real or imaginary) part-time job, in about 100 words.

# CV

You may want to include some details about yourself from your CV in the Speaking and Writing exams.

## Mein Lebenslauf

| | |
|---|---|
| persönliche Daten (pl) | personal details |
| Geburtsdatum (n) und -ort (m) | date and place of birth |
| Schulbildung (f) | education |
| Berufsausbildung (f) | training |
| Arbeitserfahrung (f) | work experience |
| Zukunftsträume (pl) | future dreams |
| Sonstiges | other |

## Etwas, nichts, wenig + adjective

Try to include some of these higher level phrases, which convert an adjective into a noun.

| | |
|---|---|
| viel Interessantes | a lot of interesting things |
| etwas Spannendes | something exciting |
| wenig Gutes | not much / little good |
| nichts Besonderes | nothing special |

## Worked example

**Dein neuer Job**

Dein Brieffreund interessiert sich für deine Arbeitserfahrung.

Schreib eine Antwort an ihn.

Du **musst** über diese Punkte schreiben:
- wo du jetzt arbeitest
- deine Arbeitserfahrung
- dein Charakter
- deine Zukunftsträume für die Arbeit.

Schreib ungefähr 80–90 Wörter **auf Deutsch**.

Nach der Schule habe ich eine Stelle als Fremdsprachenassistent/in gefunden. Das finde ich toll, weil ich Fremdsprachen sehr gern lerne. Im Arbeitspraktikum habe ich letztes Jahr in einem Gartenbetrieb gearbeitet. Ich interessiere mich sehr für Pflanzen und arbeite am liebsten im Freien. Sonnabends bin ich immer im Hallenbad zu finden, wo ich kleinen Kindern das Schwimmen beibringe. Ich finde das toll, weil ich gut mit jungen Leuten auskomme. Ich würde sagen, dass ich freundlich, geduldig, sportlich und ziemlich selbstbewusst bin. Ich bin aber auch ehrgeizig und möchte eines Tages eine erfolgreiche Karriere machen.

## Writing strategies

The best answers use structures that show your level of knowledge and application.

- ✗ **Don't** overcomplicate your work – stick to structures you are familiar with and get them (and the word order) right.
- ✗ **Don't** overuse the same verbs: ist / war, hat / hatte and es gibt / gab are great, but don't use them all the time.
- ✗ Regard long lists as verboten (banned!) because a top answer will **never** include long lists of nouns. Here, the student mentions four character traits, and leaves it at that.
- ✓ Make sure you include a good variety of grammatical structures and idioms – make every word count.

## Now try this

Now write 80–90 words about the bullet points to complete the activity.

Ich arbeite jetzt als ... in ...
Ich habe Erfahrung als ... Ich habe ...
In den Sommerferien habe / bin ich ...
Nächstes Jahr werde ich ...

# Global sports events

World sports events touch everyone these days, so make sure you are prepared to talk about them.

## Sportveranstaltungen

| | |
|---|---|
| Besucher (m) | visitor |
| Eintrittskarte (f) | entry ticket |
| Fernsehkanal (m) | television channel |
| Gastfreundschaft (f) | hospitality |
| Meisterschaft (f) | championship |
| Nationalmannschaft (f) | national team |
| Olympische Spiele (pl) | Olympic Games |
| Publikum (n) | audience |
| Schiedsrichter (m) | referee |
| Sportausrüstung (f) | sports equipment |
| Stadion (n) | stadium |
| Turnier (n) | tournament |
| Zuschauer (m) | spectator |

In meiner Stadt haben sie ein enormes Stadion gebaut.
They have built a huge stadium in my town.

Hier fehlt es an Sportevents.
There is a lack of sports events here.

Kein Einwohner hat von der Meisterschaft profitiert.
No inhabitant has benefited from the championship.

## Using als

Use als to mean 'when' in the **past** tense. It sends the verb to the end of the clause, then there is a **comma** before the next verb.

Als ich jünger war, habe ich die Olympischen Spiele in London besucht.
When I was younger I went to the Olympic Games in London.

Als er für die Nationalmannschaft gespielt hat, hat er viele Tore geschossen. When he played for the national team, he scored lots of goals.

## Worked example

**Sport**
Übersetze **ins Deutsche**.

> Countries across the world can benefit from sports events. When I went to the Olympic Games in Brazil, it was a wonderful experience.

Länder überall auf der Welt können von Sportveranstaltungen profitieren. Als ich zu den Olympischen Spielen in Brasilien gefahren bin, war das ein wunderbares Erlebnis.

## Making the translation suit you

It is unlikely that you will know **every** word or phrase in any given translation, so you need to work on strategies to adapt words to the knowledge you **do** have. Here are some examples:

| Forgotten ... | | Why not use ... ? |
|---|---|---|
| plural of 'country' | ➡ | jedes Land (every country) |
| 'across' | ➡ | in or auf |
| 'world' | ➡ | Planet (m) |
| 'events' | ➡ | Spiele, Feste, Wettbewerbe |

## Now try this

Now complete the translation **into German**.

> Although it was very expensive, Brazil had built a wonderful stadium for athletics and lots of people had bought tickets. The aim of a sportsman or a sportswoman is certainly to win a medal at a championship.

- 'had built' = pluperfect tense!
- 'aim' could also be 'wish' or 'desire'.

# Global music events

Music festivals and concerts are shared around the world, thanks to the internet. Have you ever been to or watched one yourself?

## Musikfeste

|  |  |
|---|---|
| Eintrittsgeld (n) | entry fee |
| Kleidung (f) | clothes |
| Musiker/in (m/f) | musician |
| Prominente (m/f) | celebrity |
| Tanzen (n) | dancing |
| Welt (f) | world |
| Werbung (f) | advert |
| Zelt (n) | tent |
| ermüdend | tiring |
| unglaublich | unbelievable |
| unvorstellbar | unimaginable |
| zusammen | together |

Das Musikfest war ein unvergessliches Erlebnis. The music festival was an unforgettable experience.

## 24-hour clock

The 24-hour clock is easy if you know your numbers. It is used for opening times, train times or to say when an event is taking place.

|  |  |
|---|---|
| 09:30 | neun Uhr dreißig |
| 12:45 | zwölf Uhr fünfundvierzig |
| 16:15 | sechzehn Uhr fünfzehn |
| 20:40 | zwanzig Uhr vierzig |
| 23:00 | dreiundzwanzig Uhr |

## Worked example

SPEAKING

**Instructions to candidate:**
You are buying tickets for an international music festival. Your teacher will play the role of the ticket seller and will speak first. You must address the ticket seller as *Sie*.

**Task**
Sie telefonieren mit der Musikorganisation. Sie wollen Eintrittskarten kaufen.

**1 Eintrittskarte**
– Was möchten Sie kaufen?
– Zwei Eintrittskarten für ein Konzert.

**2 Tag und Uhrzeit**
– Wann ist das Konzert?
– Es ist am Dienstag um halb neun.

**3 !**
– Warum wollen Sie es sehen?
– Ich liebe die Band.
– Prima.

## Exam alert

**You** have to use **your initiative** in these role play situations – as long as your questions and statements are relevant to the situation, they will be OK. Play to your own strengths and use language you are comfortable with.

See also page 9 for more on role plays.

Number of tickets + event is enough to cover the two details needed here.

This student knows the time expression: am + day / date and um + time.

This response answers the unexpected question – more is not needed.

## Now try this

LISTENING TRACK 50

Now practise the whole role play yourself, including the final two prompts. Listen to the audio file containing the teacher's part and fill in the pauses with your answers:
4 Transport – was und Grund
5 ? Preis

Listen carefully to the recording to help improve your pronunciation.

Listen to the recording

79

# Being green

Make sure you can say what you do and do **not** do in respect of the environment.

## Grünes Leben

| | |
|---|---|
| Energie sparen | to save energy |
| weniger Strom / Gas benutzen | to use less electricity / gas |
| Wasser nicht verschwenden | not to waste water |
| Lichter ausschalten | to turn off lights |
| Fenster und Türen zumachen | to close windows and doors |
| sich wärmer anziehen | to dress more warmly |
| die richtige Mülltonne benutzen | to use the correct rubbish bin |
| den Müll trennen | to separate the rubbish |
| Dosen / Flaschen recyceln | to recycle cans / bottles |
| Speisereste kompostieren | to compost leftover food |
| mit dem Rad fahren | to go by bike |
| mit den öffentlichen Verkehrsmitteln fahren | to travel by public transport |
| eine Fahrradwoche organisieren | to organise a cycling week |
| an einer Umweltaktion teilnehmen | to take part in an environmental campaign |

## Negatives

If you want to say what you do **not** do to help the environment, use kein (not a / none) or nicht (not) with a verb.

Unser Haus hat keine Solarenergie.
Our house has no solar energy.
Er recycelt nicht gern.
He does **not** like recycling.

## Listening tips

- The listening passages are not very long, so concentrate hard on **every word** to find the answers.
- If you do not understand every word, try to pick up on key words, cognates and parts of words, which may lead you to the answer.

---

## Worked example

LISTENING TRACK 51

### Umweltaktion

You hear a report about the environment. What does it say?

**(i)** Listen to the recording and put a cross ✗ in the correct box.

This report is about …

Listen to the recording

☐ **A** traffic.
☐ **B** energy.
☒ **C** living creatures.
☐ **D** recycling.

> — Letztes Jahr haben wir an unserer Schule keine Aktion für Menschen gemacht. Stattdessen haben wir uns auf die Natur konzentriert und daher auf dem Schulhof Nistkästen für Vögel entworfen.

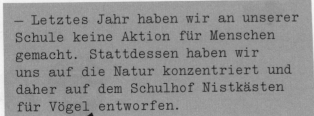

Watch out for **kein** here! This campaign had nothing to do with people!

## Now try this

LISTENING TRACK 52

Now complete the listening activity by putting a cross ✗ in the correct box for each of these reports.

**(ii)** This report is about …

Listen to the recording

☐ **A** traffic.
☐ **B** recycling.
☐ **C** acting responsibly.
☐ **D** walking to school.

**(iii)** This report is about …

☐ **A** eating healthily.
☐ **B** growing vegetables.
☐ **C** acting responsibly.
☐ **D** rubbish.

**(iv)** This report is about …

☐ **A** reducing food bills.
☐ **B** energy.
☐ **C** endangered animals.
☐ **D** second-hand clothes.

# Protecting the environment

Having a good selection of idioms will help you across the topics, so learn a few from this page to have up your sleeve!

## Umweltschutz

| | |
|---|---|
| globale Erwärmung (f) | global warming |
| Klimawandel (m) / Klimawechsel (m) | climate change |
| Pflanze (f) | plant |
| Regenwald (m) | rainforest |
| Schutz (m) | protection |
| Tierart (f) | animal species |
| Tiere (pl) | animals |
| Verschmutzung (f) | pollution |
| retten | to save |
| schützen | to protect |
| umweltbewusst | environmentally aware |
| umweltfeindlich | environmentally damaging |
| umweltfreundlich | environmentally friendly |

## Idioms

| | |
|---|---|
| Viel Glück! | Good luck! |
| Es ist mir egal. | I don't mind / care. |
| Meiner Meinung nach ... | In my opinion ... |
| Es kommt darauf an. | It depends. |
| Es macht nichts. | It doesn't matter. |
| Es lohnt sich (nicht). | It is (not) worth it. |
| Das ist in Ordnung. | That is OK. |
| Das ist schade. | That is a shame. |
| Genug davon. | Enough of that. |

Hals- und Beinbruch! Break a leg!

## Worked example

*50 einfache Dinge, die Sie tun können, um die Welt zu retten* by **Andreas Schlumberger**

Lies diesen Text über den Klimawandel.

### Mit Energie gegen den Klimakollaps

Der Klimawechsel – da sind sich die Experten einig – kommt, ja ist schon im Gange. Wir stehen nicht mehr vor der Aufgabe, ihn zu vermeiden, sondern vielmehr, seinen Effekt zu begrenzen und Strategien zu entwickeln, um uns daran anzupassen.

Jeder weiß, dass der Mensch einen großen Anteil an der Klimaerwärmung hat und dass die Folgen sich negativ auf die Menschheit auswirken werden. Für Mitteleuropa sind extreme Wetterereignisse wie Stürme oder Starkregen und auch extremes Wetter wie zum Beispiel Dürren oder Überschwemmungen zu erwarten. Hitzewellen werden zur Norm. Besonders stark könnten auch die Alpenregionen unter dem Klimawandel leiden.

Beantworte die Frage **auf Deutsch**. Vollständige Sätze sind nicht nötig.

**(a)** Wer glaubt fest an den Klimawechsel? **(1 mark)**

jeder Experte / alle Experten

## Prepositions

Make sure less common prepositions don't catch you out! Here are some you may come across:

| | |
|---|---|
| außer + dative | except for |
| bei + dative | at, at the home of |
| gegen + accusative | against |
| ohne + accusative | without |
| trotz + genitive | in spite of |
| wegen + genitive | because of |

## Now try this

Now read the extract again and complete the reading activity.

gelingen is a dative verb meaning 'to succeed'.

**(b)** Was ist uns nicht gelungen? **(1 mark)**

**(c)** Was ist das Einzige, was wir dagegen machen können? **(1 mark)**

**(d)** Warum sind wir daran schuld? **(1 mark)**

**(e)** Was wird die größte Auswirkung des Klimawandels sein? **(1 mark)**

**(f)** Welches Gebiet wird besonders unter dem Klimawandel leiden? **(1 mark)**

# Natural resources

When discussing or writing about certain topics, it is extremely useful to use the man form to express what people do generally.

## Naturschätze

 Kohle (f)     Gas (n)     Öl (n)     Tiere (pl)

 Salzwasser (n)    Pflanzen (pl)     Erde (f)

| | |
|---|---|
| Bauer (m) / Bäuerin (f) | farmer |
| Meer (n) | ocean |
| Obst und Gemüse (n) | fruit and vegetables |
| Umwelt (f) | environment |
| drohen | to threaten |
| retten | to save |
| vergiften / kontaminieren | to poison |

Der Bauer muss immer auf die Natur auf seinen Feldern aufpassen.
The farmer always has to look after nature in his fields.

Der Klimawandel bedroht unsere Inseln und Meere.
Climate change threatens our islands and oceans.

Man sollte immer Obst und Gemüse aus der Gegend kaufen.
You should always buy fruit and vegetables from the area.

Wir müssen unsere Umwelt retten.
We have to save our environment.

## Using man

- Man is used in German much more than 'one / you' is used in English.
- Use man to mean 'one / you / they / we / somebody / people'.
- Man takes the er / sie part of the verb (man hat).

## Present tense

Man hilft bei Problemen.
They help with problems.

## Past tense

Man hat einen Brief geschrieben.
Somebody wrote a letter.

## Future tense

Man wird das verbessern.
We will improve that.

Don't confuse **man** with **der Mann** (the man).

## Worked example

**Deine Umwelt**

Schreib eine Präsentation für deine Klasse über umweltfreundliches Leben.

Schreib:
- wie man umweltfreundlich einkauft
- wie man unterwegs Energie spart
- wie man die Umwelt schützen kann
- Pläne für eine Umweltaktion für nächstes Jahr.

Schreib ungefähr 40–50 Wörter **auf Deutsch**.    **(16 marks)**

- This is a short informal writing task – you only need to write about ten words for each bullet point, so don't go over the top with your response. Concentrate on writing simple, accurate sentences in German – capital letters for nouns, words spelled accurately and punctuation where required.
- If you are addressing your class, you must use the informal **du / ihr** register throughout. **Sie** forms have no place here.

**Unsere Umwelt**
Am besten kauft ihr immer frisches Gemüse auf dem Markt ein. Fahrt mit öffentlichen Verkehrsmitteln oder dem Rad, um Energie zu sparen. Wenn ihr zu Hause seid, macht die Fenster und Türen zu, um weniger Strom zu benutzen. Nächstes Jahr können wir eine Umweltaktion organisieren, um Pflanzenarten zu schützen.

## Now try this

Now complete the writing activity for yourself.

# Campaigns

You may well come across a reading or listening passage about campaigns across the globe. Make sure you know these key words and phrases, so you are prepared.

**Grammar page 94**

## Aktionen

| | |
|---|---|
| Armut (f) | poverty |
| Krieg (m) | war |
| Mangel (m) | lack |
| Menschen / Leute (pl) | people |
| Menschenrechte (pl) | human rights |
| Sicherheit (f) | security |
| Umweltorganisation (f) | environmental organisation |
| helfen | to help |
| bedürftig | needy |
| unglücklich | unfortunate |
| fairer Handel (m) | fair trade |
| freiwillig arbeiten | to work voluntarily |

## Um ... zu ...

Place a comma before um ... zu + infinitive verb to convey 'in order to' do something.

Ich sammele Geld, um Kindern in Afrika **zu** helfen.

I am collecting money (in order) to help children in Africa.

Ich mache Poster, um Leute auf das Problem aufmerksam **zu** machen.

I am making posters (in order) to make people aware of the problem.

> In English you don't always need to say 'in order to', but just 'to'.

## Worked example

**TRACK 53** — Listen to the recording

### Global campaigns

You hear a radio report about the organisation 'Kind International'.

What does it say?

Listen to the recording and put a cross ✗ in the correct box.

- ☒ **A** The charity has been going for ten years.
- ☐ **B** 'Kind International' campaigns to provide education.
- ☐ **C** The charity only supports girls.
- ☐ **D** Boys choose to go and fight.
- ☐ **E** The charity raises money for Europe.
- ☐ **F** The charity raises awareness in Europe.

> — Bei „Kind International"
> kämpfen wir seit zehn Jahren für
> Menschenrechte in aller Welt.

## Reading options carefully

✓ Don't miss small words in the answer options, such as 'only'. This is key to getting the answer correct, so don't misread statement **C** as 'The charity supports girls.' 'Only' is the word you need!

✓ Similarly, the prepositions 'for' and 'in' in statements **E** and **F** are crucial.

- **als** can mean 'as' (as well as 'when' in the past)!
- **je mehr ... desto** + comparative = the more ... the ...

## Now try this

**TRACK 54**

Now listen to the rest of the recording and choose the **two** correct answers from above. **(2 marks)**

Listen to the recording

# Good causes

Practise the sounds of the alphabet when you are working to improve your German pronunciation.

## Wohltätigkeitsverein

| | |
|---|---|
| Dürre (f) | drought |
| Erdbeben (n) | earthquake |
| Hungersnot (f) | famine |
| Orkan (m) | hurricane |
| Trinkwasser (n) | drinking water |
| Überschwemmung (f) | flood |
| Unglück (n) | catastrophe |
| Vulkan (m) | volcano |
| leiden (an) | to suffer (from) |
| sterben | to die |
| überleben | to survive |
| Briefe schreiben | to write letters |
| Geld sammeln | to raise money |
| Leuten helfen | to help people |
| Menschen unterstützen | to support people |

## The alphabet

Try to speak German words clearly and with a good accent. Use the listening passages from this book to help practise pronunciation.

LISTENING TRACK 55

Listen to the recording

| A ah | B beh | C tseh | D deh | E eh | F eff |
|---|---|---|---|---|---|
| G geh | H hah | I ee | J yot | K kah | L ell |
| M emm | N enn | O oh | P peh | Q kuh | R err |
| S ess | T teh | U oo | V fow | W veh | X iks |
| Y upsilon | Z tsett | Ä ah umlaut | Ö oh umlaut | ü uh umlaut | ß ess-tsett |

Make sure you are familiar with the German alphabet, so that if a word is spelled out you know the letters.

## Worked example

  WRITING

**Globale Probleme**

Du teilst dieses Foto online mit deinen Freunden.

Beschreib das Foto **und** schreib deine Meinung über globale Probleme.

Schreib ungefähr 20–30 Wörter **auf Deutsch**.

**(12 marks)**

Das Bild zeigt eine Katastrophe und viele Leute sind im Freien und wohnen in Zelten. Meiner Meinung nach sind diese Probleme schrecklich, weil so viele Kinder leiden.

Use **diese** instead of **die** to emphasise 'these' problems when writing or talking about a photo.
You can adapt descriptions such as these to use in more detailed writing or speaking tasks on this topic.

## Short writing task

- The task asks you to describe the photo **and** give an opinion. You **must** do both.
- Do not repeat language – always think of a different way of expressing something to avoid repetition.
- Accuracy is key here – check your work at the end for spellings, capital letters and sense!

## Now try this

  WRITING

Now write 20–30 words **in German** for your answer to the photo task.

# Gender and plurals

When you are learning a German noun, always learn it with its word for 'the' (gender).
All German words are masculine, feminine or neuter.

## Der, die, das (the)

Every German noun is masculine (m – der),
feminine (f – die) or neuter (n – das).

Der Mann ist groß.
The man is tall.
Die Frau ist klug.
The woman is clever.
Das Kind ist nervig.
The child is annoying.
Die Katzen sind süß.
The cats are cute.

|  | masc | fem | neut | pl |
|---|---|---|---|---|
| nominative | der | die | das | die |

If you don't know the gender of a word, you
can look it up in a dictionary.

**Frau** *f* woman, wife

## Der, die, das as the subject

The definite articles der, die, das, die are
used when the noun is the **subject** of the
sentence. That means it is doing the action of
the verb.

Der Lehrer spielt Fußball.
The teacher is playing football.

This is called the **nominative** case.

## Der, die, das as the object

**But** if the teacher becomes the
**object** of the verb, e.g. is seen
by someone else, then der changes to den.
Ich sehe den Lehrer.   I see the teacher.
I = subject, as it is doing the seeing.
The teacher = object, as he is being seen.
This is called the **accusative** case – die and
das stay the same when used in this way.

Grammar
pages 86–87

|  | masc | fem | neut | pl |
|---|---|---|---|---|
| accusative | den | die | das | die |

## Plurals

German nouns have different plurals. Not
sure what they are? Check in a dictionary.

**Mann** (¨er) *m* man

The part in brackets tells you what to add to
make the word plural. The umlaut before the -er
ending tells you that an umlaut is added to the
vowel before the ending, so the plural of **Mann**
is Männer.

## Now try this

Which definite article – **der**, **die** or **das**? Use a
dictionary to find the gender and plural of these
nouns.

(a) Anmeldung
(b) Fahrer
(c) Rührei
(d) Haltestelle
(e) Fernseher
(f) Brötchen

The gender is taken from the last
word in compound nouns: der Abend
+ das Brot = das Abendbrot.

# Cases and prepositions

Prepositions such as durch (through) and zu (to) trigger a change in der, die or das, as they have to be followed by a specific case – the accusative, dative or genitive.

## Changes to 'the'

|  | masc | fem | neut | pl |
|---|---|---|---|---|
| nominative | der | die | das | die |
| accusative | den | die | das | die |
| dative | dem | der | dem | den |
| genitive | des | der | des | der |

## Changes to 'a'

|  | masc | fem | neut | pl |
|---|---|---|---|---|
| nominative | ein | eine | ein | keine |
| accusative | einen | eine | ein | keine |
| dative | einem | einer | einem | keinen |
| genitive | eines | einer | eines | keiner |

> The genitive is not used very often, but it looks impressive if you can use it correctly!

> keine – not a / no

## Prepositions + accusative

Prepositions that trigger a change to the **accusative** case:

| für | for |
|---|---|
| um | around |
| durch | through |
| gegen | against / towards |
| entlang | along (after the noun) |
| bis | until |
| ohne | without |

> FUDGEBO = first letters of all accusative prepositions!

Ich kaufe ein Geschenk für einen Freund.
I am buying a present for a friend.

Geh um die Ecke.
Go round the corner.

## Prepositions + dative

Prepositions that trigger a change to the **dative** case:

| aus | from | nach | after |
|---|---|---|---|
| außer | except | seit | since |
| bei | at, at the home of | von | from |
| gegenüber | opposite | zu | to |
| mit | with | | |

nach einer Weile
after a while
Fahr mit dem Bus.
Go by bus.

> zu + dem = zum
> zu + der = zur
> bei + dem = beim

You need to add -n to the end of a plural masculine or neuter noun in the dative case:
mit meinen Freunden = with my friends.

## Prepositions + genitive

Prepositions that trigger a change to the **genitive** case:

| trotz | in spite of / despite |
|---|---|
| während | during |
| wegen | because of |

> See page 70 for more prepositions + genitive.

| laut der Zeitung | according to the newspaper |
|---|---|
| wegen des Wetters | because of the weather |

> You also need to add an -s to the end of a masculine or neuter noun in the genitive case.

## Now try this

Translate these phrases **into German** by adding the preposition and changing the word for 'the' or 'a'.

**(a)** against the wall (*die Mauer*)
**(b)** except one child (*ein Kind*)
**(c)** despite the snow (*der Schnee*)
**(d)** after an hour (*eine Stunde*)
**(e)** to the shops (*die Geschäfte – pl*)
**(f)** without a word (*ein Wort*)
**(g)** during the summer (*der Sommer*)
**(h)** at the doctor's (*der Arzt*)

# Dative and accusative prepositions

Movement **towards** or not? That is the key question! Dual-case prepositions can be followed by either the accusative or the dative case.

## Dual-case prepositions

| | |
|---|---|
| an | at |
| auf | on |
| hinter | behind |
| in | in |
| neben | next to |
| über | over |
| unter | under |
| vor | in front of |
| zwischen | between |

- If there is **movement towards** a place, these prepositions trigger a change to the **accusative** case.
  Ich gehe ins Haus. = I go into the house.
- If there is **no movement** towards a place, these prepositions trigger a change to the **dative** case.
  Ich bin im Haus. = I am in the house.

> in + das = ins
> in + dem = im

## Verbs + accusative

Some verbs work with a preposition followed by the accusative case.

| | |
|---|---|
| aufpassen auf | to look after |
| sich ärgern über | to be annoyed about |
| sich gewöhnen an | to get used to |
| sich streiten über | to argue about |
| sich erinnern an | to remember |
| sich freuen auf | to look forward to |
| warten auf | to wait for |

Ich muss auf **den** Hund aufpassen.
I have to look after the dog.
Ich freue mich auf **den** Sommer.
I am looking forward to the summer.
Ich habe mich an **die** Arbeit gewöhnt.
I have got used to the work.

## Prepositional phrases

Die Katze springt auf den Tisch. (acc)    The cat jumps onto the table.
Die Katze sitzt auf dem Tisch. (dat)    The cat is sitting on the table.
Ich surfe gern im Internet. (dat)    I like surfing the net.
Sie wohnt auf dem Land. (dat)    She lives in the countryside.
auf der linken Seite (dat)    on the left-hand side

> As you can see here, where there is no movement the dual-case preposition is generally followed by the dative case, and where there is a sense of movement it is followed by the accusative.

## Now try this

Complete the sentences with the correct definite article ('the').
(a) Ich wohne an .............. Küste (f).
(b) Sie streiten sich über .............. Fernseher (m).
(c) Was gibt es hinter .............. Haus (n)?
(d) Wie finden Sie die Geschichte über .............. Jungen (pl)?
(e) Die Nacht vor .............. Hochzeit (f).
(f) Man muss zwischen ..............Zeilen (pl) lesen.
(g) Denke an .............. Namen (m).
(h) Erinnerst du dich an .............. Person (f)?

# Dieser / jeder, kein / mein

Other groups of words, such as adjectives, also change according to case.

## Words that follow the der, die, das pattern

These words follow the pattern of der, die, das:

dieser (this)    jeder (each)    jener (that)
mancher (some)    solcher (such)    welcher (which)

dieser Mann                this man
bei jeder Gelegenheit      at every opportunity
jedes Mal                  every time

|            | masc   | fem    | neut   | pl     |
|------------|--------|--------|--------|--------|
| nominative | dieser | diese  | dieses | diese  |
| accusative | diesen | diese  | dieses | diese  |
| dative     | diesem | dieser | diesem | diesen |

### Ways to use these words

| dieses und jenes | this and that |
|---|---|
| in dieser Hinsicht | in this respect |
| jeder Einzelne | every individual |
| jeder Zweite | every other |
| zu jener Zeit / Stunde | at that time / hour |
| mancher Besucher | many a visitor / some visitors |
| Mit solchen Leuten will ich nichts zu tun haben. | I don't want to have anything to do with such people. |
| Welche Größe haben Sie? | What size are you? |

## Words that follow the ein pattern

These words follow the pattern of ein:

kein (not a)

mein (my)      unser (our)
dein (your)    euer (your, plural)
sein (his)     Ihr (your, polite)
ihr (her)      ihr (their)

|            | masc   | fem    | neut   | pl     |
|------------|--------|--------|--------|--------|
| nominative | kein   | keine  | kein   | keine  |
| accusative | keinen | keine  | kein   | keine  |
| dative     | keinem | keiner | keinem | keinen |

### Ways to use these words

| keine Ahnung | no idea |
|---|---|
| mein Fehler | my mistake |
| gib dein Bestes | do your best |
| sein ganzes Leben | his whole life |
| ihr Ziel ist es ... | it's her / their aim ... |
| als unser Vertreter | as our representative |
| auf euren Handys | on your mobiles |
| Ihr Zeichen | your reference |
| für ihre Schularbeit | for her / their schoolwork |

ich habe keine Lust – I don't want to + infinitive with zu

meiner Meinung nach (dat) – in my opinion

## Now try this

Translate the sentences **into English**.
(a) Ich habe keine Lust, einkaufen zu gehen.
(b) Sie hat ihr ganzes Taschengeld für Kleidung ausgegeben.
(c) Solche Leute werden schnell unhöflich.
(d) Ich finde mein Leben langweilig.
(e) Dieses Mal fahren wir mit dem Zug.
(f) Seine Eltern sind arbeitslos.
(g) Solche Regeln finde ich dumm.
(h) Welches Buch liest du?

# Adjective endings

Refer to the tables on this page to check you are using adjective endings correctly in your exam preparation work.

## Adjective endings with the definite article 'the'

You can also use these endings after dieser (this), jener (that), jeder (each), mancher (some), solcher (such) and welcher (which). The endings are either -e or -en!

|  | masc | fem | neut | pl |
|---|---|---|---|---|
| nominative | der kleine Hund | die kleine Maus | das kleine Haus | die kleinen Kinder |
| accusative | den kleinen Hund | die kleine Maus | das kleine Haus | die kleinen Kinder |
| dative | dem kleinen Hund | der kleinen Maus | dem kleinen Haus | den kleinen Kindern |

Siehst du den kleinen Hund? Can you see the little dog?

## Adjective endings with the indefinite article 'a'

You can also use these endings after kein (not a), mein (my), dein (your), sein (his), ihr (her / their), unser (our), euer (your, pl) and Ihr (your, polite).

|  | masc | fem | neut | pl |
|---|---|---|---|---|
| nominative | ein kleiner Hund | eine kleine Maus | ein kleines Haus | meine kleinen Kinder |
| accusative | einen kleinen Hund | eine kleine Maus | ein kleines Haus | meine kleinen Kinder |
| dative | einem kleinen Hund | einer kleinen Maus | einem kleinen Haus | meinen kleinen Kindern |

Ich wohne in einem kleinen Haus. I live in a little house.

## Adjective endings with no article

|  | masc | fem | neut | pl |
|---|---|---|---|---|
| nominative | kleiner Hund | kleine Maus | kleines Haus | kleine Kinder |
| accusative | kleinen Hund | kleine Maus | kleines Haus | kleine Kinder |
| dative | kleinem Hund | kleiner Maus | kleinem Haus | kleinen Kindern |

Kleine Kinder sind oft süß. Little children are often cute.

> Many of these are similar to the definite articles:
> das Haus – kleines Haus,
> der Mann – großer Mann.

## Now try this

Complete the sentences using the adjectives in brackets with their correct endings.

(a) Ich habe ................................................ Noten in Deutsch. (ausgezeichnet) (pl)

(b) Im Jugendklub kann ich ................................................ Essen kaufen. (warm) (n)

(c) Ich suche ein ................................................ Bett. (preisgünstig) (n)

(d) Die ................................................ Lage war sehr praktisch. (zentral) (f)

(e) Spanien ist ein ................................................ Urlaubsziel der Deutschen. (beliebt) (n)

(f) Das ist eines der ................................................ Lieder des Jahres. (meistverkauft) (pl)

(g) Letztes Wochenende gab es einen ................................................ Sonntag. (verkaufsoffen) (m)

(h) Stell keine ................................................ Daten ins Netz. (persönlich) (pl)

# Comparisons

To aim high, you will need to use comparatives and superlatives, so always think of a way to include them in your speaking and writing work.

## Formation

Add -er for the comparative, as in English (loud ➡ louder).

Add -(e)ste for the superlative 'most'.

Ich bin laut.   I am loud.

Ich bin lauter als du.
I am louder than you.

Ich bin die **lauteste** Person.
I am the loudest person.

- Adjectives are the same as adverbs, so you can compare how somebody does something very easily.

  Ich schreie laut.      I shout loudly.
  Ich schreie lauter      I shout more loudly
   als du.                than you.
  Ich schreie am          I shout the loudest.
   lautesten.

- Comparative and superlative adjectives have to agree with the noun they are describing.

  die schöneren          the prettier earrings
   Ohrringe
  der lustigste Junge    the funniest boy

## Irregular comparatives

Some adjectives have small changes in the comparative and superlative forms.

| | | |
|---|---|---|
| alt | ➡ älter | ➡ älteste |
| old | older | oldest |
| jung | ➡ jünger | ➡ jüngste |
| young | younger | youngest |
| groß | ➡ größer | ➡ größte |
| big | bigger | biggest |
| gut | ➡ besser | ➡ beste |
| good | better | best |
| lang | ➡ länger | ➡ längste |
| long | longer | longest |
| hoch | ➡ höher | ➡ höchste |
| high | higher | highest |

## Gern, lieber, am liebsten

Use gern (like), lieber (prefer) and am liebsten (like most of all) to compare your likes and dislikes.

gern and lieber go after the verb:
Ich spiele gern Schach.
I like playing chess.
Ich schwimme lieber.
I prefer swimming.
Use am liebsten to start your sentence:
Am liebsten fahre ich Ski.
Most of all I like skiing.

Lieblingssport (m) – favourite sport
Lieblingsgruppe (f) – favourite group

## Now try this

Complete the sentences with a comparative or superlative form.

(a) Mathe ist viel ............................................... als Chemie. (einfach)

(b) Mein Bruder ist.............................................. als meine Schwester. (jung)

(c) Dieses Lied ist doch.................................................. als der letzte Schlager. (gut)

(d) Meiner Meinung nach ist Physik ........................................................ als Chemie. (nützlich)

(e) Ich habe das ........................................... Zimmer im Haus. (winzig)

(f) Das ............................................ Fach in der Schule ist Informatik. (langweilig)

(g) Meine Stadt ist das.......................................... Urlaubsziel in Deutschland. (beliebt)

(h) Letztes Jahr hatte ich die .............................................. Noten in der Klasse. (schlecht)

Look at page 89 to check your endings.

# Personal pronouns

Just like der, die and das, pronouns change depending on which case they are in – the nominative, accusative or dative case.

### Pronouns

Pronouns = he, him, their, her, she, etc.

| nominative | accusative | dative |
|---|---|---|
| ich | mich | mir |
| du | dich | dir |
| er / sie / es | ihn / sie / es | ihm / ihr / ihm |
| wir | uns | uns |
| ihr | euch | euch |
| Sie / sie | Sie / sie | Ihnen / ihnen |

- Use pronouns to avoid repeating nouns:
  Ich mag Dieter, weil er nett ist.
  I like Dieter because he is nice.
- When a noun is the **accusative object** of the sentence, you need to use the **accusative pronoun**:
  Ich sehe ihn.      I see him.
- Use the correct pronoun after a preposition, depending on whether the preposition takes the accusative or dative case:
  bei mir (dat)      at my house
  für ihn (acc)      for him

---

### Dative pronoun phrases

These expressions need a dative pronoun:

| | | | |
|---|---|---|---|
| Es tut mir leid. | I am sorry. | Wie geht's dir / Ihnen? | How are you? |
| Es gefällt ihm. | He likes it. | Es geht uns gut. | We are well. |
| Es fällt mir schwer. | I find it difficult. | Es gelingt mir. | I succeed. |
| Es tut ihr weh. | It hurts her. | Es hilft ihnen. | It helps them. |
| Das schmeckt mir. | That tastes good / I like the taste. | Es scheint ihnen, dass ... | It seems to them that ... |
| Sport macht ihr Spaß. | She finds sport fun. | Das ist uns egal. | We don't mind about that. |

---

### Sie or du?

**Familiar**

du = 'you' to another young person, family member / friend, animal
ihr = 'you' plural of du (more than one young person, etc.)

**Formal**

Sie = 'you' to adult(s), teacher(s), official(s)
Sie = singular and plural

Sie   du

---

### Now try this

Choose the correct pronoun to complete each sentence.
(a) Nina ist sympathisch, obwohl ................. manchmal auch launisch ist.
(b) Es tut ................. leid, aber ich kann nicht zur Party kommen.
(c) Seit wann geht es ................. schlecht, Leon?
(d) Wir sind ins Theater gegangen, aber leider hat .................das Stück nicht gefallen.
(e) Mein Freund geht ................. auf die Nerven, aber ich will nicht mit .................
Schluss machen.
(f) Hast du Zeit, ................. bei den Hausaufgaben zu helfen?

# Word order

German word order follows rules – learn the rules and your sentences will be in the correct order.

---

### Verb in second place

The **verb** never comes first – it is always in second place!

**❶** Ich    **❷** fahre    **❸** mit dem Auto.

**❶** Jeden Tag    **❷** fahre ich    **❸** mit dem Auto.

---

### Perfect tense

Form of haben / sein goes in second position:

**❶** Gestern    **❷** bin ich    **❸** mit dem Auto    **❹** gefahren.

### Future tense

Form of werden goes in second position:

**❶** Morgen    **❷** werde ich    **❸** mit dem Auto    **❹** fahren.

---

### Modals

Form of modal goes in second position:

**❶** Ich    **❷** will    **❸** mit dem Auto    **❹** fahren.

◄ Remember:
**ich werde** – I will / I am going to
**ich will** – I want to

---

### Time – Manner – Place

A detail of transport counts as Manner, so put it **after** a Time expression, but **before** a Place.

**T** gestern / heute / letzte Woche / in Zukunft

**M** mit dem Zug / zu Fuß / mit meiner Familie

**P** nach London / in die Stadt / über die Brücke

**T** Ich fahre heute    **M** mit dem Zug    **P** nach Bonn.
Today I am going    by train    to Bonn.

### Linking words

No word order change here!

| aber | but | oder | or |
| denn | because | und | and |

Ich spiele gern Tennis **und** ich fahre gern Rad.
I like playing tennis and I like cycling.
Ich esse gern Pommes, **aber** ich esse nicht gern Bratkartoffeln.
I like eating chips but I don't like eating roast potatoes.

---

## Now try this

Order the sentences following the above rules.
(a) fahre / ich / ins Ausland / gern
(b) Verkehrsamt / findet / Informationen / beim / man
(c) gesund / ich / normalerweise / esse
(d) sehen / manchmal / Filme / wir / im Jugendklub
(e) arbeiten / ich / im Sportzentrum / möchte / im Juli
(f) habe / gearbeitet / ich / in einem Büro / letztes Jahr
(g) gehen / ins Kino / werde / mit meiner Mutter / morgen / ich

◄ Try to invert your sentences by starting with a time expression rather than **ich**, **du**, etc.

# Conjunctions

You will be expected to use plenty of conjunctions, such as weil, wenn and als, in your speaking and writing work – and you will **have** to show that you can use them correctly.

## Verb to the end

Weil (because) sends the verb ➡ to the **end** of the clause.

Ich rede über Adele, weil sie meine Lieblingssängerin ist.

I am talking about Adele because she is my favourite singer.

Ich gehe nicht gern ins Kino, weil das zu teuer ist.

I don't like going to the cinema because it is too expensive.

All these conjunctions send the verb to the end of the clause, just like weil:

| | | | |
|---|---|---|---|
| als | when (one occasion, past tense) | nachdem | after |
| | | ob | whether |
| | | obwohl | although |
| bevor | before | während | while |
| bis | until | was | what |
| da | because / since | wie | how |
| | | wenn | when / if (present or future) |
| damit | so that | | |
| dass | that | | |
| | | wo | where |

## Perfect tense

- In the **perfect** tense, the form of haben / sein is **last** in a clause.

  Ich kann nicht zur Party kommen, obwohl ich meine Hausaufgaben **gemacht habe**.

  I can't come to the party although I have done my homework.

- Watch out for the **verb, comma, verb** structure.

  Als ich klein war, habe ich viel im Garten gespielt.

  When I was small I played in the garden a lot.

Form of **haben / sein** in the perfect tense ➡ right to the end.

## Future tense and modals

- In the **future** tense, it is the form of werden which goes last.

  Da ich nach Afrika reisen werde, muss ich zum Arzt.

  Because I am going to travel to Africa, I have to go to the doctor.

- With **modal** verbs, it is the modal itself which is last in the clause.

  Ich bin immer glücklich, wenn ich ins Konzert gehen darf.

  I am always happy when I am allowed to go to the concert.

Form of **werden** ➡ right to the end.
Form of **modal** ➡ right to the end.

## Now try this

Join each pair of sentences using the subordinating conjunction in brackets.

(a) Ich habe bei meiner Großmutter gewohnt. Meine Mutter war im Krankenhaus. (während)

(b) Ich bin ins Café gegangen. Ich habe ein T-Shirt gekauft. (nachdem)

(c) Ich war in Spanien im Urlaub. Ich habe einen neuen Freund kennengelernt. (als)

(d) Er ist sehr beliebt. Er ist nicht sehr freundlich. (obwohl)

(e) Ich werde für eine neue Gitarre sparen. Ich finde einen Nebenjob. (wenn)

(f) Ich bin froh. Ich habe gute Noten in der Schule bekommen. (dass)

(g) Ich muss meine Eltern fragen. Ich darf ins Konzert gehen. (ob)

(h) Er hat mir gesagt. Er will mit mir ins Kino gehen. (dass)

# More on word order

There are a few more structures here that you should try to fit into your work to improve your writing and speaking. They also affect word order, so be careful!

## Using um ... zu ...

Um ... zu ... means 'in order to' and is used in German where English might just say 'to'. It requires an infinitive verb at the end of the clause.

Ich trage Zeitungen aus,
  um Geld zu verdienen. 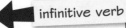 infinitive verb
I deliver newspapers, (in order) to earn money.

- Only use um ... zu ... where you would say 'in order to' in English, even if you drop the 'in order' bit.
- The verb after um ... zu ... is always in the infinitive and at the **end**.
- Add a comma before um.

ohne ... zu ... means without. It works in the same way:
Ich bin in die Schule gegangen, ohne ihn zu sehen. I went to school without seeing him.

## Infinitive expressions

These expressions with zu need an infinitive.

| ich ... (I ...) | hoffe, ... (hope) | + zu + infinitive |
|---|---|---|
| | versuche, ... (try) | |
| | beginne / fange an, ... (begin) | |
| | habe vor, ... (intend) | |
| | nutze die Chance, ... (use the opportunity) | |

Ich hoffe, Deutsch zu studieren.
I hope to study German.
Ich versuche, einen guten Job zu bekommen.
I am trying to get a good job.

With separable verbs, zu goes after the prefix.
Ich habe vor, fernzusehen.    I intend to watch TV.

## Relative pronouns

Relative pronouns send the verb to the end of the clause.

They are used to express **who** or **that** or **which**.

**m**   Der Mann, der im Café sitzt, ist Millionär.
     The man who is sitting in the café is a millionaire.

**f**   Die Katze, die unter dem Tisch schläft, ist sehr süß.
     The cat that is sleeping under the table is very sweet.

**n**   Das Mädchen, das einen roten Rock trägt, singt in einer Band.
     The girl who's wearing a red skirt sings in a band.

## Now try this

1 Combine the sentences with **um ... zu ...** .
  **(a)** Ich fahre nach Italien. Ich besuche meine Verwandten.
  **(b)** Ich gehe zum Sportzentrum. Ich nehme 5 Kilo ab.
2 Combine the clauses with **zu**.
  **(a)** Ich versuche – ich helfe anderen.
  **(b)** Ich habe vor – ich gehe auf die Uni.
3 Combine the sentences with a relative pronoun.
  **(a)** Das ist das Geschäft. Das Geschäft verkauft tolle Kleidung.
  **(b)** Hier ist eine Kellnerin. Die Kellnerin ist sehr unhöflich.

# The present tense

There are regular and irregular present tense verbs for you here, but look at page 100 for the super-irregular verbs haben (to have) and sein (to be).

## Present tense regular

Verbs change according to who is doing the action, just like in English: I drink ➡ he drinks.

The present tense describes what is happening now and can be translated as 'drink' or 'am drinking'.

| machen – to do / to make | | _infinitive verb_ |
|---|---|---|
| ich | mache | I do / make |
| du | machst | you do / make |
| er / sie / es | macht | he / she / it does / makes |
| wir | machen | we do / make |
| ihr | macht | you do / make |
| Sie / sie | machen | you / they do / make |

_wir / Sie / sie forms = same as infinitive_

- The present tense is used to describe what you are **doing now** or what you **do** regularly.
- Present tense time expressions include:

  | | |
  |---|---|
  | jetzt (now) | heute (today) |
  | im Moment | (at the moment) |
  | dienstags | (on Tuesdays) |

- You can use the present tense with a time phrase to indicate the **future**:

  Morgen fahre ich nach London.
  Tomorrow I am going to London.

## Present tense vowel changes

Some verbs have a vowel change in the du and er / sie / es forms of the present tense, but they still have the same endings (-e, -st, -t, etc.).

| geben – to give | | | _infinitive verb_ |
|---|---|---|---|
| ich | gebe | wir | geben |
| du | gibst | ihr | gebt |
| er / sie /es | gibt | Sie / sie | geben |

_vowel change_

| nehmen – to take | |
|---|---|
| ich | nehme |
| du | nimmst |
| er / sie / es | nimmt |

| essen – to eat | |
|---|---|
| ich | esse |
| du | isst |
| er / sie / es | isst |

| schlafen – to sleep | |
|---|---|
| ich | schlafe |
| du | schläfst |
| er / sie / es | schläft |

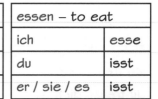

Sie schläft.

## Now try this

Complete the sentences with the correct form of the present tense verb in brackets.

(a) Ich ................................................... gern Musik. (hören)

(b) Meine Schwester ................................................... in ihrem eigenen Zimmer. (schlafen)

(c) Ihr ................................................... montags schwimmen, oder? (gehen)

(d) ................................................... du gern Wurst mit Senf? (essen)

(e) Wir ................................................... nie mit dem Auto. (fahren)

(f) Was ................................................... Sie in den Sommerferien? (machen)

(g) ................................................... es eine Ermäßigung für Senioren? (geben)

(h) Mein Bruder ................................................... heute im Bett, weil er krank ist. (bleiben)

# Separable and reflexive verbs

To aim for a higher grade, include separable and reflexive verbs in your speaking and writing work.

## Separable verbs

These verbs have two parts: a prefix + the main verb. They go their separate ways when used in a sentence.

Ich sehe oft fern.   I often watch TV.
Ich mache immer die Türen zu.
I always close the doors.

| | |
|---|---|
| aufwachen | to wake up |
| aussteigen | to get off |
| einsteigen | to get on |
| fernsehen | to watch TV |
| herunterladen | to download |
| hochladen | to upload |
| umsteigen | to change (trains, trams, buses) |
| zumachen | to close |

Make sure you can use separable verbs in all the tenses.

**Present:**   Ich steige in Ulm um.
I change in Ulm.

**Perfect:**   Ich bin in Ulm umgestiegen.
I changed in Ulm.

> Separable verbs form the past participle as one word with **-ge-** sandwiched in the middle: **zugemacht** (closed), **ferngesehen** (watched TV).

**Future:**   Ich werde in Ulm umsteigen.
I will change in Ulm.

**Modals:**   Ich muss in Ulm umsteigen.
I have to change in Ulm.

## Reflexive verbs

Reflexive verbs need a reflexive pronoun – **mich, dich,** etc.

| sich freuen – to be happy / pleased | |
|---|---|
| ich freue mich | wir freuen uns |
| du freust dich | ihr freut euch |
| er / sie / es freut sich | Sie / sie freuen sich |

- Note that **sich** never has a capital letter.
- **sich freuen auf ...** (acc) – to look forward to ...

| | |
|---|---|
| sich amüsieren | to enjoy oneself |
| sich befinden | to be located |
| sich entscheiden | to decide |
| sich erinnern an | to remember |
| sich langweilen | to be bored |
| sich interessieren für | to be interested in |

Ich interessiere mich für Geschichte.
I am interested in history.

> All reflexive verbs use **haben** in the perfect tense.
> **Er hat sich angezogen.**   He dressed.
> **Wir haben uns gelangweilt.**   We were bored.

## Now try this

1 Translate the sentences **into German**.
   (a) I watch TV. I watched TV.
   (b) I change trains at six o'clock. I changed trains at six o'clock.
   (c) I download music. I will download music.
   (d) I got on. I have to get on.

2 Complete the sentences with the correct reflexive pronoun.
   (a) Ich erinnere ........... kaum an meinen Vater.
   (b) Wir interessieren ........... für Mode.
   (c) Habt ihr ........... im Jugendklub gelangweilt?
   (d) Meine Schule befindet ........... am Stadtrand.

# Commands

Use this page to help you give commands and orders accurately.

## Sie commands

Swap the present tense round so that the verb comes before the pronoun:

Sie hören (you listen) ➡ Hören Sie! Listen!

Schreiben Sie das auf Deutsch auf.
Write that down in German.

Gehen Sie hier links.　　Go left here.

- Separable verbs separate and the prefix goes to the end of the sentence.
  Tauschen Sie nicht Ihre Telefonnummer aus.
  Don't swap your phone number.

- Sein (to be) is irregular.
  Seien Sie nicht aggressiv.
  Don't be aggressive.

## Du commands

Use the present tense du form of the verb minus the -st ending:

gehen ➡ du gehst ➡ du gehst ➡ Geh!

Bleib anonym.　　Stay anonymous.

Triff niemanden allein.
Don't meet anyone on your own.

Beleidige andere nicht.
Don't insult others.

Such dir einen Spitznamen aus.
Choose a nickname.

> This is a separable verb so it splits.

Some verbs are irregular in the present tense, so make sure you get them right when giving commands.

| | | |
|---|---|---|
| haben – to have | ➡ | Hab (Spaß)! – Have (fun)! |
| sein – to be | ➡ | Sei (ruhig)! – Be (quiet)! |
| essen – to eat | ➡ | Iss! – Eat! |
| fahren – to drive | ➡ | Fahr! – Drive! |
| geben – to give | ➡ | Gib das her! – Give me that! |
| lassen – to leave | ➡ | Lass! – Leave! |
| nehmen – to take | ➡ | Nimm! – Take! |

## Other Sie commands

| | |
|---|---|
| **Gas weg!** | Reduce your speed! |
| **Gefahr!** | Danger! |
| **Warnung!** | Warning! |
| **Achtung!** | Attention! / Watch out! |
| **Vorsicht!** | Be careful! |
| **Verboten!** | Forbidden! |
| **Kein Eintritt!** 🚫 | Keep off! / Keep out! |
| **Nicht betreten!** | No entry! |
| **Ausfahrt freihalten!** | Keep exit clear! |
| ⚠ **Lebensgefahr!** | Danger of death! |
| **Privatgrundstück** | Private land |

## Now try this

What is this sign asking dog owners to do?

**Liebe Hundehalter,**
**bitte achten Sie auf Ihre Lieblinge und benutzen Sie Grünflächen und Wege nicht als Hundetoilette.**

**Vielen Dank!**

# Present tense modals

Modal verbs need another verb in the infinitive form, e.g. gehen (to go), kaufen (to buy).
The modal verb comes second in the sentence, while the infinitive is shifted to the very end.

## Können (to be able to)

| | |
|---|---|
| ich / er / sie / es | kann |
| du | kannst |
| ihr | könnt |
| wir / Sie / sie | können |

Ich kann nicht schwimmen.   I can't swim.

## Müssen (to have to / must)

| | |
|---|---|
| ich / er / sie / es | muss |
| du | musst |
| ihr | müsst |
| wir / Sie / sie | müssen |

Du musst deine Hausaufgaben machen.
You have to do your homework.

## Wollen (to want to)

| | |
|---|---|
| ich / er / sie / es | will |
| du | willst |
| ihr | wollt |
| wir / Sie / sie | wollen |

Er will nicht umsteigen.
He doesn't want to change (trains).

## Dürfen (to be allowed to)

| | |
|---|---|
| ich / er / sie / es | darf |
| du | darfst |
| ihr | dürft |
| wir / Sie / sie | dürfen |

Wir dürfen in die Disko gehen.
We are allowed to go to the disco.

## Sollen (to be supposed to)

| | |
|---|---|
| ich / er / sie / es | soll |
| du | sollst |
| ihr | sollt |
| wir / Sie / sie | sollen |

Germans most often use the imperfect
tense of sollen to express the sense of
'should' or 'ought'.

Ich sollte meine Großeltern besuchen.
I should visit my grandparents.

## Mögen (to like)

The present tense of mögen no longer
tends to be used in the present tense
with another verb to express liking.
Instead, the subjunctive form is far more
likely to be used in the sense of 'would
like to'.

| | |
|---|---|
| ich / er / sie / es | möchte |
| du | möchtest |
| ihr | möchtet |
| wir / Sie / sie | möchten |

Sie möchte Rollschuhlaufen gehen.
She would like to go rollerblading.
Ich möchte nicht ins Kino gehen.
I would not like to go to the cinema.

## Now try this

Write modal sentences using the verbs given in brackets.
(a) Ich gehe um einundzwanzig Uhr ins Bett. (müssen)
(b) In der Schule raucht man nicht. (dürfen)
(c) Du sparst Energie. (sollen)
(d) Hilfst du mir zu Hause? (können)
(e) Ich fahre in den Ferien Ski. (wollen)
(f) Ich sehe nicht fern. (mögen)
(g) Ich löse das Problem nicht. (können)

Note that separable verbs come
together as infinitives: ich sehe
fern = fernsehen.

# Imperfect modals

Using modals and an infinitive in different tenses is a great way to incorporate a variety of tenses into your work.

---

### Imperfect modals

**Infinitive**: können – to be able to

**Present tense:**
ich kann + infinitive at end – I can ...

**Imperfect tense:**
ich konnte + infinitive at end – I was able to ...

Ich konnte nicht mehr warten.
I couldn't wait any more.

*infinitive at the end*

The endings change, depending on the subject of the verb.

| | |
|---|---|
| ich | konnte |
| du | konntest |
| er / sie / es / man | konnte |
| wir | konnten |
| ihr | konntet |
| Sie / sie | konnten |

---

## Other modals in the imperfect

- These modals work in the same way as konnte – just add the correct ending.
- There are no umlauts on imperfect tense modals.

| | | |
|---|---|---|
| müssen | ➡ musste | had to |
| wollen | ➡ wollte | wanted to |
| dürfen | ➡ durfte | was allowed to |
| sollen | ➡ sollte | was supposed to |
| mögen | ➡ mochte | liked |

Was musstet ihr gestern in Mathe machen?
What did you have to do in maths yesterday?

Er wollte doch nur helfen.
He only wanted to help.

Sie durfte ihn nicht heiraten.
She wasn't allowed to marry him.

Du solltest eine Tablette nehmen.
You should take a pill.

---

## Subjunctive modals (Higher)

Add an umlaut to konnte and mochte and you have the subjunctive. This allows you to talk about things you **could / would** do.

| imperfect | ➡ | subjunctive | |
|---|---|---|---|
| konnte | ➡ | könnte (could) | + infinitive |
| mochte | ➡ | möchte (would like) | |

The subjunctive has the same structure as imperfect modals with the infinitive at the end.

Möchtest du ins Kino gehen?
Would you like to go to the cinema?

Das Schwimmbad könnte geschlossen sein.
The swimming pool could be closed.

---

### Now try this

**1** Rewrite these sentences with an imperfect tense modal.
   (a) Ich mache Hausaufgaben. (müssen)
   (b) Sie helfen mir nicht. (können)
   (c) Er kauft eine neue Hose. (wollen)
   (d) Wir laden die Fotos hoch. (sollen)
   (e) In der Schule kaut man nie Kaugummi. (dürfen)
   (f) Alle Schüler bleiben bis sechzehn Uhr. (müssen)

**2** Rewrite these with a subjunctive modal.
   (a) Es wird schwierig. (können)
   (b) Ich tausche die gelbe Jacke um. (mögen)

# The perfect tense 1

The perfect tense is the tense most used to talk about the past in German – using it is a necessity at any level of your GCSE.

## The perfect tense

- Use the perfect tense to talk about something you have done in the **past**.
- The perfect tense is made up of **two parts**:

  the correct form of **haben** or **sein** + past participle at the end.

  Ich **habe** Musik **gehört**.   I listened to music.

Past participles generally start with ge-.

spielen ➡ gespielt (played)

lachen ➡ gelacht (laughed)

fahren ➡ gefahren (drove)

Hast du den Film gesehen?
Have you seen the film?

## The perfect tense – haben

Most verbs use haben (to have) in the perfect tense:

form of haben + sentence + past participle at the end.

| ich habe | |
| --- | --- |
| du hast | gekauft (bought) |
| er / sie / es hat | gemacht (made) |
| wir haben | besucht (visited) |
| ihr habt | gesehen (saw) |
| Sie / sie haben | |

Er **hat** im Reisebüro **gearbeitet**.
He worked at the travel agency.

Wir **haben** Frühstück **gegessen**.
We ate breakfast.

## The perfect tense – sein

Some verbs of movement use sein (to be) to make the perfect tense:

form of sein + sentence + past participle at the end.

| ich bin | |
| --- | --- |
| du bist | gegangen (went) |
| er / sie / es ist | geflogen (flew) |
| wir sind | gefahren (drove / went) |
| ihr seid | geblieben (stayed) |
| Sie / sie sind | |

Sie **ist** zu Fuß **gegangen**.
She went on foot.

Ich **bin** nach Freiburg **gefahren**.
I went to Freiburg.

There are some verbs that use **sein** in the perfect tense where there is no apparent movement: **bleiben** (to stay) is an example.

## Now try this

Write these sentences in the perfect tense.
- **(a)** Ich kaufe eine Jacke.
- **(b)** Wir fliegen nach Portugal.
- **(c)** Ich sehe meinen Freund.
- **(d)** Lena und Hannah gehen in die Stadt.
- **(e)** Ich besuche meine Tante.
- **(f)** Ich bleibe im Hotel.
- **(g)** Was isst du zu Mittag?
- **(h)** Am Samstag hört er Musik.

Put the form of **haben** / **sein** in second position and the past participle at the end of the sentence.

# The perfect tense 2

Spotting past participles will help you to identify when a text is in the past tense – but watch out for the hidden ge- in separable verbs such as ferngesehen (watched TV).

## Regular past participles

- Begin with ge-.
- End in -t.

Remove -en from the infinitive and replace with -t: machen ➡ macht ➡ gemacht

Das hat ihr Spaß gemacht.
That was fun for her.

## Some exceptions

Verbs starting with be-, emp- or ver- do not add ge- to form the past participle.

| Ich habe ... | I ... |
|---|---|
| besucht | visited |
| empfohlen | recommended |
| vergessen | forgot |
| verloren | lost |

Separable verbs add **ge-** between the prefix and the main verb:
**hochgeladen** – uploaded    **heruntergeladen** – downloaded

## Irregular past participles

There are no rules for forming irregular past participles – but here are some common ones to learn.

| Ich habe ... | gegessen | ate |
|---|---|---|
| | getrunken | drank |
| | genommen | took |
| | geschlafen | slept |
| | geschrieben | wrote |
| | gesungen | sang |
| | getragen | wore / carried |
| | getroffen | met |
| | gestanden | stood |
| Ich bin ... | gerannt | ran |
| | geschwommen | swam |
| | gewesen | have been |
| | gestiegen | climbed |
| | gestorben | died |
| | geworden | became |

## Word order

The past participle goes at the **end** of the sentence and the form of haben or sein is in **second** position:

**①** **②** **③**

Er        ist   ins Kino   gegangen.
He went to the cinema.

**①** **②** **③**

Am Montag   habe ich Fußball   gespielt.
I played football on Monday.

When the verb has already been sent to the end by a conjunction such as weil (because) or als (when), the part of haben or sein comes **after** the past participle:

Ich war dankbar, weil er mein Portemonnaie gefunden hat.
I was grateful because he found my purse.
Als er angekommen war, war er erschöpft.
When he arrived, he was exhausted.

## Now try this

Complete the sentences with the correct past participle of the verb in brackets.
- **(a)** Ich habe zu viele Kekse ................................................................. . (essen)
- **(b)** Haben Sie gut ................................................................. ? (schlafen)
- **(c)** Wir haben uns am Bahnhof ................................................................. . (treffen)
- **(d)** Ich war krank, weil ich den ganzen Tag ................................................................. habe. (stehen)
- **(e)** Ich weiß, dass du ................................................................. bist. (umsteigen)
- **(f)** Warum hast du die E-Mail ................................................................. ? (schreiben)
- **(g)** Ich habe ihr ................................................................. , dass sie nicht mitkommen sollte. (empfehlen)
- **(h)** Ich war traurig, als er ................................................................. ist. (sterben)

# The imperfect tense

If you are telling a story about the past or recounting a series of events in the past, use the imperfect tense.

## Forming the imperfect tense

- Take the infinitive, e.g. hören (to hear).
- Take off the final -en ➡ hör~~en~~ = hör.
- Add these endings:

| | |
|---|---|
| ich hörte | I heard / was hearing |
| du hörtest | you heard / were hearing |
| er / sie / es / man hörte | he / she / it / one heard / was hearing |
| wir hörten | we heard / were hearing |
| ihr hörtet | you heard / were hearing |
| Sie / sie hörten | you / they heard / were hearing |

Ich hörte gar nichts.  I didn't hear a thing.

Sie spielten drei Jahre lang in der Gruppe.
They played for three years with the group.

> Don't forget to use the imperfect modals – see page 99 for a reminder.

## 'To have' and 'to be' in the imperfect

**haben**

| | |
|---|---|
| ich hatte | I had |
| du hattest | you had |
| er / sie / es / man hatte | he / she / it / one had |
| wir hatten | we had |
| ihr hattet | you had |
| Sie / sie hatten | you / they had |

Ich **hatte** Glück.  I was lucky.

**sein**

| | |
|---|---|
| ich war | I was |
| du warst | you were |
| er / sie / es / man war | he / she / it / one was |
| wir waren | we were |
| ihr wart | you were |
| Sie / sie waren | you / they were |

Es war teuer.  It was expensive.

## Irregular verbs

- Some verbs have irregular stems in the imperfect tense.
- Add the same basic endings as above to the irregular stems on the right:
  ich ging – wir gingen (I went – we went)
  ich fuhr – wir fuhren (I drove – we drove)

Im Stück **ging** es um eine Beziehung.
The play was about a relationship.
Die Kinder **sahen** blass aus.
The children looked pale.
Es **fand** in Hamburg **statt**.
It took place in Hamburg.

| | | |
|---|---|---|
| gehen | ➡ ging | went |
| fahren | ➡ fuhr | drove |
| finden | ➡ fand | found |
| kommen | ➡ kam | came |
| nehmen | ➡ nahm | took |
| sehen | ➡ sah | saw |
| sitzen | ➡ saß | sat |
| stehen | ➡ stand | stood |
| tut weh | ➡ tat weh | hurt |

Es gab is an impersonal verb and so does not change:

Es gab ein Haus.  There was a house.
Es gab zwei Häuser.  There were two houses.

## Now try this

Put these sentences into the imperfect tense.
(a) Sie hat Angst.
(b) Es ist hoffnungslos.
(c) Es gibt Toiletten im Erdgeschoss.
(d) Hörst du das?
(e) Plötzlich kommt uns der Mann entgegen.
(f) Das ist eine Überraschung, nicht?
(g) Es ist niemand zu Hause.
(h) Sie spielen gern Tischtennis.

> Spielen is a regular verb like hören.

# The future tense

As well as using the future tense, you can also express future intent using the present tense. Use this page to check you can do both!

## The future tense

Use the future tense to talk about things you **will** do or things that **will** happen in the future:

form of werden (to become) + sentence + infinitive at the end.

| ich werde | |
|---|---|
| du wirst | holen (collect) |
| er / sie / es / man wird | klopfen (knock) |
| wir werden | mieten (rent) |
| ihr werdet | zelten (camp) |
| Sie / sie werden | |

## Word order in the future tense

Form of werden in second position:

❶        ❷        ❸        ❹

Nächste Woche werde ich in Urlaub fahren.

Ich werde erfolgreich sein.
I will be successful.
Wie groß wirst du werden?
How tall will you get?
Morgen wird es kalt sein.
It will be cold tomorrow.
Werden sie auf die Uni gehen?
Will they go to university?
Ich bin froh, dass du zu Besuch kommen wirst.
I am happy that you will come to visit.

## Reflexive and separable verbs

- Reflexive verbs – add the pronoun after part of werden:
  Ich werde mich schnell rasieren.
  I will shave quickly.

- Separable verbs – stay together at the end of the sentence:
  Er wird das Lied herunterladen.
  He will download the song.

## Present tense with future intent

You can use the present tense to express what you are **going to** do. Include a time marker to make it clear that the intent is based in the future.

| morgen | tomorrow |
| übermorgen | the day after tomorrow |
| nächste Woche | next week |

Nächsten Sommer fahren wir nach Amerika.
We are going to America next summer.

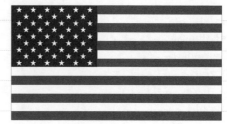

## Now try this

Rewrite the sentences in the future tense with **werden**.

(a) Ich gewinne das Spiel.
(b) Wir gehen in den Freizeitpark.
(c) Sie mieten eine große Wohnung.
(d) Ihr habt große Schwierigkeiten.
(e) Er besteht die Prüfung.
(f) Nächste Woche ziehen wir um.
(g) Trefft ihr euch später?
(h) Ich ziehe mich um sechs Uhr an.

# The conditional

The conditional is very similar in structure to the future tense and using it will improve your writing and speaking.

## Conditional

Use the conditional to talk about things you **would** do or things that **would** happen in the future:
part of würde (would) + sentence + infinitive at the end.

| ich würde | |
| du würdest | |
| er / sie / es / man würde | + infinitive |
| wir würden | |
| ihr würdet | |
| Sie / sie würden | |

Ich würde gern nach Italien fahren.
I would like to go to Italy.
Würden Sie lieber Geschäftsmann oder Klempner werden?
Would you rather become a businessman or a plumber?
Würdest du je rauchen?
Would you ever smoke?
Man würde nie ein Auto kaufen.
We would never buy a car.

würde sein = wäre – would be
würde haben = hätte – would have
es würde geben = es gäbe – there would be

## Using wenn

• You often use wenn (if) with the conditional.
• Remember: verb, comma, verb!

Wenn ich reich wäre, würde ich keine Designerkleidung kaufen.
If I were rich, I wouldn't buy designer clothes.

Wenn sie ein Vorstellungsgespräch hätte, würde sie rechtzeitig ankommen.
If she had an interview, she would arrive on time.

## Making requests

Use the conditional to make a request for something you **would** like:
Ich möchte Pommes essen.
I would like to eat chips.

The plural form adds -n:
wir möchten — we would like
sie hätten gern — they would like to have

Sie hätte gern ein neues Handy.
She would like a new mobile.

## Now try this

Rewrite these sentences using the conditional.
(a) Ich gehe gern ins Theater.
(b) Er kommt nie spät an.
(c) Wir trinken nie Bier.
(d) Helfen Sie mir bitte?
(e) Zum Geburtstag bekommt sie am liebsten Geld.
(f) Nächstes Jahr heiraten sie vielleicht.
(g) Wenn Latein Pflicht ist, gehe ich auf eine andere Schule.
(h) Wenn ich das mache, gibt es Krach mit meinen Eltern.

# The pluperfect tense

The pluperfect tense is used to say you **had** done something. Use it to aim for a top grade!

## Forming the pluperfect

- Use the pluperfect tense to talk about events which **had** happened.
- It is made from the **imperfect** of haben or sein + past participle.

| | |
|---|---|
| ich hatte <br> du hattest <br> er / sie / es / man hatte <br> wir hatten <br> ihr hattet <br> Sie / sie hatten | Pause gemacht (had had a break) <br><br> Freunde gesehen (had seen friends) |

| | |
|---|---|
| ich war <br> du warst <br> er / sie / es / man war <br> wir waren <br> ihr wart <br> Sie / sie waren | Ski gefahren (had been skiing) <br><br> zu Hause geblieben (had stayed at home) |

## Haben or sein?

- Some participles take haben and some sein. The rules are the same as for the perfect tense.
  Sie hatte kein Wort gesagt.
  She had not said a word.

| ich hatte <br> (I had) | angefangen / begonnen (begun) |
|---|---|
| | gearbeitet (worked) |
| | gebracht (brought) |
| | eingeladen (invited) |
| | erreicht (reached) |
| | geholt (fetched) |
| | gelogen (lied) |

Er war nicht gekommen.    He had not come.

| ich war <br> (I had) | geblieben (stayed) |
|---|---|
| | hineingegangen (entered) |
| | eingeschlafen (fallen asleep) |
| | vorbeigegangen (gone by) |
| es war | geschehen (it had happened) |

## The pluperfect and perfect tenses

Look how similar the pluperfect tense is to the perfect tense.

| | | |
|---|---|---|
| Ich habe Basketball gespielt. | ➡ | Ich hatte Basketball gespielt. |
| I played basketball. | | I had played basketball. |
| Es hat ihm Spaß gemacht. | ➡ | Es hatte ihm Spaß gemacht. |
| It was fun for him. | | It had been fun for him. |
| Wir sind zur Eishalle gegangen. | ➡ | Wir waren zur Eishalle gegangen. |
| We went to the ice rink. | | We had gone to the ice rink. |

## Now try this

Write these sentences in the pluperfect tense.
- **(a)** Ich habe zu Mittag gegessen.
- **(b)** Sie haben als Stadtführer gearbeitet.
- **(c)** Bist du schwimmen gegangen?
- **(d)** Wir sind in Kontakt geblieben.
- **(e)** Sie sind mit dem Rad in die Stadt gefahren.
- **(f)** Ich habe sie vor einigen Monaten besucht, aber damals war sie schon krank.
- **(g)** Bevor ich ins Haus gegangen bin, habe ich ein Gesicht am Fenster gesehen.
- **(h)** Obwohl ich kaum mit ihm gesprochen habe, schien er sehr freundlich zu sein.

# Questions

In the role play task, you will **have** to ask at least one question, so make sure you can do just that by studying this page carefully!

## Asking questions

You can swap the pronoun and verb round to form a question:

Du hast einen Hund.    You have got a dog.

Hast du einen Hund?    Have you got a dog?

Make sure you use a variety of tenses when you ask questions about events at different times:

Sie sind nach Spanien geflogen.
You flew to Spain.

Sind Sie nach Spanien geflogen?
Did you fly to Spain?

## Key question words

Wann?        When?

Warum?       Why?

Was?         What?

Wer?         Who?

Wie?         How?

Wo(hin)?     Where (to)?

Wohin werden Sie in Urlaub fahren?
Where will you go on holiday?

Wann sind Sie dorthin gefahren?
When did you go there?

Warum hat Ihnen der Film nicht gefallen?
Why didn't you like the film?

## Other question words

Was für ...?          What sort of ...?

Was für Bücher lesen   What sort of books
 Sie gern?               do you like reading?

Wie viele?            How many?

Wie viele Stunden pro Woche treiben Sie Sport?
How many hours a week do you do sport?

Wessen?              Whose?

Wessen Idee war das?  Whose idea was that?

*Wessen never changes case.*

*Welchen is in the accusative case.*

Wen? Wem?            Who(m)?

Wen finden Sie besser?  Who do you find better?

Mit wem spielen Sie Squash?
Who do you play squash with?

*Wen is in the accusative case.*

*Wem is in the dative case after mit.*

## Using welcher (which)

Welcher agrees with the noun it is asking about.

| masc | Welcher Sport? Which sport? |
| fem | Welche Aufgabe? Which activity? |
| neut | Welches Fach? Which subject? |
| pl | Welche Fächer? Which subjects? |

Welchen Sport finden Sie am einfachsten?
Which sport do you find the easiest?

Welches Fach machst du am liebsten?
Which subject do you like doing best?

## Now try this

1 Turn the sentences into questions.
   (a) Sie lesen gern Science-Fiction-Bücher.
   (b) Sie finden Ihre Arbeit anstrengend.
   (c) Sie möchten nur teilzeit arbeiten.
   (d) Nächsten Sommer werden Sie nach Australien auswandern.

2 Write questions **in German** to ask in your role play.
   (a) Who could help me?
   (b) When does the restaurant open?
   (c) Why is there a bag here?
   (d) How can I get to the cathedral?
   (e) What can one do in the evenings?

# Time markers

Here are some ideas to introduce a variety of time expressions into your work – remember to put the verb in **second** position if you are starting with one of these.

## Present tense

| | |
|---|---|
| aktuell | current(ly) |
| heute | today |
| heutzutage | these days |
| jetzt | now |
| seit | since / for |

Jetzt, wo ich noch Schülerin bin, muss ich viel lernen.

Now, while I am still a pupil, I must work hard.

## Past tenses

| | |
|---|---|
| gestern | yesterday |
| vorgestern | the day before yesterday |
| vor drei Monaten | three months ago |
| letzte Woche | last week |
| letztes Wochenende | last weekend |
| früher | previously |
| als (kleines) Kind | as a (small) child |
| neulich | recently |

Vor sechs Wochen habe ich mir das Bein gebrochen.

I broke my leg six weeks ago.

## Future tense

| | |
|---|---|
| bald | soon |
| in Zukunft | in future / in the future |
| morgen (früh) | tomorrow (morning) |
| übermorgen | the day after tomorrow |
| nächste Woche | next week |
| am nächsten Tag | on the next day |

In Zukunft werde ich eine gute Stelle finden.

In the future, I will find a good job.

## General

| | |
|---|---|
| jeden Tag / täglich | every day / daily |
| wöchentlich | weekly |
| eines Tages | one day |
| immer | always |
| immer noch | still |
| schon immer | always |
| am Anfang | at the start |
| von Zeit zu Zeit | from time to time |
| sofort | immediately |
| rechtzeitig | on time |
| regelmäßig | regularly |

Ich habe schon immer in Wales gewohnt.

I have always lived in Wales.

## Now try this

Rewrite these sentences with the time expressions provided in brackets.

(a) Ich spiele Klavier. (*for three years*)

(b) Er hat die Hausaufgaben nicht gemacht. (*last week*)

(c) Wir werden in den Bergen wandern gehen. (*next summer*)

(d) Wir wollten das Betriebspraktikum nicht machen. (*at the start*)

(e) Man wird alle Lebensmittel elektronisch kaufen. (*in future*)

(f) Ich hoffe, Disneyland zu besuchen. (*one day*)

(g) Ich hatte Halsschmerzen. (*the day before yesterday*)

(h) Sie spielen oft Tennis. (*earlier*)

Watch the tense!

# Numbers

Numbers are really important in a variety of contexts so make sure you know them!

## Numbers

| | | | |
|---|---|---|---|
| 1 eins | 11 elf | 21 einundzwanzig | 100 hundert |
| 2 zwei | 12 zwölf | 22 zweiundzwanzig | 101 hunderteins |
| 3 drei | 13 dreizehn | | 200 zweihundert |
| 4 vier | 14 vierzehn | | 333 dreihundertdreiunddreißig |
| 5 fünf | 15 fünfzehn | | |
| 6 sechs | 16 sechzehn | 30 dreißig | |
| 7 sieben | 17 siebzehn | 40 vierzig | |
| 8 acht | 18 achtzehn | 50 fünfzig | 1000 tausend |
| 9 neun | 19 neunzehn | 60 sechzig | |
| 10 zehn | 20 zwanzig | 70 siebzig | ein Tausend — a thousand |
| | | 80 achtzig | eine Million — a million |
| | | 90 neunzig | eine Milliarde — a billion |
| | | | eine Billion — a trillion |

all one word – however long!

no und after hundert

## Ordinal numbers

| | | | |
|---|---|---|---|
| 1st erste | 11th elfte | am vierzehnten März | on 14 March |
| 2nd zweite | 12th zwölfte | ab dem achten Juni | from 8 June |
| 3rd dritte | 13th dreizehnte | vom ersten bis zum | from 1 to 13 |
| 4th vierte | 14th vierzehnte | dreizehnten Dezember | December |
| 5th fünfte | | nach / vor dem zehnten April | after / before 10 April |
| 6th sechste | 20th zwanzigste | | |
| 7th siebte | 21st einundzwanzigste | seit dem dritten Februar | since 3 February |
| 8th achte | 30th dreißigste | **Years** | |
| 9th neunte | 31st einunddreißigste | (im Jahr) neunzehnhundertachtundachtzig | in 1988 |
| 10th zehnte | | (im Jahr) zweitausendzwanzig | in 2020 |

## Now try this

LISTENING TRACK 56

Listen to the recording

Listen and fill in the numbers.

(a) ☐ . – ☐ . Mai

(b) ☐ : ☐

(c) € ☐ , ☐

(d) ☐ . Januar ☐

(e) € ☐ Millionen

(f) ☐ % Ermäßigung

(g) ☐ : ☐

(h) ☐ Grad

# Vocabulary

These pages cover key German vocabulary that you need to know. This section starts with general terms that are useful in a wide variety of situations and then divides into vocabulary for each of the five main topics covered in this revision guide:

**1** High frequency language     **2** Identity and culture     **3** Local area, holidays and travel
**4** School     **5** Future aspirations, study and work     **6** International and global dimension

Sections marked **Aiming Higher** are only needed if you are studying for the Higher tier paper. Learning vocabulary is essential preparation for all four skills of reading, writing, listening and speaking but don't try to learn too much at once – concentrate on learning and testing yourself one page at a time.

# **1** High frequency language

| Verbs A–E | | Verbs E–K | | Verbs L–S | |
|---|---|---|---|---|---|
| abfahren | to depart | enden | to finish, end | lächeln | to smile |
| anfangen | to begin | erklären | to explain | lachen | to laugh |
| ankommen | to arrive | erlauben | to allow | lassen | to leave |
| annehmen | to accept | erreichen | to reach | laufen | to walk, run |
| anrufen | to phone | erzählen | to tell | leben | to live |
| antworten | to answer | fallen | to fall | legen | to lay |
| arbeiten | to work | fallen lassen | to drop | leihen | to borrow, hire |
| aufhören | to stop | fehlen | to miss | lesen | to read |
| aufmachen | to open | fernsehen | to watch TV | lieben | to love |
| ausgeben | to spend | finden | to find | liegen | to lie |
| ausleihen | to lend | fliehen | to escape | lügen | to tell a lie |
| bedienen | to serve | folgen | to follow | meinen | to think, say |
| befehlen | to order | fragen | to ask | mieten | to rent |
| begegnen | to meet | fühlen | to feel | mitteilen | to inform |
| beginnen | to begin | führen | to lead | nachsehen | to check |
| begleiten | to accompany | füllen | to fill | nehmen | to take |
| bekommen | to receive | geben | to give | nennen | to call |
| benutzen | to use | gefallen | to please | notieren | to note |
| beraten | to advise | gehören | to belong | öffnen | to open |
| beschließen | to decide | gelingen | to succeed | organisieren | to organise |
| beschreiben | to describe | geschehen | to happen | passieren | to happen |
| besprechen | to discuss | gewinnen | to win | planen | to plan |
| bestellen | to order | glauben | to think, believe | plaudern | to chat |
| besuchen | to visit | haben | to have | raten | to advise |
| bevorzugen | to prefer | halten | to stop, hold | rechnen | to count |
| bleiben | to stay | hassen | to hate | reden | to talk |
| brauchen | to need | heißen | to be called | reparieren | to repair |
| bringen | to bring | helfen | to help | retten | to save |
| danken | to thank | hineingehen | to enter | sagen | to say |
| dauern | to last | hoffen | to hope | schauen | to look |
| denken | to think | holen | to fetch | scheinen | to seem, shine |
| drücken | to push | hören | to hear | schenken | to give (gift) |
| eilen | to hurry | kaufen | to buy | schicken | to send |
| einkaufen | to shop | kennen | to know | schlagen | to knock, hit |
| einladen | to invite | kleben | to stick | schließen | to shut |
| einschalten | to turn on | klettern | to climb | schreiben | to write |
| einschlafen | to fall asleep | klingeln | to ring | sehen | to see |
| eintreten | to enter | klopfen | to knock | sich ärgern | to get angry |
| empfehlen | to recommend | kommen | to come | sich beeilen | to hurry |
| | | kosten | to cost | sich befinden | to be located |

**Now try this**

Pick five verbs at random from each column and see if you can write each one in the present, perfect and future tense for the **ich** form. Check your answers by looking at pages 95–103.

# ❶ High frequency language

## Verbs S–Z

|  |  |
|---|---|
| sich entscheiden | to decide |
| sich erinnern an | to remember |
| sich freuen auf | to look forward to |
| sich langweilen | to get bored |
| sich streiten | to argue |
| sitzen | to sit |
| spazieren | to walk |
| sprechen | to speak |
| springen | to jump |
| stecken | to place |
| stehlen | to steal |
| steigen | to climb, get on |
| stellen | to put |
| stoppen | to stop |
| streiten | to argue |
| studieren | to study at uni |
| tippen | to type |
| tragen | to wear, carry |
| treffen | to meet |
| trinken | to drink |
| unterschreiben | to sign |
| verbessern | to improve |
| verbringen | to spend (time) |
| verdienen | to earn |
| vergeben | to forgive |
| vergessen | to forget |
| verhindern | to prevent |
| verkaufen | to sell |
| verlassen | to leave |
| verlieren | to lose |
| vermeiden | to avoid |
| versprechen | to promise |
| verstehen | to understand |
| versuchen | to try |
| verzeihen | to forgive |
| vorbeigehen | to pass by |
| vorhaben | to intend |
| vorstellen | to introduce |
| wählen | to choose, dial |
| warten auf | to wait for |
| wechseln | to change |
| werden | to become |
| wiederholen | to repeat |
| wissen | to know |
| wohnen | to live |
| wünschen | to wish |
| zahlen | to pay |
| zählen | to count |
| zeigen | to show |

fahren  to drive

schlafen  to sleep

gehen  to walk, go

weinen  to cry

essen  to eat

werfen  to throw

|  |  |
|---|---|
| zuhören | to listen |
| zumachen | to close |
| zurückfahren | to return (by car) |
| zurückgehen | to return (on foot) |
| zurückkommen | to come back |
| zurückstellen | to put back |
| zusehen | to watch |

## Modal verbs

|  |  |
|---|---|
| dürfen | to be allowed to |
| können | to be able to |
| mögen | to like |
| müssen | to have to |
| sollen | to be supposed to |
| wollen | to want to |

## Adverbs

|  |  |
|---|---|
| besonders | especially |
| da | there |
| da drüben | over there |
| dort | there |
| fast | almost |
| gern | willingly |
| hier | here |
| immer | always, still |
| irgendwo | somewhere |
| jedoch | however |
| leider | unfortunately |
| lieber | rather |
| manchmal | sometimes |
| mehr | more |
| mitten | in the middle of |
| neulich | recently |
| nie | never |
| oben | above, upstairs |
| oft | often |
| regelmäßig | regularly |
| rückwärts | backwards |
| schnell | quickly |
| schon | already |
| sehr | very |
| sofort | immediately |
| unten | below |
| unterwegs | en route |
| vielleicht | perhaps |
| vorwärts | forwards |
| wahrscheinlich | probably |
| wirklich | really |
| ziemlich | rather, quite |
| zu | too |
| zusammen | together |

### Now try this

Choose 20 words you didn't know from this page and the previous page and write them in German. Close the book and try to write the English next to each one. Check back, then test yourself again on any you didn't get right.

# ① High frequency language

## Adjectives A–F

| | |
|---|---|
| aktuell | current |
| alle / alles | all |
| allein | alone |
| allgemein | general |
| anders | other |
| ärgerlich | annoying |
| artig | well behaved |
| aufregend | exciting |
| ausgezeichnet | excellent |
| bequem | comfortable |
| bereit | ready |
| beschäftigt | busy |
| bestimmt | definite |
| böse | angry |
| breit | broad |
| dankbar | grateful |
| dick | fat |
| dicht | dense |
| draußen | outside |
| dreckig | dirty |
| drinnen | inside |
| dumm | stupid |
| dünn | thin |
| dynamisch | dynamic |
| echt | real |
| ehemalig | old, former |
| eigen | own |
| eilig | in a hurry |
| einzig | only |
| ekelhaft | disgusting |
| eng | narrow, tight |
| erfreut | pleased |
| ermüdend | tiring |
| ernst | serious |
| erschöpft | exhausted |
| erst | first |
| erstaunt | astonished |
| falsch | false |
| fantastisch | great |
| faul | lazy |
| fertig | ready |
| fleißig | hard-working |
| flexibel | flexible |
| frei | free |

## Adjectives G–N

| | |
|---|---|
| gebrochen | broken |
| gefährlich | dangerous |
| genau | exact |
| geöffnet | open |
| geschlossen | closed |
| gesund | healthy |
| gleich | similar, same |
| glücklich | happy |
| großartig | magnificent |
| gültig | valid |
| gut | good |
| gut gelaunt | in a good mood |
| hart | severe, unkind / hard, unripe |
| hässlich | ugly |
| heiß | hot |
| hoch | high |
| hübsch | pretty |
| jung | young |
| kaputt | broken |
| klar | clear |
| klasse | sensational |
| komisch | funny |
| kostenlos | free (cost) |
| krank | ill |
| kurz | short |
| lang | long |
| langweilig | boring |
| launisch | moody |
| laut | noisy |
| lautlos | silent |
| leer | empty |
| leicht | easy |
| leise | quiet |
| letzte | last |
| Lieblings | favourite |
| lustig | funny |
| müde | tired |
| nächst | next |
| nah | near |
| nett | kind, nice |
| neu | new |
| niedrig | low |

| Farbe (f) | colour |
|---|---|
| hell | light |
| dunkel | dark |
| blau | |
| braun | |
| gelb | |
| grau | |
| grün | |
| lila | |
| rosa | |
| rot | |
| schwarz | |
| weiß | |
| gepunktet | |
| gestreift | |

## Adjectives N–R

| | |
|---|---|
| nötig | necessary |
| notwendig | necessary |
| nützlich | useful |
| offen | open |
| perfekt | perfect |
| prima | great, marvellous |
| reich | rich |
| reif | mature, ripe |
| richtig | true, right |
| ruhig | peaceful, calm |
| rund | round |

jung   alt        groß   klein

## Now try this

Look around the room you are in. Try to use 10 German adjectives to describe the room or the objects in it. Then think of a friend you have seen today. Try to use 10 German adjectives to describe their appearance, their personality and their clothing.

# ① High frequency language

## Adjectives S–Z

| | |
|---|---|
| satt | full |
| sauber | clean |
| schlecht | bad |
| schmal | narrow |
| schmutzig | dirty |
| schnell | fast, quick |
| schön | beautiful |
| schrecklich | awful, terrible |
| schüchtern | shy |
| schwach | weak |
| schwer | heavy, difficult |
| schwierig | difficult |
| spannend | exciting |
| stark | strong |
| steil | steep |
| stolz | proud |
| streng | strict |
| teuer | expensive |
| toll | great |
| traurig | sad |
| typisch | typical |
| überrascht | surprised |
| umweltfeindlich | eco-unfriendly |
| umweltfreundlich | eco-friendly |
| unglaublich | unbelievable |
| unterschiedlich | variable |
| unvorstellbar | unimaginable |
| verantwortlich | responsible |
| voll | full |
| wahr | true |
| weich | soft |
| weit | far |
| wertvoll | valuable |
| wichtig | important |
| wirklich | real |
| wunderbar | marvellous |
| zahlreich | numerous |
| zornig | angry |
| zufrieden | pleased, satisfied |

## Connecting words

| | |
|---|---|
| aber | but |
| also | so |
| auch | also, too |
| außerdem | moreover |
| dafür | from that |
| dann | then |
| deshalb | for this reason |
| deswegen | for this reason |
| nachher | afterwards |
| oder | or |
| übrigens | moreover |
| und | and |
| vorher | beforehand |
| zuerst | first of all |

## Quantities

| | |
|---|---|
| ein bisschen | a little (of) |
| ein Drittel | a third of |
| ein Dutzend | a dozen |
| ein Glas | a jar of |
| ein Stück | a piece of |
| eine Dose | a tin, box of |
| eine Flasche | a bottle of |
| eine Packung | a packet of |
| eine Scheibe | a slice of |
| eine Tafel | a bar of |
| eine Tüte | a bag of |
| genug | enough |
| mehrere | several |
| viele | many |

## Time expressions

| | |
|---|---|
| ab | from |
| ab und zu | from time to time |
| Abend (m) | evening |
| am Anfang | at the start |
| bald | soon |
| früh | early |
| gestern | yesterday |
| heute | today |
| heutzutage | nowadays |
| immer | always |
| immer noch | still |
| jetzt | now |
| meistens | mostly |
| Minute (f) | minute |
| Mittag (m) | midday |
| Mitternacht (f) | midnight |
| morgen | tomorrow |
| Morgen (m) | morning |
| morgen früh | tomorrow a.m. |
| Nachmittag (m) | afternoon |
| nächst | next |
| Nacht (f) | night |
| pünktlich | on time |
| rechtzeitig | on time |
| seit | since |
| sofort | immediately |
| spät | late |
| später | later |
| Tag (m) | day |
| täglich | every day |
| übermorgen | the day after tomorrow |
| von Zeit zu Zeit | from time to time |
| Vormittag (m) | morning |
| Woche (f) | week |
| Wochenende (n) | weekend |
| wöchentlich | weekly |

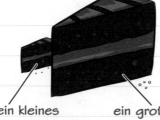

ein kleines Stück Kuchen     ein großes Stück Kuchen

ein Glas Marmelade

eine Tafel Schokolade

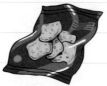

eine Packung Chips

eine Flasche Medizin

eine Scheibe Toast

eine Dose Erbsen

## Now try this

Test yourself on the time expressions above by covering up the English column and then writing down the English translations yourself. Compare your answers with the list above. How many have you got right?

# ① High frequency language

## Questions

| | |
|---|---|
| wann? | when? |
| warum? | why? |
| was? | what? |
| was für? | what sort of? |
| wen? wem? | whom? / who? |
| wer? | who? |
| wessen? | whose? |
| wie? | how? |
| wie viel(e)? | how much / many? |
| wo? | where? |

| | Montag<br>Monday | Dienstag<br>Tuesday | Mittwoch<br>Wednesday | Donnerstag<br>Thursday | Freitag<br>Friday | Samstag /<br>Sonnabend<br>Saturday | Sonntag<br>Sunday |
|---|---|---|---|---|---|---|---|
| 07.00 | | | | | | | |
| 08.00 | | | | | | | |

## Other high frequency words

| | |
|---|---|
| alle | everyone |
| Art (f) | type |
| das | that |
| Ding (n) | thing |
| Ende (n) | end |
| Form (f) | shape |
| Frau (f) | Mrs |
| Gegenstand (m) | object |
| Herr (m) | Mr |
| irgendetwas | something |
| ja | yes |
| jeder | everybody |
| jemand | someone |
| Mal (n) | time |
| Mitte (f) | middle |
| nein | no |
| Nummer (f) | number |
| ob | whether |
| Sache (f) | thing |
| weil | because |
| Weise (f) | way |
| wenn | if |
| wie | as, like |
| Zahl (f) | figure (number) |
| zum Beispiel | for example |

## 12-hour clock

Viertel nach zwei    halb drei    zehn vor drei

## 24-hour clock

 zwölf Uhr fünfundvierzig

 zwanzig Uhr vierzig

 dreiundzwanzig Uhr

## Social conventions

| | | | |
|---|---|---|---|
| alles Gute | all the best | danke schön | thank you |
| auf Wiedersehen | goodbye | Entschuldigung | excuse me |
| bis bald | see you soon | grüß Gott | hello |
| bis morgen | see you tomorrow | gute Nacht | goodnight |
| | | guten Abend | good evening |
| bis später | see you later | guten Tag | hello, good day |
| bitte | please | | |
| bitte schön | you're welcome | hallo | hello |
| | | mit bestem Gruß | best wishes |
| | | wie bitte? | pardon? |

## Months

Januar · Faschung Februar · März · April · Mai · Juni

Juli · August · September · Oktober · November · Dezember

## Now try this

Practise the days of the week and the months of the year by translating the birthdays of family and friends into German.

# ① High frequency language

## Prepositions

| | |
|---|---|
| an | at |
| auf | on |
| aus | out of |
| außer | except |
| bei | with, at (house) |
| bis | until |
| durch | through |
| entlang | along |
| für | for |
| gegen | towards |
| gegenüber | opposite |
| hinter | behind |
| in | in, into |
| mit | with |
| nach | after |
| neben | next to |
| ohne | without |
| seit | since |
| statt | instead of |
| trotz | despite |
| über | above, over |
| um | around |
| unter | beneath, under |
| von | from |
| vor | in front of |
| während | during |
| wegen | because of |
| zu | to |
| zwischen | between |

## Continents

| | |
|---|---|
| Afrika | Africa |
| Asien | Asia |
| Australien | Australia |
| Europa | Europe |
| Nordamerika | North America |
| Südamerika | South America |

## Countries

| | |
|---|---|
| Belgien | Belgium |
| Dänemark | Denmark |
| Griechenland | Greece |
| die Niederlande | Netherlands |
| Russland | Russia |
| Deutschland | |
| die Schweiz | |
| die Türkei | |
| die Vereinigten Staaten | |
| England | |
| Frankreich | |
| Großbritannien | |
| Indien | |
| Irland | |
| Italien | |
| Österreich | |
| Schottland | |
| Spanien | |
| Wales | |

## Nationalities

The first line of each entry in this sec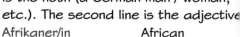 is the noun (a German man / woman, etc.). The second line is the adjective

| | |
|---|---|
| Afrikaner/in afrikanisch | African |
| Amerikaner/in amerikanisch | American |
| Belgier/in belgisch | Belgian |
| Brite/Britin britisch | British |
| Däne/Dänin dänisch | Danish |
| Deutsche(r) deutsch | German |
| Engländer/in englisch | English |
| Europäer/in europäisch | European |
| Franzose/Französin französisch | French |
| Grieche/Griechin griechisch | Greek |
| Inder/Inderin indisch | Indian |
| Ire/Irin irisch | Irish |
| Italiener/in italienisch | Italian |
| Niederländer/in niederländisch | Dutch |
| Österreicher/in österreichisch | Austrian |
| Russe/Russin russisch | Russian |
| Schotte/Schottin schottisch | Scottish |
| Schweizer/in schweizerisch | Swiss |
| Spanier/in spanisch | Spanish |
| Waliser/in walisisch | Welsh |

## Now try this

Match the German place names to their English equivalents.

| | | |
|---|---|---|
| (a) | Bayern | Vienna |
| (b) | der Ärmelkanal | Bavaria |
| (c) | der Bodensee | Geneva |
| (d) | der Schwarzwald | Danube |
| (e) | die Alpen | Black Forest |
| (f) | die Donau | Cologne |
| (g) | Genf | English Channel |
| (h) | Köln | Lake Constance |
| (i) | München | Munich |
| (j) | Wien | Alps |

# ❷ Identity and culture

## Food and drink

|  |  |
|---|---|
| Abendessen (n) | evening meal |
| Apfelsine (f) | orange |
| Appetit (m) | appetite |
| Aprikose (f) | apricot |
| Aufschnitt (m) | cold sliced meat |
| Auswahl (f) | choice, selection |
| bedienen | to serve |
| Besteck (n) | cutlery |
| bestellen | to order |
| bezahlen | to pay |
| Blumenkohl (m) | cauliflower |
| Bockwurst (f) | frankfurter |
| Bohne (f) | bean |
| Braten (m) | roast meat |
| Bratwurst (f) | fried sausage |
| Brot (n) | bread |
| Brötchen (n) | roll |
| Butterbrot (n) | sandwich |
| Champagner (m) | champagne |
| Chips (pl) | crisps |
| Ei (n) | egg |
| Eisdiele (f) | ice cream parlour |
| Erfrischungen (pl) | refreshments |
| Essig (m) | vinegar |
| Fertiggericht (n) | ready meal |
| Fleisch (n) | meat |
| Frikadelle (f) | meatball |
| Fruchtsaft (m) | fruit juice |
| Frühstück (n) | breakfast |
| Gabel (f) | fork |
| Gasthaus (n) | inn |
| Gebäck (n) | biscuits / pastries |
| Geld (n) | money |
| gemischt | mixed |
| Gemüse (n) | vegetables |
| Getränk (n) | drink |
| Gurke (f) | cucumber |
| Hähnchen (n) | chicken |
| Hauptgericht (n) | main course |
| Himbeere (f) | raspberry |
| hungrig | hungry |
| Imbissstube (f) | snack bar |
| Kakao (m) | cocoa |
| Kännchen (n) | pot |
| Käse (m) | cheese |
| Kebab (m) / Döner (m) | kebab |
| Keks (m) | biscuit |
| Kellner (m) / Kellnerin (f) | waiter / waitress |
| Kohl (m) | cabbage |
| Kotelett (n) | chop (e.g. pork) |
| Krapfen (m) | doughnut |
| Kuchen (m) | cake |
| Leberwurst (f) | liver sausage |
| lecker | tasty |

 Zitrone (f)   Ananas (f)   Apfel (m)   Birne (f)   Erdbeere (f)

 Kirsche (f)   Pflaume (f)   Karotte (f)   Champignon / Pilz (m)

 Erbsen (pl)   Paprika (f)   Kartoffel (f)   Tomate (f)

|  |  |
|---|---|
| Löffel (m) | spoon |
| Mahlzeit (f) | meal |
| Marmelade (f) | jam |
| Menü (n) | set meal |
| Messer (n) | knife |
| Milch (f) | milk |
| Mineralwasser (n) | mineral water |
| Mittagessen (n) | lunch |
| Nachspeise (f) | dessert |
| Nachtisch (m) | dessert |
| Nudeln (pl) | pasta |
| Obst (n) | fruit |
| Obsttorte (f) | fruit pie |
| Pfirsich (m) | peach |
| Pommes (frites) (pl) | chips |
| probieren | to try |
| Rechnung (f) | bill |
| Rindfleisch (n) | beef |
| roh | raw |
| Ruhetag (m) | day off |
| Saft (m) | juice |
| Sahne (f) | cream |
| Salat (m) | lettuce, salad |
| Salz (n) | salt |
| satt | full up |
| scharf | hot (spicy) |
| Schinken (m) | ham |
| Schnellimbiss (m) | snack bar |
| Schnitzel (n) | escalope |
| Schokolade (f) | chocolate |
| Schweinefleisch (n) | pork |
| Selbstbedienung (f) | self-service |
| Senf (m) | mustard |
| Soße (f) | gravy, sauce |
| Speisekarte (f) | menu |
| Speisesaal (m) | dining room |
| Spezialität (f) | speciality |
| Steak (n) | steak |
| Suppe (f) | soup |
| süß | sweet |
| Tagesgericht (n) | dish of the day |
| Tasse (f) | cup |
| Teelöffel (m) | teaspoon |
| Teller (m) | plate |
| Thunfisch (m) | tuna |

|  |  |
|---|---|
| Tisch (m) | table |
| Tischtuch (n) | tablecloth |
| Torte (f) | gateau |
| trinken | to drink |
| Trinkgeld (n) | tip (money) |
| Vegetarier/in (m/f) | vegetarian (person) |
| vegetarisch | vegetarian (food) |
| voll | full |
| Vorspeise (f) | starter |
| Wein (m) | wine |
| Weintraube (f) | grape |
| Wurst (f) | sausage |
| Zucker (m) | sugar |
| Zwiebel (f) | onion |

### Aiming Higher

|  |  |
|---|---|
| Bier vom Fass (n) | draught beer |
| blutig | rare (steak) |
| durch | well-done (steak) |
| Ente (f) | duck |
| Forelle (f) | trout |
| gedämpft, gedünstet | steamed |
| geräuchert | smoked |
| hausgemacht | home-made |
| Honig (m) | honey |
| Kalbfleisch (n) | veal |
| Knoblauch (m) | garlic |
| Kräutertee (m) | herbal tea |
| Lachs (m) | salmon |
| Meeresfrüchte (pl) | seafood |
| Pute (f) | turkey |
| Rührei (n) | scrambled egg |
| scharf | sharp, spicy |
| schmackhaft | tasty |
| Sekt (m) | sparkling wine |
| Spiegelei (n) | fried egg |
| Spinat (m) | spinach |
| Tablett (n) | tray |
| Truthahn (m) | turkey |
| Untertasse (f) | saucer |
| Vollmilch (f) | full-fat milk |
| würzig, pikant | spicy |

### Now try this

Look at the pictures on this page and memorise the items. Then close the book and see how many you can remember – in German! Open the book and check your spelling carefully.

# ❷ Identity and culture

## Dress and style

|  |  |
|---|---|
| altmodisch | old-fashioned |
| angezogen | dressed |
| Anzug (m) | suit |
| Armband (n) | bracelet |
| Badeanzug (m) | swimming costume |
| Badehose (f) | trunks |
| aus Baumwolle | (made of) cotton |
| gepflegt, schick | smart |
| Halskette (f) | necklace |
| Halstuch (n) | scarf |
| Handschuh (m) | glove |
| Juwelen (pl) | jewels |
| Klamotten (pl) | clothes (slang) |
| Kleidung (f) | clothing |
| Lippenstift (m) | lipstick |
| Marke (f) | make, brand |
| Mode (f) | fashion |
| modisch | fashionable |
| Mütze (f) | cap |
| Nachthemd (n) | nightdress |
| Ohrring (m) | earring |
| Pantoffel (m) | slipper |
| Pullover, Pulli (m) | pullover |
| Regenschirm (m) | umbrella |
| Schlafanzug (m) | pyjamas |
| Schlips (m) | tie |
| Schminke (f) | make-up |
| Slip (m) | pants, briefs |
| Stiefel (m) | boot |
| Strumpfhose (f) | tights |
| Trainingsanzug (m) | tracksuit |
| Unterhose (f) | underpants |

### Aiming Higher

|  |  |
|---|---|
| eng | tight |
| gefärbt | dyed |
| Morgenmantel (m) | dressing gown |
| aus Seide / Samt | made from silk / velvet |
| sich schminken | to put on make-up |
| Wolljacke (f) | cardigan |

Gürtel (m)

Hemd (n)

Hut (m)

Bluse (f)

Mantel (m)

Kleid (n)

Krawatte (f) / Schlips (m)

Rock (m)

Jacke (f)

Shorts (pl)

Schal (m)

Schuh (m)

Socke (f)

Jeans (f)

Sportschuhe (pl)

## Family, friends and home

|  |  |  |  |
|---|---|---|---|
| allein | alone | bevorzugen | to prefer |
| alt | old | Beziehung (f) | relationship |
| älter | older | Bild (n) | picture |
| Alter (n) | age | blöd | foolish, silly |
| arbeitslos | unemployed | böse | angry, cross |
| arm | poor | Brieffreund (m) | penfriend |
| auf die Nerven gehen | to annoy | Brille (f) | glasses |
| | | Bruder (m) | brother |
| Augen (pl) | eyes | charmant | charming |
| auskommen mit | to get on with | Cousin/e (m/f) | cousin |
| aussehen | to look (appearance) | Doppelhaus (n) | semi-detached house |
| babysitten | to babysit | egoistisch | selfish |
| Badezimmer (n) | bathroom | Ehe (f) | marriage |
| Bart (m) | beard | Ehemann (m) | husband |
| bequem, gemütlich | comfortable, cosy | Ehering (m) | wedding ring |
| | | ehrlich | honest |
| berühmt | famous | einladen | to invite |
| Besuch (m) | visit | Einladung (f) | invitation |
| besuchen | to visit | einsam | lonely |

### Now try this

Think of all the clothes items on this page that you have worn during the past week. Make a list in English, then try to write the German equivalents without looking at the page. Check back to see how many you got right. Learn the ones you got wrong!

# ❷ Identity and culture

| | | | | | |
|---|---|---|---|---|---|
| einverstanden | agreed | hübsch | pretty | rechthaberisch | bossy |
| Einzelkind (n) | only child | humorlos | no sense of | reich | rich |
| Eltern (pl) | parents | | humour | Reihenhaus (n) | terraced house |
| Enkelkind (n) | grandchild | humorvoll | humorous | Respekt haben vor | to respect |
| ernst | serious | Hund (m) | dog | sauer | sour, cross |
| Erwachsene (m/f) | adult | Jahr (n) | year | Schlafzimmer (n) | bedroom |
| Esszimmer (n) | dining room | Jugend (f) | youth (time | schlank | thin |
| Familie (f) | family | | of life) | Schnurrbart (m) | moustache |
| Feier (f) | party | Jugendliche (m/f) | young person | schön | beautiful |
| feiern | to celebrate | jung | young | schüchtern | shy |
| Frau (f) | wife, woman | Junge (m) | boy | schwätzen | to chat |
| frech | cheeky | Katze (f) | cat | Schwester (f) | sister |
| Freund (m) | male friend | kennen | to know | Schwiegersohn (m) | son / |
| Freundin (f) | female friend | Kind (n) | child | /-tochter (f) | daughter- |
| freundlich | friendly | klug, intelligent | intelligent | | in-law |
| Freundschaft (f) | friendship | komisch | funny (strange) | selbst | self |
| Garten (m) | garden | kritisieren | to criticise | Sessel (m) | armchair |
| Garage (f) | garage | Küche (f) | kitchen | sich freuen auf | to look |
| geboren | born | Kuss (m) | kiss | | forward to |
| Geburtsdatum (n) | date of birth | küssen | to kiss | sich kümmern um | to look after |
| Geburtsort (m) | birthplace | Laune (f) | mood | sich streiten | to argue |
| Geburtstag (m) | birthday | Leben (n) | life | sich trennen | to separate |
| geduldig | patient | lebendig | lively | sich verloben | to get |
| Gefühl (n) | feeling | ledig | unmarried | | engaged |
| gemein | mean, nasty | leiden | to suffer, bear | sich verstehen | to get on |
| gern haben | to like | nicht leiden | to dislike, not | sich vorstellen | to introduce |
| Geschenk (n) | present | können | be able to | Sohn (m) | son |
| geschieden | divorced | | bear | sorgen für | to care for |
| Geschwister (pl) | siblings | Leute (pl) | people | spenden | to donate |
| Gesicht (n) | face | lieb | likeable | Spitzname (m) | nickname |
| gesprächig, | | lockig | curly | Stief- | step- |
| schwatzhaft | chatty | lustig | funny | still | quiet |
| getrennt | separated | Mädchen (n) | girl | Streit (m) | argument |
| glatt | straight (hair) | Mann (m) | man, husband | Stuhl (m) | chair |
| eine Glatze haben | to be bald | Meerschweinchen | | sympathisch | nice, likeable |
| gratulieren | to | (n) | guinea pig | Tante (f) | aunt |
| | congratulate | Möbel (pl) | furniture | Tochter (f) | daughter |
| großartig | magnificent | multikulturell, | | tot | dead |
| Großeltern (pl) | grandparents | multikulti | multicultural | Traum (m) | dream |
| Großmutter (f) | grandmother | Mund (m) | mouth | traurig | sad |
| Großvater (m) | grandfather | Mutter (f) | mother | Typ (m) | guy, bloke |
| gut / schlecht | in a good / | Nachbar (m) | neighbour | Umfrage (f) | survey |
| gelaunt | bad mood | nett | nice, kind | unerträglich | unbearable |
| Haar (n) | hair | Oma (f) | grandma | unternehmungslustig | |
| Halb- | half- | Onkel (m) | uncle | | adventurous |
| hässlich | ugly | Opa (m) | grandad | unterstützen | to support |
| Haus (n) | house | ordentlich | tidy | Vater (m) | father |
| Haustier (n) | pet | Person (f) / | | verheiratet | married |
| Heim (n) | home | Mensch (m) | person | verliebt | in love |
| heiraten | to get married | Persönlichkeit (f) | personality | verlobt | engaged |
| heißen | to be called | pessimistisch | pessimistic | Vorname (m) | first name |
| Hochzeit (f) | wedding | Piercing (n) | body piercing | Wohnblock (m) | block of flats |
| höflich | polite | Postleitzahl (f) | postcode | Wohnort (m) | home location |
| | | Prominente (m/f) | celebrity | Wohnung (f) | flat |

## Now try this

To help you learn the personality adjectives, write out the German words in three lists: positive, negative and neutral. Then memorise five adjectives that could describe you.

# ② Identity and culture

|  |  |
|---|---|
| Wohnzimmer (n) | sitting room |
| zufrieden | satisfied |
| Zuhause (n) | home |
| Zwillinge (pl) | twins |

### Aiming Higher

|  |  |
|---|---|
| ähnlich | similar |
| Alleinerziehende (m/f) | single parent |
| Alleinstehende (m/f) | single person |
| (hohes) Alter (n) | old age |
| Altersheim (n) | old people's home |
| angeberisch | pretentious |
| ausgeglichen, ausgewogen | well-balanced |
| aussehen wie | to resemble |
| benachteiligen | to disadvantage |
| leiden | to suffer |
| minderjährig | underage |
| Pickel (m) | spot (acne) |
| rassistisch | racist |
| Rentner/in (m/f) | pensioner |
| schikanieren, mobben | to bully |
| selbstsicher, selbstbewusst | self-confident |
| sensibel, empfindlich | sensitive |
| stur, dickköpfig | stubborn |
| Treffen (n) | meeting |
| verständnisvoll | understanding |
| Verwandte (m/f) | relative |
| verwöhnt, verdorben | spoilt |
| Vorbild (n) | role model |
| zuverlässig | reliable |

## Lifestyle: healthy living and exercise

|  |  |
|---|---|
| abnehmen | to lose weight |
| Alkohol (m) | alcohol |
| alkoholisch | alcoholic |
| alt | old |
| Alter (n) | age |
| Angst haben | to be afraid |
| Arm (m) | arm |

|  |  |
|---|---|
| atmen | to breathe |
| aufgeben | to give up |
| aufhören | to stop |
| Bauch (m) | stomach |
| Bein (n) | leg |
| betrunken | drunk |
| brechen | to break |
| Diät machen | to diet |
| dick | fat |
| Droge (f) | drug |
| dünn | thin |
| Durchfall (m) | diarrhoea |
| Durst (m) | thirst |
| durstig | thirsty |
| Erkältung (f) | cold |
| Erste Hilfe | first aid |
| fettig | fatty, greasy |
| Fieber (n) | temperature |
| Finger (m) | finger |
| Fuß (m) | foot |
| gebrochen | broken |
| gesund | healthy |
| Gesundheit (f) | health |
| glücklich | happy |
| Grippe (f) | flu |
| Hals (m) | neck, throat |
| Hand (f) | hand |
| Herz (n) | heart |
| husten | to cough |
| Knie (n) | knee |
| Kopf (m) | head |
| Körper (m) | body |
| köstlich | delicious |
| laufen | to run |
| lebendig | lively |
| Leber (f) | liver |
| Lunge (f) | lung |
| Magen (m) | stomach |
| mager | low-fat |
| Medikament (n) | medicine |
| nervös | nervous |
| rauchen | to smoke |
| Raucher (m) | smoker |
| riechen | to smell |
| Rücken (m) | back (body) |
| Ruhe (f) | calm, peace |
| schlimm | bad |
| schmecken | to taste |
| Schmerz (m) | pain |
| Schulter (f) | shoulder |
| sich entspannen | to relax |
| sich fit halten | to keep fit |
| sich fühlen | to feel |
| sich verletzen | to harm, injure |

|  |  |
|---|---|
| sportlich | sporty |
| Spritze (f) | injection |
| spritzen | to inject |
| sterben | to die |
| stressig | stressful |
| übel | sick, ill |
| Unfall (m) | accident |
| ungesund | unhealthy |
| Vegetarier/in (m/f) | vegetarian |
| Verletzung (f) | injury |
| Verstopfung (f) | constipation |
| vorbereiten | to prepare |
| weh tun | to hurt |
| Zahn (m) | tooth |
| Zigarette (f) | cigarette |
| zunehmen | to put on weight |

### Aiming Higher

|  |  |
|---|---|
| abhängig | addicted |
| Ballaststoff (m) | dietary fibre |
| Behandlung (f) | treatment |
| bewusstlos | unconscious |
| Biokost (f) | organic food |
| Blut (n) | blood |
| Entziehungskur (f) | rehab |
| ermüdend | tiring |
| fettarm | low-fat |
| Fettleibigkeit (f) | obesity |
| Fußgelenk (n) | ankle |
| Gehirn (n) | brain |
| Geruch (m) | smell |
| Geschmack (m) | taste |
| Heuschnupfen (m) | hay fever |
| Krebs (m) | cancer |
| magersüchtig | anorexic |
| Mehl (n) | flour |
| Nahrung (f) | food |
| Nuss (f) | nut |
| Rauschgift (n) | drug(s) |
| Schnupfen (m) | cold |
| schwindlig | dizzy |
| sich erholen | to recover |
| sich gewöhnen an | to get used to |
| sich trimmen | to keep fit |
| Sucht (f) | addiction |
| süchtig | addicted |
| übergewichtig | overweight |
| verstauchen | to sprain |

### Now try this

Write at least 10 body parts in German from memory. Look at the page and check your spelling.

# ❷ Identity and culture

## Cultural life

|  |  |
|---|---|
| Agentenroman (m) | spy novel |
| Bräutigam (m) | bridegroom |
| Buch (n) | book |
| Bühne (f) | stage |
| Computerspiel (n) | computer game |
| Disko / Disco (f) | disco |
| Dokumentarfilm (m) | documentary |
| Dreikönigsfest (n) | Epiphany |
| Ehe (f) | marriage |
| Ehering (m) | wedding ring |
| Fantasyfilm (m) | fantasy film |
| Fastenzeit (f) | Lent |
| Feier / Party (f) | party |
| Fernsehkanal (m) | TV channel |
| Fotoapparat (m) | camera |
| Freizeit (f) | free time, leisure |
| Freizeitbeschäftigung (f) | leisure activity |
| gratulieren | to congratulate |
| Gruppe / Band (f) | band |
| Handy (n) | mobile phone |
| Heiligabend (m) | Christmas Eve |
| heiraten | to get married |
| Hobby (n) | hobby |
| Hochzeit (f) | wedding |
| Horrorfilm (m) | horror film |
| Jugendklub (m) | youth club |
| Karfreitag (m) | Good Friday |
| Kino (n) | cinema |
| Konzert (n) | concert |
| Krimi (m) | detective story |
| Lesen (n) | reading |
| Liebesfilm (m) | love film |
| Lied (n) | song |
| MP3-Datei (f) | MP3 file |
| Muttertag (m) | Mother's Day |
| Nachrichten (pl) | news |
| Neujahr (n) | New Year |
| Ostermontag (m) | Easter Monday |
| Ostern (n) | Easter |

Ich spiele ...
I play ...

Geige (f)   Trompete (f)   Flöte (f)

Schlagzeug (n)

Klarinette (f)   Klavier (n)   Blockflöte (f)

|  |  |
|---|---|
| Popmusik (f) | pop music |
| Quizsendung (f) | quiz show |
| romantisch | romantic |
| sammeln | to collect |
| Sammlung (f) | collection |
| Sänger/in (m/f) | singer |
| Schau (f) | show |
| Seifenoper (f) | soap opera |
| Sender (m) | (TV) channel |
| Sendung (f) | (TV) programme |
| Serie (f) | series |
| Silvester (n) | New Year's Eve |
| Spielkonsole (f) | games console |
| Spielzeug (n) | toy |
| Spionageroman (m) | spy novel |
| Taschengeld (n) | pocket money |
| Theaterstück (n) | play |
| Unterhaltung (f) | entertainment |
| Vergnügen (n) | pleasure |
| Volksmusik (f) | folk music |
| Weihnachten (n) | Christmas |
| Wettbewerb (m) | competition |
| Zeichentrickfilm (m) | cartoon |
| Zeitschrift (f) | magazine |

**Aiming Higher**

|  |  |
|---|---|
| Brettspiel (n) | board game |
| Fernbedienung (f) | remote control |
| Fernsehkomödie (f) | sitcom |
| Heimwerken (n) | DIY |
| Hochzeitsfeier (f) | wedding ceremony |
| Melodie (f) | melody, tune |
| Originalfassung (f) | original version |
| Publikum (n) | audience |
| Satellitenfernsehen (n) | satellite TV |

|  |  |
|---|---|
| synchronisiert | dubbed |
| Untertitel (pl) | subtitles |
| Verlobung (f) | engagement (pre-marriage) |
| Wissen (n) | knowledge |
| Zuhörer (m/pl) | listener(s) |
| Zuschauer (m/pl) | viewer(s) |

## Cultural life (sports)

|  |  |
|---|---|
| (asiatische) Kampfsportarten (pl) | martial arts |
| Ausrüstung (f) | equipment |
| Bergsteigen (n) | mountaineering |
| Bodybuilding (n) | bodybuilding |
| Bogenschießen (n) | archery |
| Boxen (n) | boxing |
| bummeln | to go for a stroll |
| Extremsport (m) | extreme sport |
| Fallschirmspringen (n) | parachuting |
| Fan (m) | fan (supporter) |
| Federball (m) | badminton |
| Fußball (m) | football |
| Gleitschirmfliegen (n) | paragliding |
| Halle (f) | hall |
| Handball (m) | handball |
| Hockey (n) | hockey |
| Inlineskaten (n) | rollerblading |
| Judo (n) | judo |
| Kanufahren (n) | canoeing |
| Karate (n) | karate |
| kegeln gehen | to go bowling |
| Klettern (n) | climbing |
| Mannschaft (f) | team |
| Mitglied (n) | member |
| Radfahren (n) | cycling |
| reiten | to ride a horse |
| Rollschuh laufen | to rollerskate |

**Now try this**

Choose five compound nouns from this page and write them as their separate nouns. That way you can expand your vocabulary!

# ❷ Identity and culture

| Schach (n) | chess |
| Schiedsrichter (m) | referee |
| Schlittschuhlaufen (n) | ice skating |
| Schwimmen (n) | swimming |
| Segeln (n) | sailing |
| Skateboard fahren (n) | to go skateboarding |
| spazieren gehen | to go for a stroll |
| Spiel (n) | game |
| Sport (m), Sportart (f) | sport |
| sportlich | sporty |
| Sportplatz (m) | sports ground |
| Sport treiben | to do sport |
| Surfen (n) | surfing |
| Tanz (m), Tanzen (n) | dance, dancing |
| teilnehmen an | to take part in |
| Tennis (n) | tennis |
| Tischtennis (n) | table tennis |
| ein Tor schießen | to score a goal |
| trainieren | to exercise |
| Trampolinspringen (n) | trampolining |
| Turnen (n), Gymnastik (f) | gymnastics |
| Verein (m) | club |
| wandern | to hike |
| Wasserskifahren (n) | waterskiing |
| Windsurfen (n) | windsurfing |

**Aiming Higher**

| Angelrute (f) | fishing rod |
| Fechten (n) | fencing |
| Halbzeit (f) | half time |

[Image labels:]
| Bildschirm (m) | screen |
| Tastatur (f) | keyboard |
| Taste (f) | key |
| Drucker (m) | printer |
| Computer (m) | computer |

| Liga (f) | league |
| Meisterschaft (f) | championship |
| Rudern (n) | rowing |
| Segelboot (n) | sailing boat |
| Sporttauchen (n) | scuba diving |
| Turnier (n) | tournament |
| Umkleidekabine (f) | changing rooms |

## Using social media

| Anschluss (m) | connection |
| Blog (m/n) | blog |
| brennen | to burn |
| Chatroom (m), Chatraum (m) | chatroom |
| chatten | to chat (online) |
| Computervirus (m/n) | computer virus |
| E-Mail (f) | email |
| drucken | to print |
| Festplatte (f) | disk |
| Gefahr (f) | danger |
| herunterladen, downloaden | to download |
| hochladen, heraufladen, uploaden | to upload |
| Homepage (f) | homepage |

| Internet-Mobbing (n) | cyberbullying |
| Internetseite (f) | website, web page |
| mailen | to email |
| löschen | to delete, remove |
| Passwort (n) | password |
| Progammierer (m), Programmiererin (f) | programmer |
| Schrägstrich (m) | forward slash |
| Sicherheit (f) | security |
| sichern, speichern, absaven | to save, store |
| soziales Netzwerk (n) | social network |
| tippen | to type |
| Verbindung (f) | connection |
| Web (n) | web |
| Webcam (f), Netzkamera (f) | webcam |
| Website / Webseite (f) | website, web page |

**Now try this**

Make two lists of the sports from this page and page 119: ones you have played and ones you have never played.

# ❸ Local area, holiday and travel

## Local area

|  |  |
|--------|---------|
| Abfalleimer (m) | rubbish bin |
| Apotheke (f) | chemist's |
| Bäckerei (f) | baker's |
| Bauernhof (m) | farm |
| Bibliothek (f) | library |
| Buchhandlung (f) | bookshop |
| Busbahnhof (m) | bus station |
| Eishalle (f) | ice rink |
| Fabrik (f) | factory |
| Freizeitpark (m) | theme park |
| Freizeitzentrum (n) | leisure centre |
| Gebäude (n) | building |
| Geschäft (n) | shop |
| Hafen (m) | port |
| Hallenbad (n) | indoor pool |
| Hochhaus (n) | tower block |
| Kaufhaus (n) | department store |
| Kino (n) | cinema |
| Kirche (f) | church |
| Kneipe (f) | pub |
| Krankenhaus (n) | hospital |
| Kunstgalerie (f) | art gallery |
| Laden (m) | shop |
| Lebensmittelgeschäft (n) | grocer's |
| Markt (m) | market |
| Metzgerei (f) | butcher's |
| Museum (n) | museum |
| Nachtklub (m) | nightclub |
| Palast (m) | palace |
| Platz (m) | square |
| Polizeiwache (f) | police station |
| Rathaus (n) | town hall |
| Schloss (n) | castle |
| Schnellimbiss (m) | snack bar |
| Schwimmbad (n) | swimming pool |
| Spielplatz (m) | playground |
| Sportzentrum (n) | sports centre |
| Supermarkt (m) | supermarket |

das Stadion
the stadium

der Dom
the cathedral

der Flughafen
the airport

der Bahnhof
the railway station

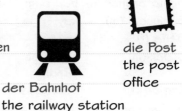
die Post
the post office

|  |  |
|--------|---------|
| Tankstelle (f) | petrol station |
| Treffpunkt (m) | meeting place |
| Turm (m) | tower |
| Unterhaltungsmöglichkeiten (pl) | entertainment, things to do |
| Waschsalon (m) | launderette |
| Zeitungskiosk (m) | news kiosk |

### Aiming Higher

|  |  |
|--------|---------|
| Denkmal (n) | monument |
| Flohmarkt (m) | flea market |
| Geldautomat (m) | cashpoint |
| Grünanlage (f) | park |
| Reinigung (f) | dry cleaner's |

## Holiday accommodation

|  |  |
|--------|---------|
| ankommen | to arrive |
| Ankunft (f) | arrival |
| Anmeldung (f) | booking in |
| Aufenthaltsraum (m) | games room |
| Aufzug (m) | lift |
| Ausgang (m) | exit |
| auspacken | to unpack |
| Aussicht (f) | view |
| Bad (n) | bath |
| Badetuch (n) | towel |
| Badewanne (f) | bathtub |
| Badezimmer (n) | bathroom |
| Balkon (m) | balcony |
| besetzt | occupied |
| Besitzer (m) | owner |
| Betttuch (n) | sheet |
| Bettwäsche (f) | bed linen |
| Campingplatz (m) | campsite |

|  |  |
|--------|---------|
| Doppelzimmer (n) | double room |
| Dorf (n) | village |
| Dusche (f) | shower |
| Einzelzimmer (n) | single room |
| Empfang (m) | reception |
| Erdgeschoss (n) | ground floor |
| Esszimmer (n) | dining room |
| Etage (f) | floor (1st, 2nd) |
| Fahrstuhl (m) | lift |
| Fenster (n) | window |
| Fernsehapparat (n) | TV set |
| frei | free, available |
| funktionieren | to work |
| Gepäck (n) | luggage |
| Halbpension (f) | half board |
| Heizung (f) | heating |
| Hotelverzeichnis (n) | hotel list |
| im ersten Stock | on the first floor |
| im Voraus | in advance |
| inbegriffen | included |
| Jugendherberge (f) | youth hostel |
| Kleiderschrank (m) | wardrobe |
| Koffer (m) | suitcase |
| Kopfkissen (n) | pillow |
| Küche (f) | kitchen |
| Miete (f) | rent |
| mieten | to rent |
| mit Blick auf | with a view of |
| möbliert | furnished |
| Pension (f) | B & B |
| Preisliste (f) | price list |
| Reservierung (f) | reservation |
| Schlafsack (m) | sleeping bag |

## Now try this

Without looking at the book, think about all of the amenities in your local town or city and make a list of them in German. Open the book and then check your spelling.

# ❸ Local area, holiday and travel

| | |
|---|---|
| Schlafzimmer (n) | bedroom |
| Schlüssel (m) | key |
| Seife (f) | soap |
| Stock (m) | floor (1st, 2nd) |
| Treppe (f) | staircase |
| Trinkwasser (n) | drinking water |
| übernachten | to stay the night |
| Übernachtung (f) | overnight stay |
| Untergeschoss (n) | basement |
| Unterkunft (f) | accommodation |
| Vollpension (f) | full board |
| Wand (f) | wall (inside) |
| Waschbecken (n) | wash basin |
| Wohnwagen (m) | caravan |
| Wohnzimmer (n) | sitting room |
| Zahnbürste (f) | toothbrush |
| Zahnpasta (f) | toothpaste |
| Zelt (n) | tent |
| zelten | to camp (tent) |
| Zweibettzimmer (n) | twin room |

### Aiming Higher

| | |
|---|---|
| bestätigen | to confirm |
| Gastfreundschaft (f) | hospitality |
| Klimaanlage (f) | air conditioning |
| Notausgang (m) | emergency exit |
| unterbringen | to put someone up |

## Visitor information

| | |
|---|---|
| Andenken (n) | souvenir |
| Ausflug (m) | outing |
| Ausgang (m) | exit |
| Ausstellung (f) | exhibition |
| Berg (m) | mountain |

| | |
|---|---|
| Broschüre (f) | brochure |
| Bürgersteig (m) | pavement |
| Büro (n) | office |
| Dorf (n) | village |
| draußen | outside |
| Eingang (m) | entrance |
| Eintrittsgeld (n) | admission |
| Einwohner (m) | inhabitant |
| Ermäßigung (f) | reduction |
| Feiertag (m) | public holiday |
| Feld (n) | field |
| Fest (n) | festival |
| flach | flat |
| Fußgänger (m) | pedestrian |
| Gegend (f) | area |
| geöffnet | open |
| geschlossen | closed |
| Hauptstadt (f) | capital city |
| Hügel (m) | hill |
| im Ausland | abroad |
| im Freien | in the open air |
| im Frühling | in spring |
| im Herbst | in autumn |
| im Sommer | in summer |
| im Winter | in winter |
| Informationsbüro (n) | information office |
| Insel (f) | island |
| Küste (f) | coast |
| Land (n) | country |
| Landschaft (f) | countryside |
| malerisch | picturesque |
| Meer (n) | sea |
| Öffnungszeiten (pl) | opening hours |
| Ort (m) | place |
| ruhig | quiet |
| Rundfahrt (f) | tour |
| Rundgang (m) | tour (walking) |
| Schild (n) | sign |
| See (f) | sea |

| | |
|---|---|
| See (m) | lake |
| sehenswert | worth seeing |
| Sehenswürdigkeiten (pl) | sights |
| Stadt (f) | town |
| Stadtplan (m) | town map |
| Stadtrand (m) | outskirts |
| Stadtteil (m) | part of town |
| Stadtviertel (n) | district |
| Stadtzentrum (n) | town centre |
| Strand (m) | beach |
| Verkehrsamt (n) | tourist office |
| Vorort (m) | suburb |
| Vorstellung (f) | performance |
| Wald (m) | wood, forest |

### Aiming Higher

| | |
|---|---|
| Aufenthalt (m) | stay |
| Badeort (m) | seaside resort |
| Bodensee (m) | Lake Constance |
| Brunnen (m) | fountain |
| Erinnerung (f) | memory |
| Erlebnis (n) | experience |
| Feuerwerk (n) | fireworks |
| Gebiet (n) | area |
| Grünanlage (f) | park |
| Lärm (m) | noise |
| Pauschalreise (f) | package holiday |
| stattfinden | to take place |
| Tiergarten (m) | zoo |
| Umgebung (f) | surrounding area |
| Umzug (m) | procession |
| Veranstaltung (f) | event |
| Zoll (m) | customs |

## Now try this

Choose five words from this page which are important to you on a holiday. Write a sentence for each word in German.

# ❸ Local area, holiday and travel

## Travel (transport)

|  |  |
|---|---|
| Abfahrt (f) | departure |
| Abflug (m) | plane departure |
| Abgase (pl) | exhaust fumes |
| Abteil (n) | compartment |
| Ankunft (f) | arrival |
| Anschluss (m) | connection |
| aussteigen | to get off |
| Autobahn (f) | motorway |
| Bahn (f) | railway |
| Bahnsteig (m) | platform |
| Benzin (n) | petrol |
| einfach | single (ticket) |
| Einfahrt (f) | entrance (road) |
| einsteigen | to get on (train) |
| Einzelfahrkarte (f) | single ticket |
| entwerten | to validate (ticket) |
| Fähre (f) | ferry |
| Fahrkarte (f) | ticket |
| Fahrplan (m) | timetable |
| Fahrt (f) | journey, trip |
| Führerschein (m) | driving licence |
| Gepäckaufbewahrung (f) | left luggage |

|  |  |
|---|---|
| Gleis (n) | platform |
| Haltestelle (f) | stop (bus, train) |
| hin und zurück | return (ticket) |
| Karte (f) | ticket |
| Motor (m) | engine |
| öffentliche Verkehrsmittel (pl) | public transport |
| Panne (f) | breakdown |
| Platz (m) | seat |
| Reise (f) | journey |
| Rückfahrkarte (f) | return ticket |
| S-Bahn (f) | suburban train |
| schaden | to harm |
| schädlich | harmful |
| Schalter (m) | counter |
| Schlafwagen (m) | sleeper |
| Schließfach (n) | luggage locker |
| sich verspäten | to be late |
| Stau (m) | traffic jam |
| Straßenkarte (f) | road map |
| Tankstelle (f) | petrol station |
| U-Bahn (f) | underground railway |
| Überfahrt (f) | crossing |
| Umleitung (f) | diversion |
| umsteigen | to change |
| Verbindung (f) | connection |

|  |  |
|---|---|
| Verkehr (m) | traffic |
| verpassen | to miss |
| Verspätung (f) | delay |
| Vorfahrt (f) | priority |
| Wagen (m) | car, carriage |
| Wartesaal (m) | waiting room |

### Aiming Higher

|  |  |
|---|---|
| Autobahnkreuz (n) | motorway junction |
| bremsen | to brake |
| Fahrzeug (n) | vehicle |
| Geschwindigkeit (f) | speed |
| Hubschrauber (m) | helicopter |
| Raststätte (f) | motorway services |
| sich beeilen | to hurry |
| Sicherheitsgurt (m) | safety belt |
| Stoßzeit (f) | rush hour |
| überholen | to overtake |

Auto (n)

Zug (m)

Boot (n)

Bus (m)

Fahrrad (n)

Flugzeug (n)

Lastwagen (m)

Mofa (n)

Motorrad (n)

Straßenbahn (f)

## Now try this

Make a list of all the forms of transport you have used in the past year. Memorise the words, then test yourself on the German spellings.

# ❸ Local area, holiday and travel

## Travel (directions)

| | |
|---|---|
| Ampel (f) | traffic lights |
| Brücke (f) | bridge |
| Ecke (f) | corner |
| Einbahnstraße (f) | one-way street |
| Fluss (m) | river |
| Kreisverkehr (m) | roundabout |
| Kreuzung (f) | crossroads |
| Landkarte (f) | map |
| Richtung (f) | direction |
| sich befinden | to be situated |
| überqueren | to cross |
| weit | far |
| zu Fuß | on foot |

auf der linken Seite
on the left

auf der rechten Seite
on the right

links
left

rechts
right

geradeaus
straight on

## Weather

| | |
|---|---|
| bedeckt | overcast |
| bewölkt | cloudy |
| es donnert | it's thundering |
| es friert | it's freezing |
| frostig | frosty |
| Gewitter (n), Sturm (m) | thunderstorm |
| Grad (m) | degree |
| heiß | hot |
| heiter | bright |
| Himmel (m) | sky |
| Hitze (f) | heat |
| Höchsttemperatur (f) | highest temperature |
| Jahreszeit (f) | season |
| kalt | cold |
| Klima (n) | climate |
| nass | wet |
| neblig | foggy |
| Regen (m) | rain |
| regnerisch | rainy |
| schlecht | bad |
| Schnee (m) | snow |

die Sonne scheint

es blitzt

es ist windig

es regnet

es schneit

es ist kalt

im Norden
im Westen — im Osten
im Süden

| | |
|---|---|
| sonnig | sunny |
| Sturm (m) | storm |
| Tiefsttemperatur (f) | lowest temperature |
| trocken | dry |
| Wolke (f) | cloud |
| wolkig | cloudy |

**Aiming Higher**

| | |
|---|---|
| Aufheiterung (f) | bright spell |
| aufklären | to brighten up |
| Durchschnittstemperatur (f) | average temperature |
| hageln | to hail |
| Niederschlag (m) | rainfall |
| stürmisch | stormy |
| wechselhaft | changeable |

## Dealing with problems

| | |
|---|---|
| Bedienung (f) | service |
| Beschwerde (f) | complaint |
| Diebstahl (m) | theft |
| Ersatzteil (n) | replacement part |
| ersetzen | to replace |
| Farbe (f) | colour |
| Fehler (m) | mistake, fault |
| Formular (n) | form |
| kaputt | broken |
| Kundendienst (m) | customer service |
| Lieferung (f) | delivery |
| Menge (f) | quantity |
| Panne (f) | breakdown |
| Quittung (f) | receipt |
| Rechnung (f) | bill (invoice) |
| Reparatur (f) | repair |
| reparieren | to repair |
| Schaden (m) | damage |
| sich beschweren | to complain |
| umtauschen | to exchange |
| Unfall (m) | accident |
| Wartezeit (f) | waiting time |
| zahlen | to pay |

**Now try this**

Test this vocabulary, and your knowledge of tenses, by trying to describe the weather yesterday, the weather today and what you hope the weather will be like tomorrow.

**Aiming Higher**

| | |
|---|---|
| (Auto)unfall (m) | crash / collision |
| Gebrauchsanweisung (f) | instructions for use |
| versichern | to insure |
| Versicherung (f) | insurance |

# ④ School

|  |  |  |  |  |  |
|---|---|---|---|---|---|
| Abitur (n) | equivalent of A levels | Kunst (f) | art | Taschenrechner (m) | calculator |
| abwesend | absent | Kurs (m) | course | Theater (n) | drama |
| anwesend | present | Labor (n) | laboratory | Trimester (n) | term |
| Aula (f) | school hall | Latein | Latin | Turnen (n) | gymnastics |
| Austausch (m) | exchange | Lehrer/in (m/f) | teacher | Turnhalle (f) | gym |
| Berufsberater/in (m/f) | careers adviser | Lehrerzimmer (n) | staffroom | üben | to practise |
| bestehen | to pass (exam) | Leistung (f) | achievement | Übung (f) | exercise |
| Bildung (f) | education | lernen | to learn | ungerecht | unfair |
| Biologie (f) | biology | Lineal (n) | ruler | Unterricht (m) | lesson |
| Bleistift (m) | pencil | Mannschaft (f) | team | unterrichten | to teach |
| Chemie (f) | chemistry | Mathe(matik) (f) | maths | weitermachen | to carry on |
| Chor (m) | choir | Medienwissen- | media studies | Werken (n) | DT |
| dauern | to last | schaft (f) | | wiederholen | to repeat |
| Deutsch | German | Mittlere Reife (f) | GCSE equivalent | Wörterbuch (n) | dictionary |
| Direktor (m), Schulleiter (m) | head teacher | mündlich | oral | zeichnen | to draw |
| durchfallen | to fail (exam) | nachsitzen | to have a detention | | |
| Englisch | English | | | | |
| Erdkunde (f) | geography | Naturwissenschaften (pl) | sciences | **Aiming Higher** | |
| Erfolg (m) | success | Note (f) | grade | abschreiben | to copy |
| erfolgreich | successful | Oberstufe (f) | sixth form | Aufsatz (m) | essay |
| Etui (n) | pencil case | Pause (f) | break | ausfallen | to be cancelled (lesson) |
| Fach (n) | subject | Physik (f) | physics | begabt | gifted |
| faul | lazy | Privatschule (f) | private school | erklären | to explain |
| Ferien (pl) | holidays | Prüfung (f) | exam | Erlaubnis (f) | permission |
| Filzstift (m) | felt tip | Radiergummi (m) | rubber | Internat (n) | boarding school |
| fleißig | hard-working | rechnen | to calculate | Klassenbuch (n) | class register |
| Fortschritt (m) | progress | Rechner (m) | calculator | Kopfhörer (m) | headphones |
| Frage (f) | question | Regel (f) | rule | lehren | to teach |
| Französisch | French | Resultat (n) | result | Leistungsdruck (m) | pressure to achieve (good grades) |
| Fremdsprachen (pl) | languages | Schere (f) | scissors | | |
| Füller (m) | fountain pen | Schreibtisch (m) | desk | notwendig | necessary |
| Gang (m) | corridor | schriftlich | written | Pflichtfach (n) | core subject |
| gerecht | fair | Schule besuchen | to attend school | schwänzen | to skive |
| Gesamtschule (f) | comprehensive school | Schüler/in (m/f) | pupil | Strafarbeit (f) | lines (punishment) |
| Geschichte (f) | history | Schülerzeitung (f) | school newspaper | Studium (n) | studies |
| Grundschule (f) | primary school | Schulhof (m) | playground | übersetzen | to translate |
| Gymnasium (n) | grammar school | Schultasche (f) | school bag | Übersetzung (f) | translation |
| | | schwach | weak (subject) | vereinbaren | to agree |
| Hauptschule / Realschule(f) | secondary school | schwer | hard, difficult | Wahlfach (n) | optional subject |
| Hausaufgaben (pl) | homework | Seite (f) | page | Wirtschaftslehre (f) | economics |
| Hausmeister (m) | caretaker | Sekretariat (n) | school office | | |
| Heft (n) | exercise book | sitzen bleiben | to repeat a year | | |
| Informatik (f) | ICT | Sommerferien (pl) | summer holidays | | |
| Kantine (f) | canteen | | | | |
| Klassenarbeit (f) | class test | Spanisch | Spanish | | |
| Klassenfahrt (f) | school trip | Sprache (f) | language | | |
| Klassenzimmer (n) | classroom | staatlich | state | | |
| Klebstoff (m) | glue | stark | strong | | |
| klug | clever | Stunde (f) | lesson, hour | | |
| korrigieren | to correct | Stundenplan (m) | timetable | | |
| Kuli (m) | ballpoint pen | Tafel (f) | board | | |

| | |
|---|---|
| 1 = sehr gut | very good |
| 2 = gut | good |
| 3 = befriedigend | satisfactory |
| 4 = ausreichend | adequate |
| 5 = mangelhaft | unsatisfactory, poor |
| 6 = ungenügend | inadequate |

## Now try this

What GCSEs are you and your friends taking? Check that you can say / write all the subjects in German. If you're thinking of taking A levels, can you name those subjects too?

# ⑤ Future aspirations, study and work

## Further study and work

Add –in for the female word, unless given.

| | |
|---|---|
| Angestellter (m) / Angestellte (f) | employee |
| Anruf (m) | call |
| Arbeiter (m) | worker |
| Arbeitgeber (m) | employer |
| Arbeitsbedingungen (pl) | terms of employment |
| arbeitslos | unemployed |
| Arbeitspraktikum (n) | work experience |
| babysitten | to babysit |
| Bäcker (m) | baker |
| Bauarbeiter (m) | builder |
| Bauer (m) | farmer |
| Beamter (m) / Beamtin (f) | civil servant |
| Begeisterung (f) | enthusiasm |
| berufstätig | in work |
| beschäftigt | busy |
| Besitzer (m) | owner |
| Betrieb (m) | business |
| Betriebspraktikum (n) | work experience |
| Bezahlung (f) | pay |
| Bildung (f) | education |
| Blumenhändler (m) | florist |
| Briefmarke (f) | stamp |
| Briefträger (m) | postman |
| Chef (m) | boss |
| einstellen | to appoint |
| Elektriker (m) | electrician |
| Fabrik (f) | factory |
| Fähigkeiten (pl) | skills |
| Fehler (m) | mistake |
| Ferienjob (m) | holiday job |
| Feuerwehrfrau (f) | firefighter |
| Feuerwehrmann (m) | firefighter |
| Fleischer (m) | butcher |
| Ganztagsjob (m) | full-time job |
| Gehalt (n) | salary |
| Gelegenheit (f) | opportunity |
| geplant | planned |
| Hausfrau (f) | housewife |
| Hausmann (m) | house husband |
| Hochschulabschluss (m) | degree |

| | |
|---|---|
| Informatik (f) | computer science |
| jobben | to do casual work |
| Kassierer (m) | cashier |
| Kauffrau (f) | businesswoman |
| Kaufmann (m) | businessman |
| Klempner (m) | plumber |
| Kollege / Kollegin | colleague |
| Künstler (m) | artist |
| einen Kurs besuchen | to attend a course |
| Lehre (f) | apprenticeship |
| lehrreich | educational |
| Lkw-Fahrer (m) | lorry driver |
| Lohn (m) | wage(s) |
| Maler (m) | painter |
| Maurer (m) | builder |
| Messe (f) | trade fair |
| Metzger (m) | butcher |
| Mitteilung (f), Nachricht (f) | message |
| Teilzeitjob (m) | part-time job |
| Polizei (f) | police |
| Reisebüro (n) | travel agency |
| Schauspieler (m) | actor |
| Schichtarbeit (f) | shiftwork |
| schlecht bezahlt | badly paid |
| selbstständig | independent |
| Soldat (m) | soldier |
| Sorge (f) | worry |
| Stadtführer (m) | city guide |
| Streik (m) | strike |
| Student (m) | student (university) |
| studieren | to study |
| Teilzeit (f) | part time |
| Tellerwäscher (m) | washer-upper |
| Tierarzt (m) / Tierärztin (f) | vet |
| Tischler (m) | joiner |
| Universität (f) | university |
| verdienen | to earn |
| Verkäufer (m) | sales assistant |
| Vertreter (m) | representative |
| Werkstatt (f) | workshop |
| Zeitungen austragen | to deliver newspapers |
| Ziel (n) | aim |
| zurückrufen | to call back |

| | |
|---|---|
| Arbeitnehmer (m) | employee |
| Arbeitsamt (n) | job centre |
| ausrichten | to give a message |
| Auszubildende (m/f) | trainee |
| Bewerber (m) | applicant |
| Dolmetscher (m) | interpreter |
| Einzelhändler (m) | retailer |
| Fließband (n) | conveyer belt |
| freiwillig | voluntary |
| Gelegenheitsarbeit (f) | casual work |
| Gesetz (n) | law |
| Gleichheit (f) | equality |
| Gleitzeit (f) | flexitime |
| Hochschulbildung (f) | higher education |
| Jura | study of law |
| kündigen | to resign |
| Landwirt (m) | farmer |
| Lehrling (m) | apprentice |
| Medizin (f) | (study of) medicine |
| Praktikum (n) | internship |
| Qualifikation (f) | qualification |
| qualifiziert / ausgebildet | qualified |
| Rechtsanwalt (m) | lawyer |
| Schriftsteller (m) | author |
| sich entschließen | to decide |
| Unternehmen (n) | firm |
| vereinbaren | to agree |

## Volunteering

| | |
|---|---|
| beschäftigt | busy |
| freiwillig arbeiten | to work voluntarily |
| geplant | planned |
| im Ausland | abroad |
| Nähen (n) | sewing |
| organisieren | to organise |
| Plan (m) | plan |
| Projekt (n) | project |
| Schneiderei (f) | tailoring |
| Sprache (f) | language |
| Traum (m) | dream |
| Wohltätigkeit (f) | charity |

### Now try this

Pick 10 words from this page that you would use when applying for a job. Memorise them and then test yourself later.

# ⑤ Future aspirations, study and work

**Aiming Higher**

| | |
|---|---|
| freiwillige Arbeit (f) | voluntary work |
| Freiwilliger (m) / Freiwillige (f) | volunteer |
| Spendenaktion (f) | charity sale |
| zu Gunsten | in aid of |

der Arzt   die Ärztin

die Krankenschwester
der Krankenpfleger

der Bauer   die Bäuerin

der Polizist   die Polizistin

der Künstler   die Künstlerin

die Zahnärztin   der Zahnarzt

## Work

| | |
|---|---|
| abheften | to file |
| Akte (f) | file |
| Aktenmappe (f) | folder |
| Angestellter (m) / Angestellte (f) | employee |
| Anrufbeantworter (m) | answerphone |
| Anzeige (f) | advert |
| Arbeit (f) | work |
| Arbeitgeber/in (m/f) | employer |
| Arbeitsbedingungen (pl) | terms of employment |
| Arbeitslosigkeit (f) | unemployment |
| auflegen | to hang up (phone) |
| Besprechung (f) | meeting |
| Ehrgeiz (m) | ambition |
| erfahren | experienced |
| Formular (n) | form |
| Gehalt (n) | salary |
| Gesellschaft (f) | society / company |
| gut / schlecht bezahlt | well / badly paid |
| Job (m) / Stelle (f) | job |
| Kaffeepause (f) | coffee break |
| Kollege (m) / Kollegin (f) | colleague |
| Konferenz (f) | conference |
| Manager/in (m/f) | manager |
| Marketing (n) | marketing |
| Mittagspause (f) | lunch break |
| Nachricht (f) | news |
| Reisebüro (n) | travel agency |

| | |
|---|---|
| sich um einen Job bewerben | to apply for a job |
| Stellengesuche (pl) | situations wanted |
| pro Stunde | per hour |
| Teepause (f) | tea break |
| Teilzeit (f) | part time |
| Telefonanruf (m) | telephone call |
| Vorstellungsgespräch (n) | interview |
| wählen | to dial (a number) |

## Jobs

| | |
|---|---|
| Apotheker/in (m/f) | pharmacist |
| Architekt/in (m/f) | architect |
| Bäcker/in (m/f) | baker |
| Bauarbeiter/in (m/f) | builder |
| Beamter (m) / Beamtin (f) | civil servant |
| Dichter/in (m/f) | poet |
| Elektriker/in (m/f) | electrician |
| Fahrer/in (m/f) | driver |
| Feuerwehrfrau (f) | firefighter |
| Feuerwehrmann (m) | firefighter |
| Flugbegleiter/in (m/f) | cabin crew |
| Informatiker/in (m/f) | computer scientist |
| Ingenieur/in (m/f) | engineer |
| Journalist/in (m/f) | journalist |

| | |
|---|---|
| Kassierer/in (m/f) | cashier |
| Klempner/in (m/f) | plumber |
| Koch (m) / Köchin (f) | chef |
| Mechaniker/in (m/f) | mechanic |
| Metzger/in (m/f) | butcher |
| Modeschöpfer/in (m/f) | fashion designer |
| Musiker/in (m/f) | musician |
| Programmierer/in (m/f) | programmer |
| Schauspieler/in (m/f) | actor |
| Techniker/in (m/f) | technician |
| Vertreter/in (m/f) | sales rep |

**Aiming Higher**

| | |
|---|---|
| Aufstiegsmöglichkeiten (pl) | promotion prospects |
| Beruf (m) | job, profession |
| Bewerbungsbrief (m) | letter of application |
| Bewerbungsformular (n) | application form |
| Eindruck (m) | impression |
| Stellenangebot (n) | job vacancy |
| Termin (m) | appointment |
| Unterschrift (f) | signature |
| Ziel (n) | goal |

## Now try this

To help you learn the jobs vocabulary, make a list of five jobs that you would like to do and five jobs that you would not like to do and then memorise them.

# ❻ International and global dimension

## Bringing the world together

| | |
|---|---|
| Aktion (f) | campaign |
| Armut (f) | poverty |
| fairer Handel (m) | fair trade |
| für / gegen | for / against |
| (Fußball)weltmeisterschaft (f) | world cup (football) |
| global / weltweit | global |
| Hunger (m) | hunger |
| Katastrophe (f) / Unglück (n) | catastrophe |
| Krieg (m) | war |
| Land (n) | country |
| leben | to live |
| Mangel (m) (an) | lack (of) |
| Menschen (pl) / Leute (pl) | people |
| Musikfest (n) | music festival |
| Nachteil (m) | disadvantage |
| die Olympischen Spiele (pl) | Olympic Games |
| Schutz (m) | protection |
| sterben | to die |
| Vorteil (m) | advantage |
| Wohltätigkeitsverein (m) | charity |

## Environmental issues

| | | | |
|---|---|---|---|
| recyceln | to recycle | die Welt | the world |

| | |
|---|---|
| Dürre (f) | drought |
| Energie (f) | energy |
| Erde (f) | earth |
| Hungersnot (f) | famine |
| Müll (m) | rubbish |
| Naturschätze (pl) | natural resources |
| Orkan (m) | hurricane |
| Planet (m) | planet |
| Regenwald (m) | rainforest |
| Schutz (m) | protection |
| schützen | to protect |
| Strom (m) | electricity |
| Trinkwasser (n) | drinking water |
| Überschwemmung (f) | flooding |
| Umwelt (f) | environment |
| Verschmutzung (f) | pollution |

**Aiming Higher**

| | |
|---|---|
| Art (f) | species |
| drohen | to threaten |
| Erdbeben (n) | earthquake |
| frisches Wasser (n) / Süßwasser (n) | fresh water |
| globale Erwärmung (f) | global warming |
| Klima (n) | climate |
| kompostieren | to compost |
| Solarenergie (f) | solar energy |
| trennen | to separate (rubbish) |
| verschmutzen, vergiften | to pollute / poison |
| Vulkan (m) | volcano |

**Aiming Higher**

| | |
|---|---|
| bedürftig | needy |
| fehlen | to lack |
| Menschenrechte (pl) | human rights |
| profitieren | to profit |
| retten | to rescue |
| Sicherheit (f) | security |
| Spionage (f) | spying |
| überleben | to survive |
| unglucklich | unfortunate |
| unmittelbar | instant |

Kohle (f)
coal

Gas (n)
gas

Öl (n)
oil

Tiere (pl)
animals

Salzwasser (n)
salt water

Pflanzen (npl)
plants

## Now try this

Choose 10 words and make learning cards for them – English or a photo on one side and German on the other.

# Answers

The answers to the Speaking activities below are sample answers – there are many ways you could answer these questions.

## Identity and culture

### 1. Physical descriptions

(a) zwanzig
(b) lang
(c) ein Piercing
(d) Kleidung
(e) sprechen

### 2. Character descriptions

(a) faul
(b) freundlich
(c) laut
(d) laut
(e) lustig

### 4. Friends

(a) Meine Freundin Carol ist klug / intelligent und sehr lustig.
(b) Ich sehe meine Freunde / Freundinnen oft nach der Schule.
(c) Letzte Woche gab mein Freund eine Party.
(d) Meine beste Freundin hat in Spanien gewohnt, als sie acht Jahre alt war.

### 5. Role models

(a) depends on favourite pastime of the person
(b) help to develop own talents / achieve sporting goals
(c) any two: teachers, environmentalists / nature protectors, scientists, authors

### 6. Relationships

(a) Lehrer
(b) 45
(c) viermal
(d) Freunde
(e) mag

### 7. When I was younger

Listen to the recording

### 9. Customs

Listen to the recording

### 10. Home

My parents are old-fashioned and we always have to have lunch together and chat because mobile phones are banned at the table. It is my dream to live alone in the city centre, so that I can have / make my own rules. As a child I lived in the countryside, but that was terribly dull.

### 11. Everyday life

(b) their everyday life has become so technical
(c) any two: managers had a secretary / office to plan for them / assistants for technical matters / were not going through puberty
(d) everything themselves

### 12. Meals at home

(a) Frühstück
(b) Kaffee und Kuchen
(c) Abendessen
(d) Mittagessen
(e) Kaffee und Kuchen

### 14. Shopping for clothes

Listen to the recording

### 15. Social media

B, D and G

### 17. Online activities

(b) her parents find it particularly important
(c) talks for hours on mobile phone
(d) any two: turns on tablet / uploads funny photos / waits for comments
(e) she only wants to get positive comments

### 19. Hobbies

(i) D
(ii) A
(iii) C

### 20. Interests

Yesterday I went with my family to the cinema. I found the film boring, because the special effects are old-fashioned.

### 22. Sport

Listen to the recording

### 23. Reading

(b) made them look tiny
(c) nothing
(d) any two: she saw so little / it was tiring / she only read one letter each day

### 25. Television

(a) lustig
(b) blöd
(c) interessant
(d) entspannend
(e) lustig

### 26. Celebrations

(a) cake
(b) often
(c) money
(d) drinks
(e) works

### 27. Festivals

Als mein Freund eine Faschingsparty gab, hat diese mir gar nicht gefallen und ich bin früh nach Hause gegangen. Heute Abend fahre ich zu Silvester in die Stadtmitte, weil eine Band auf dem Marktplatz ist und wir dort tanzen können. Ich feiere gerne mit vielen Leuten draußen.

# Local area, holiday and travel

## 29. Hotels

(a)  Bett
(b)  viel
(c)  online
(d)  regelmäßig
(e)  plant

## 30. Campsites

C, E and G

## 31. Accommodation

Listen to the recording

## 32. Holiday destinations

As a family we go every year to Tenerife, where there is / they've got the biggest water park in Europe. I would also recommend a day trip to the capital, in order to visit the wonderful markets and buy souvenirs. We have been going there for four years, and before, we used to go to the windy North Sea for our summer holiday.

## 33. Holiday experiences

(a)  fantastisch
(b)  enttäuschend
(c)  interessant

## 34. Holiday activities

(b)  any one: archery / climbing / waterskiing
(c)  go for walks
(d)  a day trip
(e)  will come back

## 35. Holiday plans

Als ich letztes Mal dort war, habe ich einige echt nette Leute kennengelernt. Wir werden uns wieder im Mai treffen und alle einen Tagesausflug zum See machen. Ich möchte lieber Urlaub mit Freunden als mit meiner / der Familie, weil mir das besser gefällt.

## 36. Holiday problems

Listen to the recording

## 37. Asking for help

Listen to the recording

## 39. Travel

(b)  much better than in England
(c)  if we invested more in trains

## 40. Directions

(i)  D
(ii)  C
(iii)  A

## 41. Eating in a café

Last time my mother ordered a fried egg. This time she is ordering something else.

## 42. Eating in a restaurant

(i)  B
(ii)  D
(iii)  A

## 43. Shopping for food

(a)  Petra
(b)  Alex
(c)  Kai
(d)  Edi
(e)  Petra

## 44. Opinions about food

(b)  waiter was very rude / not at all polite
(c)  would recommend restaurant for wonderful views and 10% reduction for students

## 45. Buying gifts

(b)  wonderful shop windows
(c)  they sell gold watches / silk linen
(d)  the very tall houses / the noise / the number of people

## 46. Weather

(i)  D
(ii)  A

## 47. Places to see

(b)  one of the most popular tourist destinations
(c)  it is a small town
(d)  one of the oldest buildings in the town (**not**: old building / historic)
(e)  in the town centre

## 48. At the tourist office

Listen to the recording

## 49. Describing a town

(a)  Das Kaufhaus ist sehr alt und teuer.
(b)  Ich gehe lieber auf dem Markt einkaufen.
(c)  Gestern bin ich ins Kino gegangen.
(d)  Mein Bruder ist zu Hause geblieben, weil er müde war / denn er war müde.

## 50. Describing a region

D, E and C

## 51. Tourism

Listen to the recording

# School

## 53. School subjects

(ii)  A
(iii)  B

## 54. Opinions about school

Listen to the recording

## 55. School day

D, E and G

## 57. School facilities

Listen to the recording

## 58. School rules

Last term a pupil / student smoked in the playground, because he thought that was cool. But the head teacher was very angry and sent the boy straight home. I would never smoke or drink alcohol at school, because I wouldn't want to get lines / a written punishment.

## 59. Pressures at school

Obwohl Schüler / Schülerinnen heutzutage oft Klassenarbeiten schreiben müssen, können wir uns noch echt auf die Klassenfahrten freuen. Wenn ich fleißig lerne, um gute Noten zu bekommen, werde ich auch vielleicht ein Geschenk von meinen Eltern bekommen – und das wäre toll!

## 60. Primary school

C

## 61. Success at school

(ii)   D

## 63. School exchange

Listen to the recording

## 64. School events

(i)   A, F      (ii)   B, D

# Future aspirations, study and work

## 65. Future study

Listen to the recording

## 66. Jobs

(b)   any one: Saturday job / cashier / in a shoe shop
(c)   any one: works long hours / exhausted after work / has no time for hobbies (**not**: she's a doctor)
(d)   works in a hut in the garden / collects original ties (**not**: he is funny / collects originals)

## 67. Professions

Last weekend she worked hard. This week she is applying for a new job.

## 68. Job wishes

(a)   variety          (b)   salary, travel

## 69. Opinions about jobs

2   Negative                    7   Positive and negative
3   Positive and negative       8   Positive and negative
4   Positive and negative       9   Negative
5   Negative                   10   Positive
6   Positive

## 70. Job adverts

(b)   Mein Freund / Meine Freundin verdient zehn Euro pro Stunde.
(c)   Er arbeitet in einem Büro in der Stadtmitte.
(d)   Letztes Jahr habe ich als Kellner gearbeitet.
(e)   Ich brauche einen Job, weil ich kein Geld habe.

## 71. Applying for a job

(a)   A       (b)   D

## 72. Job interview

Listen to the recording

## 73. Languages beyond the classroom

(b)   seine Sprachkenntnisse sind nicht gut genug / mangelnde Sprachkenntnisse / man muss in der Sprache fließend sein (not: er hat zwei Sprachen / Portugiesisch / Finnisch gelernt)
(c)   any one: mit deutlichen Pausen sprechen / zu langsam verstehen oder reagieren / undeutlich sprechen (not: sofort reagieren / Informationen schnell verarbeiten / das Gesagte klar und flüssig wiedergeben)

## 74. Volunteering

(i)   C and E          (ii)   A and E

## 75. Training

Listen to the recording

# International and global dimension

## 78. Global sports events

Obwohl es sehr teuer war, hatte Brasilien ein wunderbares Leichtathletikstadion gebaut und viele Menschen hatten Eintrittskarten gekauft. Das Ziel eines Sportlers oder einer Sportlerin ist es bestimmt, eine Medaille bei einer Meisterschaft zu gewinnen.

### 79. Global music events

Listen to the recording

### 80. Being green

**(i)** A **(ii)** D **(iii)** B

### 81. Protecting the environment

**(b)** Klimawechsel zu vermeiden (**not**: seinen Effekt zu begrenzen / Strategien zu entwickeln)

**(c)** uns daran anpassen / uns an das Klima anpassen (**not**: seinen Effekt zu begrenzen / Strategien entwickeln)

**(d)** Menschen haben eine große Rolle dabei gespielt (**not**: negative Folgen)

**(e)** extremes Wetter (**not**: any of the individual weather types)

**(f)** die Berge / die Alpen

### 83. Campaigns

B and F

## Grammar

### 85. Gender and plurals

**(a)** die Anmeldung / die Anmeldungen
**(b)** der Fahrer / die Fahrer
**(c)** das Rührei / die Rühreier
**(d)** die Haltestelle / die Haltestellen
**(e)** der Fernseher / die Fernseher
**(f)** das Brötchen / die Brötchen

### 86. Cases and prepositions

**(a)** gegen die Mauer
**(b)** außer einem Kind
**(c)** trotz des Schnees
**(d)** nach einer Stunde
**(e)** zu den Geschäften
**(f)** ohne ein Wort
**(g)** während des Sommers
**(h)** beim Arzt

### 87. Dative and accusative prepositions

**(a)** der
**(b)** den
**(c)** dem
**(d)** die
**(e)** der
**(f)** den
**(g)** den
**(h)** die

### 88. Dieser / jeder, kein / mein

**(a)** I don't want to go shopping.
**(b)** She spent all her pocket money on clothes.
**(c)** Such people quickly become impolite.
**(d)** I find my life boring.
**(e)** This time we are going by train.
**(f)** His parents are unemployed.
**(g)** I find such rules stupid.
**(h)** Which book are you reading?

### 89. Adjective endings

**(a)** ausgezeichnete
**(b)** warmes
**(c)** preisgünstiges
**(d)** zentrale
**(e)** beliebtes
**(f)** meistverkauften
**(g)** verkaufsoffenen
**(h)** persönlichen

### 90. Comparisons

**(a)** einfacher
**(b)** jünger
**(c)** besser
**(d)** nützlicher
**(e)** winzigste
**(f)** langweiligste
**(g)** beliebteste
**(h)** schlechtesten

### 91. Personal pronouns

**(a)** sie
**(b)** mir
**(c)** dir
**(d)** uns
**(e)** mir, ihm
**(f)** mir

### 92. Word order

*Possible answers:*

**(a)** Ich fahre gern ins Ausland.
**(b)** Man findet Informationen beim Verkehrsamt.
**(c)** Normalerweise esse ich gesund.
**(d)** Manchmal sehen wir im Jugendklub Filme.
**(e)** Im Juli möchte ich im Sportzentrum arbeiten.
**(f)** Letztes Jahr habe ich in einem Büro gearbeitet.
**(g)** Morgen werde ich mit meiner Mutter ins Kino gehen.

### 93. Conjunctions

**(a)** Ich habe bei meiner Großmutter gewohnt, während meine Mutter im Krankenhaus war.
**(b)** Ich bin ins Café gegangen, nachdem ich ein T-Shirt gekauft habe.
**(c)** Ich war in Spanien im Urlaub, als ich einen neuen Freund kennengelernt habe.
**(d)** Er ist sehr beliebt, obwohl er nicht sehr freundlich ist.
**(e)** Ich werde für eine neue Gitarre sparen, wenn ich einen Nebenjob finde.
**(f)** Ich bin froh, dass ich gute Noten in der Schule bekommen habe.
**(g)** Ich muss meine Eltern fragen, ob ich ins Konzert gehen darf.
**(h)** Er hat mir gesagt, dass er mit mir ins Kino gehen will.

### 94. More on word order

**1 (a)** Ich fahre nach Italien, um meine Verwandten zu besuchen.
**(b)** Ich gehe zum Sportzentrum, um 5 Kilo abzunehmen.
**2 (a)** Ich versuche, anderen zu helfen.
**(b)** Ich habe vor, auf die Uni zu gehen.
**3 (a)** Das ist das Geschäft, das tolle Kleidung verkauft.
**(b)** Hier ist eine Kellnerin, die sehr unhöflich ist.

### 95. The present tense

**(a)** höre
**(b)** schläft
**(c)** geht
**(d)** Isst
**(e)** fahren
**(f)** machen
**(g)** Gibt
**(h)** bleibt

### 96. Separable and reflexive verbs

**1 (a)** Ich sehe fern. Ich habe ferngesehen.
**(b)** Ich steige um sechs Uhr um. Ich bin um sechs Uhr umgestiegen.
**(c)** Ich lade Musik herunter. Ich werde Musik herunterladen.
**(d)** Ich bin eingestiegen. Ich muss einsteigen.
**2 (a)** mich
**(b)** uns
**(c)** euch
**(d)** sich

## 97. Commands

To pay attention to their darlings and not to use the green spaces and paths as a dog toilet.

## 98. Present tense modals

(a) Ich muss um einundzwanzig Uhr ins Bett gehen.
(b) In der Schule darf man nicht rauchen.
(c) Du sollst Energie sparen.
(d) Kannst du mir zu Hause helfen?
(e) Ich will in den Ferien Ski fahren.
(f) Ich möchte nicht fernsehen.
(g) Ich kann das Problem nicht lösen.

## 99. Imperfect modals

1 (a) Ich musste Hausaufgaben machen.
(b) Sie konnten mir nicht helfen.
(c) Er wollte eine neue Hose kaufen.
(d) Wir sollten die Fotos hochladen.
(e) In der Schule durfte man nie Kaugummi kauen.
(f) Alle Schüler mussten bis sechzehn Uhr bleiben.
2 (a) Es könnte schwierig werden.
(b) Ich möchte die gelbe Jacke umtauschen.

## 100. The perfect tense 1

(a) Ich habe eine Jacke gekauft.
(b) Wir sind nach Portugal geflogen.
(c) Ich habe meinen Freund gesehen.
(d) Lena und Hannah sind in die Stadt gegangen.
(e) Ich habe meine Tante besucht.
(f) Ich bin im Hotel geblieben.
(g) Was hast du zu Mittag gegessen?
(h) Am Samstag hat er Musik gehört.

## 101. The perfect tense 2

(a) Ich habe zu viele Kekse gegessen.
(b) Haben Sie gut geschlafen?
(c) Wir haben uns am Bahnhof getroffen.
(d) Ich war krank, weil ich den ganzen Tag gestanden habe.
(e) Ich weiß, dass du umgestiegen bist.
(f) Warum hast du die E-Mail geschrieben?
(g) Ich habe ihr empfohlen, dass sie nicht mitkommen sollte.
(h) Ich war traurig, als er gestorben ist.

## 102. The imperfect tense

(a) Sie hatte Angst.
(b) Es war hoffnungslos.
(c) Es gab Toiletten im Erdgeschoss.
(d) Hörtest du das?
(e) Plötzlich kam uns der Mann entgegen.
(f) Das war eine Überraschung, nicht?
(g) Es war niemand zu Hause.
(h) Sie spielten gern Tischtennis.

## 103. The future tense

(a) Ich werde das Spiel gewinnen.
(b) Wir werden in den Freizeitpark gehen.
(c) Sie werden eine große Wohnung mieten.
(d) Ihr werdet große Schwierigkeiten haben.
(e) Er wird die Prüfung bestehen.
(f) Nächste Woche werden wir umziehen.
(g) Werdet ihr euch später treffen?
(h) Ich werde mich um sechs Uhr anziehen.

## 104. The conditional

(a) Ich würde gern ins Theater gehen.
(b) Er würde nie zu spät ankommen.
(c) Wir würden nie Bier trinken.
(d) Würden Sie mir bitte helfen?
(e) Zum Geburtstag würde sie am liebsten Geld bekommen.
(f) Nächstes Jahr würden sie vielleicht heiraten.
(g) Wenn Latein Pflicht wäre, würde ich auf eine andere Schule gehen.
(h) Wenn ich das machen würde, gäbe es Krach mit meinen Eltern.

## 105. The pluperfect tense

(a) Ich hatte zu Mittag gegessen.
(b) Sie hatten als Stadtführer gearbeitet.
(c) Warst du schwimmen gegangen?
(d) Wir waren in Kontakt geblieben.
(e) Sie waren mit dem Rad in die Stadt gefahren.
(f) Ich hatte sie vor einigen Monaten besucht, aber damals war sie schon krank.
(g) Bevor ich ins Haus gegangen war, hatte ich ein Gesicht am Fenster gesehen.
(h) Obwohl ich kaum mit ihm gesprochen hatte, schien er sehr freundlich zu sein.

## 106. Questions

1 (a) Lesen Sie gern Science-Fiction-Bücher?
(b) Finden Sie Ihre Arbeit anstrengend?
(c) Möchten Sie nur Teilzeit arbeiten?
(d) Werden Sie nächsten Sommer nach Australien auswandern?
2 (a) Wer könnte mir helfen?
(b) Wann macht das Restaurant auf?
(c) Warum gibt es eine Tasche hier?
(d) Wie komme ich zum Dom?
(e) Was kann man abends machen?

## 107. Time markers

(a) Seit drei Jahren spiele ich Klavier.
(b) Letzte Woche hat er die Hausaufgaben nicht gemacht.
(c) Nächsten Sommer werden wir in den Bergen wandern gehen.
(d) Am Anfang wollten wir das Betriebspraktikum nicht machen.
(e) In Zukunft wird man alle Lebensmittel elektronisch kaufen.
(f) Ich hoffe, eines Tages Disneyland zu besuchen.
(g) Vorgestern hatte ich Halsschmerzen.
(h) Früher haben sie / Sie oft Tennis gespielt.

## 108. Numbers

(a) 14.–23. Mai
(b) 07:45
(c) €3,80
(d) 27. Januar 1756
(e) €185 Millionen
(f) 15% Ermäßigung
(g) 16:35
(h) 35 Grad

## 114. Vocabulary

(a) Bavaria
(b) English Channel
(c) Lake Constance
(d) Black Forest
(e) Alps
(f) Danube
(g) Geneva
(h) Cologne
(i) Munich
(j) Vienna

Published by Pearson Education Limited, 80 Strand, London, WC2R 0RL.

www.pearsonschoolsandfecolleges.co.uk

Copies of official specifications for all Pearson qualifications may be found on the
website: qualifications.pearson.com

Text and illustrations © Pearson Education Limited 2017, 2021
Produced, typeset and illustrations by Cambridge Publishing Management Ltd, Newgen KnowledgeWorks and Newgen Publishing UK
Cover illustration © Kamae Design Ltd

The rights of Harriette Lanzer to be identified as author of this work have been asserted by her in accordance with the
Copyright, Designs and Patents Act 1988.

First published 2021

24

10 9 8 7

British Library Cataloguing in Publication Data
A catalogue record for this book is available from the British Library

ISBN 978 1 2924 12252

**Copyright notice**
All rights reserved. No part of this publication may be reproduced in any form or by any means (including photocopying or storing it in
any medium by electronic means and whether or not transiently or incidentally to some other use of this publication) without the written
permission of the copyright owner, except in accordance with the provisions of the Copyright, Designs and Patents Act 1988 or under the
terms of a licence issued by the Copyright Licensing Agency, 5th Floor, Shackleton House, Hay's Galleria, 4 Battle Bridge Lane, London,
SE1 2HX (www.cla.co.uk). Applications for the copyright owner's written permission should be addressed to the publisher.

Printed in Great Britain by Bell and Bain Ltd, Glasgow

**Acknowledgements**
The publisher would like to thank the following for their kind permission to reproduce their photographs:

(Key: b-bottom; c-centre; l-left; r-right; t-top; tr-top right; bl-bottom left)

**123RF:** Dmitriy Shironosov 13, 29, NejroN 21, Graham Oliver 30, Vadim Guzhva 67, 70; **Alamy Stock Photo:** Sorge/Agencja
Fotograficzna Caro 49, Sigrid Gombert/Image Source 107; **Getty Images:** LightFieldStudios/iStock/Getty Images Plus 56, Peter Muller/
Image Source 59, Viktoriia Hnatiuk/iStock/Getty Images Plus 62; **Pearson Education Ltd:** Gareth Boden 2, 100, Lord and Leverett 69,
75tr, 98, Sophie Bluy 104l, 104r; **Photodisc:** Photodisc 55; **Shutterstock:** Shutterstock 7, Fonzales 16, 120, Dotshock 22, Dziurek 26,
IM_photo 28, Maksym Gorpenyuk 31, Martin Valigursky 32, Uellue 34, Joshua Haviv 35, Devteev 38, Infografick 45, Mikadun 47,
InnaFelker 48, Pawel Kazmierczak 51, Lucky Business 57, Fizkes 61, Salov Evgeniy 66t, Andreas33 66c, Vicki L. Miller 74, Runzelkorn
75bl, Jefferson Bernardes 78, Bjoern Deutschmann 79, Sergey Kohl 83, 87914 84, Aastock 95cr, kckate16 103.

All other images © Pearson Education

**Audio Files and Transcripts**
**Pearson Education Limited** © Pearson Education Limited 2017. **Track 6: Everyday Life:** Extract from T Krauel. Jugendliche haben einen
Alltag wie früher Manager, Die Welt, 29/06/2014. http://www. welt.de/debatte/kommentare/article129580927/Jugendliche-haben-einen-
Alltag-wie-frueher-Manager.html Accessed: 13 Aug 2021; **Track 10: Social Media:** Extract from http://www.jugendundmedien.ch/
chancenund-gefahren/soziale-netzwerke.html © Programm Jugend und Medien, 2016.

*We are grateful to the following for permission to reproduce copyright material:*

**Text**
Page 11: **Die Welt:** Worked Example and Audio Track 6: T Krauel. Jugendliche haben einen Alltag wie früher Manager, Die Welt,
29/06/2014. http://www.welt.de/debatte/kommentare/article129580927/Jugendliche-haben-einen-Alltag-wie-frueher-Manager.html
Accessed: 13 Aug 2021; Page 15: **Programm Jugend und Medien:** Worked Example and Audio Track 10 : Extract from http://www.
jugendundmedien.ch/chancenund-gefahren/soziale-netzwerke.html © Programm Jugend und Medien, 2016. Page 23: **Verlag Razamba:**
Worked Example from Paula die Leseratte,Verlag Razamba (Ebbertz, M. 2010) p.5; Page 45: **Red Fox/Oetinger Publishing Group:** Worked
Example from Emil und die Detektive, Cecilie Dressler Verlag (Kastner, E. 1991) p.67; Page 55: **Beltz & Gelberg:** Worked Example adapted
from Stundenplan, Beltz & Gelberg (Nöstlinger,C. 2014) 9; Page 73: **EU publications:** Adapted from Übersetzen und Dolmetschen: Mit
Sprachen arbeiten (2014), EU publications p1. © EU Union. Available under a Creative Commons CC-BY license; Page 81: **Westend
Verlag GmbH:** Extract from '50 einfache Dinge, die man tun kann, um die Welt zu retten', Schlumberger. Andreas. © Westend Verlag
GmbH (2006) 13.

**Notes from the publisher**

1. While the publishers have made every attempt to ensure that advice on the qualification and its assessment is accurate, the official
specification and associated assessment guidance materials are the only authoritative source of information and should always be referred
to for definitive guidance.

Pearson examiners have not contributed to any sections in this resource relevant to examination papers for which they have responsibility.

2. Pearson has robust editorial processes, including answer and fact checks, to ensure the accuracy of the content in this publication, and
every effort is made to ensure this publication is free of errors. We are, however, only human, and occasionally errors do occur. Pearson
is not liable for any misunderstandings that arise as a result of errors in this publication, but it is our priority to ensure that the content is
accurate. If you spot an error, please do contact us at resourcescorrections@pearson.com so we can make sure it is corrected.